M000219159

The Good Ghost guide

Acknowledgements
The author would like to thank Mari Roberts for her tireless efforts in making a long text readable (and for designating her own favourite hauntings); Brian Skinner for suggesting the title and helping to develop the concept of the book; to the many librarians and booksellers who gave their expertise so willingly, and to Ryz, the illustrator, whose artistic flair and goodwill were so important. The author and publisher will be pleased to hear of readers supernatural experiences so that the most interesting of these may be included in future editions.

The Good Ghost Guide

Author: John Brooks
Editor: Mari Roberts
Illustrator: Ryz Hajdul
Maps: Richard Snowball

© Jarrold Publishing
First published in 1994 by Jarrold Publishing, Norwich 1/94
ISBN 0-7117-0669-7

Printed in Great Britain

JOHN BROOKS

The Good Ghost guide

JARROLD

Contents

Keymap

WESTERN ISLES

HIGHLAND

SCOTLAND   GRAMPIAN

TAYSIDE

FIFE

CENTRAL

LOTHIAN

STRATHCLYDE

BORDERS

DUMFRIES AND
GALLOWAY

NORTHUMBERLAND

TYNE AND WEAR

CUMBRIA   DURHAM   CLEVELAND

**NORTH WEST
ENGLAND**   **NORTH EAST
ENGLAND**

NORTH YORKSHIRE

LANCASHIRE   WEST
YORKSHIRE   HUMBERSIDE

MERSEYSIDE   GREATER
MANCHESTER   SOUTH
YORKSHIRE

CHESHIRE   DERBYSHIRE   LINCOLNSHIRE

GWYNEDD   CLWYD   **NORTH
MIDLANDS**   NOTTINGHAMSHIRE

STAFFORDSHIRE   LEICESTERSHIRE   NORFOLK

SHROPSHIRE   WEST
MIDLANDS   **EASTERN
ENGLAND**

WALES   WARWICK
SHIRE   NORTHAMPTONSHIRE

POWYS   HEREFORD AND
WORCESTER   CAMBRIDGESHIRE   SUFFOLK

DYFED   **SOUTH
MIDLANDS**   BEDFORDSHIRE

BUCKINGHAM
SHIRE   HERTFORD
SHIRE   ESSEX

WEST GLAMORGAN   GLOUCESTERSHIRE

MID GLAMORGAN   GWENT   OXFORDSHIRE   **GREATER LONDON**

SOUTH GLAMORGAN   AVON   BERKSHIRE

WILTSHIRE   SURREY   KENT

SOMERSET   **SOUTHERN ENGLAND**

HAMPSHIRE   WEST
SUSSEX   EAST
SUSSEX

**SOUTH WEST
ENGLAND**   DORSET

DEVON

CORNWALL

Introduction

Our legacy of ghost stories goes as far back as prehistoric times when ancestors gathered round wood fires to hear tales told by the tribe elders. The stories would dwell on heroic achievements of the past, but would also include experiences that primitive people were unable to explain. Some inexplicable events would be put down to the vagaries of the gods, others to malevolent forces generated by the dead or by forces of nature.

The blurred distinction between religion and the supernatural lived on after the advent of Christianity which, like the earlier religions, also embraced the miracles of natural science as well as phenomena of more obscure or problematic origin. Thus Cornish fishermen seeing a glowing figure on St Michael's Mount in the year 495 automatically took it to be the vision of a saint, though today it is perhaps more likely that we would call it a ghost.

Any review of ghost stories may cast doubt on the authenticity of some hauntings. The abundance of ghosts generated by the Civil War in the seventeenth century gives rise to the suspicion that some may have been invented for political reasons, just as the prevalence of ghosts in the favourite haunts of smugglers suggests that many of these were fictions intended to keep the curious from investigating mysterious lights and sounds too closely.

Two famous hauntings in eighteenth-century London, at Cock Lane and at Stockwell, were later found to be hoaxes. In the latter case the maid wanted to have the house to herself to entertain her lover. She joined horse hairs together and fixed them to household objects to create bogus poltergeist activity, hoping in this way to frighten her old mistress away from the place. At Cock Lane the counterfeit ghost was an eleven-year-old girl who had been persuaded to imitate a ghost for financial reasons. She kept a sounding board concealed in her stays to produce the noise that was characteristic of the ghost and gave it the improbable nickname of Scratching Fanny. However, these cases should not cast doubt on the many thoroughly investigated instances of poltergeist activity, nor should the suspicion that there are a few doubtful phantom Cavaliers and Roundheads lead to the disparagement of all the hauntings of that era.

A well-established feature of ghosthunting is that those who go out expecting to see a ghost are very unlikely to do so – it is practically impossible to ambush such an entity. You are much more likely to catch a fleeting glimpse of a strange figure out of the corner of an eye when you least expect it, or to feel the chilly sensation of being watched when you are certain no one is near. It is easy to pass a lifetime believing in ghosts without ever meeting one, and although this book mentions times and places where ghosts are reputed to appear, no guarantees are offered.

The ghosts in these pages were chosen subjectively and the author can only apologise if a favourite haunting has been left out. However, it is worth pointing out that most of the ghosts here have a reason for appearing at their location and have a known identity. It would be frustrating to read of a White Lady or a Black Monk without knowing who they were or why their spirits linger.

Britain's ghost lore embraces history, sociology, psychology, and even science. You do not have to be passionately interested in the paranormal to enjoy these tales. Many display surprising elements of humour and throw light on unexpected aspects of local history. Neither is the topic wholly based in the past. New hauntings are reported all the time, though modern phenomena often quickly fade after a spectacular initial appearance. Ancient or modern, and whether undertaken seriously or with a light heart, the ghosts of Britain provide a piquant seasoning to our buildings and landscape.

How to use this book

Inclusion of an entry in this book does not mean the haunted area is open to the public. The words 'open to the public' in the text indicate places that charge an entrance fee and may be open only at specified times. It is advisable to check fees and times with the local tourist authority. Pubs and hotels present no problems (beyond, in the case of pubs, those operating to licensing hours) but visiting a church, for example, may require that you request a key locally. In all cases, ghosthunters are asked to respect privacy, even that of the ghost.

The haunted locations are listed in alphabetical order in each section. If the haunting is in a town or village, it is listed under the town or village's name. Other haunted sites are large enough, or far enough from the nearest town or village, to appear under their own name, such as Glamis Castle in Tayside, Scotland, or Annesley Hall in Nottinghamshire, North Midlands. Lesser-known haunted sites have directions to the nearest main town.

The symbols enable you to identify at a glance certain types of haunting, as well as the existence of refreshment possibilities.

Key to symbols

🏠	Hotel, pub or restaurant
✛	Church or churchyard
😈	A ghost believed to bring harm to the onlooker
🌑	A ghost that makes scheduled appearances
👑	Royalty
✕	Battlefield or spectral army
🐗	Animal or bird ghost (excluding the horses, headless or otherwise, employed by the many roaming ghosts)
🗡	World war ghost
🎵	Ghostly music, whether voice or instrument
🚂	Railway
⚓	Phantom ship

South West England

Cornwall, Devon, Somerset, Avon and Dorset

Cornwall is England's most Celtic county, its natives sharing the characteristics of the Welsh and the Irish. Thus many of its ghost stories have fairytale influences rare in other parts, though the magical city seen off Land's End would seem to owe more to meteorology than to any psychic power.

Further to the east, Devon has more traditional ghosts though it can also provide hauntings as diverse as the Hairy Hands of Dartmoor (see Plympton and Postbridge), and the cavalcade of medieval noblemen at Lustleigh. The ghost of Sir Francis Drake haunts Exeter and Buckland Abbey, while that of Sir Walter Raleigh is seen at Sherborne in the neighbouring county of Dorset.

Dorset and Somerset both have several hauntings connected with the rebellion led by the Duke of Monmouth (the bastard son of Charles II), which ended with his defeat at the Battle of Sedgemoor in 1685. James II sent his Chief Justice, Judge Jeffreys, to the West Country to bring the remaining rebels to book, and Jeffreys attacked this task with such cruelty that it left an indelible psychic echo which survives in the ghost stories of many towns and villages in this region.

Other notable ghosts include those of King Arthur (at South Cadbury), Lawrence of Arabia (at Clouds Hill, his home in Dorset), and Isambard Kingdom Brunel, who haunts a wood on the outskirts of Bristol.

Ashmore Dorset

4 miles SW of Shaftesbury

Between this village and Fontmell Magna, 3 miles to the west, there is a place called Washer's Pit, once the site of a tumulus or burial mound. This was the home of strange ghosts called Gabbygammies, noisy creatures that jabbered incessantly in an unknown tongue. When the tumulus was destroyed by farming, the Gabbygammies took off to Ashmore and now, it seems, haunt the pond there.

Athelhampton House Dorset 🐾

5 miles NE of Dorchester

 This romantic old house (open to the public) has a fine selection of ghosts, including that of a monkey. In the sixteenth century a young lady of the Martyn family, disappointed in love, committed suicide in a secret room above the Great Hall. She failed to notice that her pet monkey had followed her into the chamber, and the animal suffered a lingering death of starvation. Its frenzied scratching at the panelling may still be heard. A monkey is incorporated into the Martyn crest. Athelhampton House also has a Grey Lady, a priest robed in black, a pair of duellists, and a phantom cooper who hammers away in the cellars.

Athelhampton House

Aveton Gifford Devon

3 miles NW of Kingsbridge

South Efford House has three ghosts. There is a naval officer who loathed courting couples and used to curse them from his window – his spectre continues the tradition. Then there is the shade of a manservant who hanged himself from a beam over the staircase. Finally, there lingers the spirit of a ferryman who died brokenhearted. He lost his livelihood when the well-intentioned landowner blocked steps to the river from the ferryman's cottage, fearing for the old man's safety.

Badbury Rings Dorset

3 miles NW of Wimborne

Magic generated in prehistoric times remains here, cultivated by modern Druids who often hold their festivals in the Iron Age fort. A dwarfish, hairy figure lurks around the perimeter and seems to enjoy spying on courting couples. Some say his face is distorted by terrible wounds, so he may be the ghost of a warrior slain in battle, or he is possibly the custodian of the golden coffin said to be buried beneath the fort.

Bath Avon 🍺

Assembly Rooms

The figure of a man in a black hat has haunted the Assembly Rooms almost since they opened in 1771. He has also been seen in Saville Row.

Gay Street

Predictably it is a homosexual ghost that has been reported from Gay Street, the apparition of a man with white hair tied back into a pony tail, who appears only to men and boys.

Grosvenor Hotel

A 'misty figure', taken to be that of a lady, haunts the hotel and leaves the air feeling icy cold as she passes.

Theatre Royal

The Garrick's Head pub, next to the New Theatre Royal, was once the home of Beau Nash. The pub and theatre share a Grey Lady, the ghost of a woman who fell in love with an actor. The woman's husband killed the actor in a duel whereupon she took her own life. The ghost is felt more often than seen, the temperature dropping abruptly as the scent of jasmine fills the air. The dancer Pavlova saw a Grey Lady in one of the boxes of the theatre in 1920. The theatre has a long-standing tradition that a peacock butterfly is always seen here before the start of the annual pantomime. If the insect is alive, good fortune ensues; if it is found dead, disaster invariably follows.

Beaminster Dorset ✛ 🕐

The sad apparition of a schoolboy named John Daniel, cruelly murdered in 1728, haunts St Mary's Church on 27 June each year. The gallery of the church once served as the schoolroom and it was here that the boy's ghost first appeared to his schoolmates, standing beside a spectral coffin, seven weeks after his death. The apparition disappeared when stones were thrown at it, but its appearance led to John Daniel's body being exhumed and the discovery that he had been strangled – previously it was thought that he had died of a fit. His murderer, however, was never caught. Bridge House is haunted by a Blue Lady, and bears a murder victim's bloodstain which can never be eradicated.

Beer Devon 🍺

6 miles W of Lyme Regis

Bovey House, 2 miles north-west of Beer, was enlarged from a medieval manor to an Elizabethan mansion in 1592, and sheltered Charles II after his defeat at Worcester in 1651. It is now a hotel, the most popular guest room being the one with a remarkable plaster ceiling showing the king hiding in the Boscobel Oak. The smell of lavender water that occasionally wafts through the house for no obvious reason may be a psychic reminder of the king's visit. Bovey is also reputed to have a headless ghost, but this may have been invented by smugglers when the house was empty and they were using it for their operations.

Berry Pomeroy Castle Devon 💀

2 miles E of Totnes

Lady Eleanor Pomeroy was locked up in a dungeon here in the castle (open to the public) for nineteen years by her insanely jealous sister, Margaret, who finally starved her to death. Lady Eleanor's harmless ghost still walks the romantic crumbling ruin, but there is also an evil presence (some say it is Margaret's ghost) which tempts people to the high walls above the gorge and then urges them to jump.

Bettiscombe Dorset

6 miles NE of Lyme Regis

The manor house is famous for the skull kept here which causes havoc if it is ever removed. The skull, which probably comes from a nearby prehistoric burial-place, is said to have shed drops of blood just before the outbreak of the First World War. Bettiscombe Manor also has a ghostly funeral procession which makes its stately way past the south front of the house.

Bolventor Cornwall 🍺

8 miles SW of Launceston

Daphne du Maurier's novel made the Jamaica Inn Britain's most famous pub, but Bodmin Moor can no longer be called remote and its romance is diluted by the presence of tourists. The inn has several ghosts, the most commonly seen being the motionless figure of a sailor who sits on the wall of the courtyard, the victim of a mugger. The sailor was lured from the pub, robbed and killed.

Boscastle Cornwall ⚓

A ghostly peal of bells can be heard ringing beneath the waves at Forrabury, a hamlet situated immediately to the south of Boscastle, notable for its finely proportioned, isolated church. The bells for Forrabury church were originally brought by sea from the foundry. However, almost at the end of the voyage, the captain uttered a blasphemous curse with the result that a terrible storm engulfed his ship, which went down with all hands. Spectral vessels, both large and small, have been seen where the bell boat sank.

Bovington Camp Dorset

5 miles W of Wareham

Keepers at the Tank Museum have described 'Herman the German' (though some call him Fried Fritz), who is often seen peering through the high windows at a Tiger tank. He probably died in this tank when it was hit by shell-fire in the Second World War.

Bristol Avon ✚ 🍺

All Saints' Church

The apparition of a black-robed monk has often been seen in and around the church, which is situated on the junction of Corn Street with High Street. All Saints' was one of the wealthiest of the West Country churches and it has been suggested that the monk guards treasure hidden from those despoiling churches and monasteries for Henry VIII.

Cathedral

The cathedral is haunted by a grey-robed monk who also visits the library next door, where he is seen consulting theological volumes.

Leigh Woods

These woods on the western side of Clifton Gorge are haunted by the ghost of Isambard Kingdom Brunel, who died before Clifton Suspension Bridge (which he designed to span the gorge) was erected. Weird screams sometimes emanate from the woods for no apparent reason, and dogs have sometimes shown symptoms of extreme fear here. The bridge itself holds a morbid attraction for would-be suicides.

Llandoger Trow Inn

This King Street pub is named after the type of flat-bottomed boat which used to ply the rivers Severn and Avon. The pub dates from

Leigh Woods

13

1664 and was visited by Defoe (who met Alexander Selkirk there) and Robert Louis Stevenson (who described it in *Treasure Island*). It has the ghost of a boy with a lame leg whose faltering footsteps are heard as he limps across the floor. Occasionally he is seen carrying a white enamel pail.

Pembroke Road
This road was formerly known as Gallows Lane because of the gibbet that stood here. It is haunted by the figure of a dwarf named Jenkins Protheroe, a beggar who turned to murder to supplement his income, and was executed on 31 March 1783.

Purdown
The large lady dressed in white on horseback is the ghostly form of a duchess of Beaufort, who died when she was struck by lightning while out riding.

Brixham Devon
The fourteenth-century Black House harbours the ghost of Squire Hilliard who endlessly seeks his son to ask his forgiveness. The squire prevented him from wedding the girl he loved and subsequently the young man committed suicide.

Brockley Combe Avon ✠☠
7 miles SW of Bristol

This village, with its combe, is one of the most haunted villages in the West Country. The ghost to avoid is that of an old woman who appears every twenty-six years and is next due in 2016. You will either die or go mad if you see her. The road up to the combe from the village has several hauntings: a phantom coach; an occasional 'leader light' – a weird oval of unnatural yellowish-green light that is said to herald death if it is encountered; a hunt led by a headless huntsman that can prove a hazard to traffic; and the ghost of a clergyman named Hibbetson who murdered a local squire for his money. Brockley church has the spirit of an old lady dressed in brown, who used to clean the church about a hundred years ago. Her ghost vanishes if it is spoken to.

Buckfastleigh Devon 🐾
The tomb of Richard Capel is in the churchyard, formidably impregnable. Capel, who died in 1677, had led a promiscuous life and was a scourge to the young women of the neighbourhood. As he lay on his deathbed the whisht hounds gathered about the house, howling horribly, waiting to take his soul to the Devil. Local children dare each other to walk thirteen times round his tomb and then insert a finger through the keyhole. Few risk the latter, fearing that Capel will rise from his grave to gnaw off the finger. On a night in early July the headless form of Capel, with a pack of hounds, rides up the drive of his home, Brook Manor. He is said to have inspired the character of Black Hugo in *The Hound of the Baskervilles*.

Buckland Abbey Devon ⚱

7 miles N of Plymouth

This was the home (now open to the public) of Sir Francis Drake, who was a magical figure in more than one sense. Locals believed that he was in league with the Devil, and that he and fellow wizards met on Devil's Point, the westernmost promontory of Plymouth, to conjure up the great storm which wrought havoc on the Armada. Drake is supposed to appear at Buckland driving a black hearse drawn by four headless horses, with attendant headless hounds. (See also the Ship Inn at Exeter, and Stogumber, below.) Drake's Drum is kept at Buckland and sounds when England is in dire peril, to awaken Drake and bring him from Heaven or Hades to help his country's cause. It was heard before Trafalgar, during the First World War and as the Battle of Britain was being fought.

Buckland Monachorum Devon 🍺

8 miles N of Plymouth

The Who'd Have Thought It inn at Milton Combe is haunted by a former landlord named Abe Beer and an erstwhile Cavalier who occasionally rings for service.

Burgh Island Devon 🕐

6 miles NW of Salcombe

Tom Crocker was a famous pirate who used the island as his headquarters until he was brought to justice and hanged in 1395. His ghost walks during the third week in August each year, undisturbed by the local celebrations organised in his memory.

Camborne Cornwall

The spectre of a man dressed in black has been seen by the shore at the appropriately named Deadman's Cove on Hudder Down.

Chard Somerset 🍺

The Chough Hotel is an old building, one of the many places in the West Country where Judge Jeffreys is supposed to have stayed when he went to try followers of Monmouth in what became known as the 'bloody assizes'. One of the hotel's traditions is the preservation of a stuffed chough (a crow-like bird) in a glass case, which is on the inventory and is passed from landlord to landlord. There is a tombstone behind the fireplace which defies efforts to photograph it – either camera or flashgun fails. Three separate manifestations have been seen here: a man in a suit of armour; an old lady; and an unpleasant-looking man who was once apprehended at the bar by the local policeman, but turned out to be a spectral villain.

Chardstock Devon

4 miles N of Axminster

The Grey Lady who walks from the vicarage to the churchyard is described as a 'vague creature'.

Charmouth Dorset

Charmouth Lodge in the main street is haunted by a ghostly monk and a White Lady. The latter is supposed to be the shade of a woman murdered in the house – her body was thrown in the well.

Chettle Dorset

6 miles NE of Blandford

The district surrounding this village is well haunted. The ghost of the first Lord Shaftesbury rides in a coach driven by a headless coachman over Thickthorn Down, while Chettle Down has the ghostly hand of a poacher, struck off in a skirmish with gamekeepers, which seeks to be re-united with the rest of the body and is likely to be seen at Bloody Shard Gate.

Chideock Dorset

3 miles W of Bridport

A Black Dog haunts the lanes around the village and usually returns to the old graveyard where it vanishes.

Chilton Cantelo Somerset

3 miles NE of Yeovil

The skull of Theophilus Broome, who died in 1670, is kept in a cupboard at Higher Farm opposite the church. Broome appears to have had a morbid fear of his head being buried and asked that his skull should be kept at the farm rather than laid to rest in the churchyard. There were many attempts to bury the skull, all of which ended in failure.

Christchurch Dorset

Although acquitted of helping to murder her elderly husband, Alma Rattenbury committed suicide four days after the end of the trial on 4 June 1935. She chose to kill herself at a spot known as Three Arches Bend, where the railway line is taken over the River Avon by a three-spanned bridge. Her body was found half-submerged in a backwater of the Avon with six stab wounds, three of which pierced her heart – a remarkable way to commit suicide. Her wraith lingers here at dusk on June evenings, a ghost redolent with a terrible sadness.

Clouds Hill Dorset

9 miles E of Dorchester

The National Trust cares for T.E. Lawrence's cottage (now open to the public), which he bought in 1925 when he rejoined the RAF after his exploits in Arabia. He was killed on the lonely road close by when he crashed his powerful Brough Superior motorbike – the opening sequence of David Lean's film, *Lawrence of Arabia*, shows an unforgettable reconstruction of the accident. Thus the sound of Lawrence's motorbike haunts the area, being abruptly cut off when the machine leaves the road, leaving the surrounding pine trees to throw back psychic echoes of his death. A figure in Arabian dress has also been seen at the cottage. This apparition usually appears when calamity threatens Britain.

Colebrooke Devon 🐾

5 miles W of Crediton

A ghost described as being that of a red monkey haunts the steep-sided lanes around the village and sometimes attacks people.

Corfe Castle Dorset

The dramatic silhouette of the ruined castle (open to the public) is one of the sights of the West Country and it would be surprising if it were not haunted, especially after the grim events that it has witnessed. In 978, King Edward was murdered here (see also Shaftesbury, below), and in the reign of King John, twenty-two French noblemen were starved to death in its dungeon. The castle suffered a long siege during the Civil War before the garrison was betrayed and it was subsequently blown up by the victorious Roundheads. A headless woman walks the approach path to the castle, but her reason for haunting is unclear.

Dartington Devon 👊

2 miles NW of Totnes

A school occupied Dartington Hall for many years and now it is an art college, but the place has maintained its supernatural fame. The famous White Lady is still to be seen, though the prime reason for her appearance is to warn of a death in the Champerknowe family, the former owners. There is also a Grey Lady who, when alive, threw herself off the old church tower, and a headless horseman who appears at the lower gate. The Countess's Room is haunted by a lady in Norman dress, supposed to be the wife of Gaven Champerknowe, and a grand piano has often been heard playing by itself in the locked drawing room.

Dartmouth Devon 🍺 👑

The Royal Castle Hotel has a royal ghost – that of Mary, wife of William III, who spent her first night in England here. On some autumnal nights her carriage rumbles into the courtyard of the hotel.

Dozmary Pool Cornwall

7 miles NW of Liskeard

This lonely spot on Bodmin Moor is one of many places where Sir Bedivere is supposed to have thrown the sword Excalibur as King Arthur lay on his deathbed (see also Trent, below). The ghost of Tregeagle, a lawyer of exceptional wickedness, was laid here, with the task of emptying the pool with a limpet shell.

Exeter Devon ✚ 🕐 👊

Cathedral

The ghost of a nun visits the cloisters of the cathedral, favouring the hour of seven in the evening and the month of July. The cathedral close is haunted by a monk.

Lord Haldon Hotel

The hotel occupies the surviving wing of Haldon House, the vast mansion built by the Palk family who owned much of Torbay, and whose male line bore the title of Lord Haldon. A sad young maidservant haunts the top floor, appearing in sodden eighteenth-century clothing. She was seduced by the master of the house who murdered her when he found out she was pregnant, throwing the body into the lake once situated in the grounds.

Ship Inn

This pub in Martin's Lane was supposed to be a favourite with Sir Francis Drake, so it comes as no surprise to find that his ghost is seen here. There is, however, another presence, less benign, which attempts to push people down the stairs.

Falmouth Cornwall

Falmouth Bay is supposed to have a Morgawr, the Cornish version of the Loch Ness monster, which was sighted on many occasions in 1976 and has been seen infrequently since.

Forde Abbey Dorset

3 miles SE of Chard

A spectral black monk haunts the cloisters and Great Hall of this grand house (open to the public). It has been suggested that this is the ghost of Thomas of Chard, abbot of the Cistercian abbey, who built the tower and Great Hall in about 1500.

Frithelstock Devon

2 miles W of Great Torrington

The ruined priory stands next to the church, on private property. In the days when the public was allowed to visit the ruins, a young boy had a remarkable experience of reincarnation here, describing how – as an old man – he used to climb twisty stairs to toll the bell. At the time there was no reason to believe that the priory had ever had a tower, but later archaeological evidence was uncovered to prove that the building had been as the boy described it.

Glastonbury Somerset 🍺

Some regard Glastonbury as the most holy place in Britain and people of many faiths are drawn here by its mystical associations. It is said that King Arthur and his queen are buried in the precincts of the abbey, and that the Holy Grail is hidden in Chalice Well, whose iron-rich waters are treasured by Christian and pagan alike. The George and Pilgrims Inn dates from 1475 and is haunted by both a fat and jovial monk, and a grinning man wearing a blue sports coat, surrounded by a halo of bright light. Both ghosts come into the 'bedroom intruder' category, where guests are made aware of the physical presence of phantoms by pressure they experience on their bedclothes.

Godolphin House Cornwall

8 miles E of Penzance

This lovely early-Tudor house (open to the public) has a 'ghost path' leading to the site of the old family chapel close by. A spectral funeral party passes down this path, which is overhung by evergreens. It is also the haunt of a White Lady, said to be the ghost of Margaret, wife of the first Earl of Godolphin, who appears on the anniversary of her funeral. The date is hard to pinpoint since, although a plaque in Breage church gives the day she died as 9 September 1678, she insisted on being buried in Cornwall, and it took two weeks to bring her lead coffin to Godolphin. Charles II stayed at Godolphin before the Restoration and his face has been seen looking down from the window of the room he occupied.

Kentisbeare Devon ●

3 miles E of Cullompton

One of the most unlikely ghosts to feature in these pages haunts the Bradfield Hall estate. It is a farmworker who rides up and down on a horse-drawn roller (a traditional farming implement) every night at midnight.

Land's End Cornwall

Some people have seen a vision of the lost land of Lyonnesse from the cliffs – one woman twice saw a vista of a great city with domes, spires and towers, far out on the horizon.

Lapford Devon ●

17 miles NW of Exeter

John Radford, a nineteenth-century vicar of Lapford, murdered his curate but managed to escape the hangman because of the reluctance of his parishioners to give evidence against him. He died in 1867 and his ghost escapes from his grave in the churchyard (he had wished to be buried inside the church) to roam the village, always leaving the cross which marks the grave awry. Lapford also has the ghost of St Thomas à Becket which gallops through the village on the eve of St John's Day (27 December) on its way to Nymet Rowland. This must be a confused ghost: not only does it appear two days before the anniversary of Becket's death, but it should be heading for the neighbouring village of Nymet Tracey, near Bovey Tracey, the home of one of Becket's murderers.

Launceston Cornwall

The churchyard at Launceston is haunted by a ghoul. Three miles to the south-west is the hamlet of Botathan, which was the scene of a famous haunting in 1665. The vicar was one of a number of people who saw the ghost of Dorothy Dingley, and his lengthy account of the haunting and of his attempts to exorcise the ghost was later edited and re-published by Defoe. The exorcism was particularly elaborate, involving the drawing of pentagrams, the use of rowan twigs following a 'magick tradition', and the adoption of the Syriac tongue, believed to be the only language understood by ghosts. For all this, Dorothy's ghost still reappears occasionally at Botathan.

Lewtrenchard Devon 🍺

7 miles E of Launceston

The Manor, owned by the Baring-Gould family, is now a hotel and is haunted by Old Madam, the redoubtable Margaret Belfield who saved the family fortunes from being squandered by her dissolute son. She is most likely to be seen in the Long Gallery. Another apparition, a White Lady, walks outside the house. This is the spirit of Susannah Gould who died of a heart attack just after her wedding ceremony on 19 March 1729.

Lidwell Devon

2 miles NW of Teignmouth

This tiny hamlet once had a holy well and a neighbouring hermit's cell. One hermit, who lived here in the fourteenth century, invited patrons of the well into his cell to hear confession and then murdered them. His ghost, the Mad Monk, still lingers here.

Locking Avon 🐇

2 miles E of Weston-super-Mare

Sir John Plumley supported Monmouth's rebellion, and after the defeat at Sedgemoor fled to his home at Locking. He hid here but was betrayed by one of his dogs and was subsequently hanged in his own park. His wife then threw herself into the well, holding her pet dog in her arms. Sir John, his wife, and both of the unfortunate dogs are said to haunt the environs of the manor house.

Lulworth Cove Dorset

The shades of a squadron of Roman soldiers have been seen marching over Bindon Hill, to the east of the cove.

Lustleigh Devon

9 miles NW of Newton Abbot

A haunting known as 'the Knights of Dartmoor' has been witnessed at the entrance to Lustleigh Cleave. This is a cavalcade of richly dressed medieval noblemen, accompanied by footmen with greyhounds, which disappears into woodland. As the woodland no longer exists this means that the vegetation is also part of the apparition. The haunting could represent a re-enactment of the Perambulation of Dartmoor in 1240 (a tour of inspection rich in pageantry), or is perhaps a ghostly royal hunt.

Lydford Devon

This village, situated on the western edge of Dartmoor, has several ghosts. The famous gorge is haunted by an old woman wearing a red handkerchief about her head (Kitty's Steps is particularly favoured); the Black Hound, which roams the village, is supposed to be the spirit of wicked Lady Howard (see Okehampton, below); and the castle harbours the ghost of Judge Jeffreys, presumably because many of his victims in the 'bloody assizes' met cruel deaths within the walls of the stronghold.

Lyme Regis Dorset 🍺

The Royal Lion Hotel stands beside the old execution-place where felons were publicly hanged, and this may be the reason why the hotel is haunted. Unnerving cold spots have frequently been reported, as well as a floating mass of mist that also bears an unnatural chill, which may be ectoplasm.

Marnhull Dorset

6 miles SW of Shaftesbury

Ghostly pall-bearers have been seen carrying a coffin from Marnhull to Todber, where a battle is supposed to have been fought long ago. However, bones found at Todber are believed to have come from a plague pit, a more probable explanation for phantom coffin-bearers. Their faces are always concealed.

Minehead Somerset

The ghost of Mrs Leakey caused considerable disturbance in the town in the seventeenth century. It is believed that Mrs Leakey was a witch who sold fair winds to sailors (a trade known as 'whistling up the wind') and this may be why the spirit was known as the Whistling Spectre. Alternatively, it may have been that her ghost caused the nuisance by whistling incessantly.

Mullion Cornwall

5 miles S of Helston

Bochym Manor is haunted by a Pink Lady, unusual in that she appears to be less than five feet tall, so she could be the ghost of a girl or of an exceptionally short woman. Since she is supposed to linger at Bochym because her lover was killed by her father in a duel, the latter seems more likely. In the First World War there was a naval Balloon Corps based close to the ancient manor house, and one of its officers wrote an account of a terrifying experience. He was walking towards Mullion on a starlit evening, and had just passed the Bochym driveway when he was 'gripped by a sudden fear akin to panic'. In a field to the right of the lane, two figures were fighting with rapiers, and after a flurry of blows one of them fell to the ground. The other man dropped to his knees beside the fallen figure and then beckoned towards a hedge. Six men bearing a coffin appeared from the shadow of the hedge and, as they approached, the kneeling swordsman looked up and seemed to become aware of the bystander, pointing his sword towards him. At this the officer fainted. When he came to, minutes later, all signs of the duel had vanished.

Norton Fitzwarren Somerset

2 miles W of Taunton

After a battle at the nearby hillfort, Norton Camp, a pile of bodies was transformed by 'spontaneous generation' into a fearsome dragon. The dragon terrorised the district until it was killed by Fulk

Fitzwarine, who became a local hero. The legend is depicted on the rood screen of the church.

Nunney Somerset 🍺

3 miles SW of Frome

The George Inn is haunted by the sound of bodies swinging from a gibbet that was erected in its grounds to hang rebels after the Battle of Sedgemoor in 1685. There were reports of a phantom hitch-hiker haunting the road to Frome in the 1970s. He was seldom seen actually thumbing a ride, but more often just appeared on the back seat of vehicles travelling along this road, usually disappearing as they approached Frome or Nunney.

Oare Devon ✠

4 miles E of Lynmouth

The church is famous for its associations with Lorna Doone. It is haunted by a former vicar, who greets new incumbents by ringing the bell and then appearing to them as they approach the church to investigate the sound.

Okehampton Devon 🐾 💀 🍺

Okehampton Castle

The castle (open to the public) is visited by a Black Dog whose glance means death to the beholder within a year. This beast is not to be confused with the skeletal hound that follows the wicked Lady Howard's macabre coach (made from the bones of her four husbands and driven by a headless coachman), which passes by the castle each night en route to her home at Fitzford, near Tavistock.

The White Hart Hotel

The hotel, in the centre of the town, is haunted by the ghost of a playful young boy named Peter, who plays hide-and-seek with the landlord's children and tinkers with their toys.

Pengersick Castle Cornwall

7 miles E of Penzance

The castle looks out of place now among the caravan sites of Praa Sands, but its history goes back to the twelfth century when it was built by Henry de Pengersick. He was notorious for his evil ways and eventually suffered 'the Greater Excommunication' (comprehensive banishment from the church), which may be why his ghost appears at the castle. The 'wicked crusader' also seen is possibly a confusion with Henry's ghost. Of the other castle ghosts the one most often seen is a man called Millington who owned the castle in Henry VIII's time. He tried to kill his wife by poisoning her wine, but she switched goblets so that he died instead.

Penryn Cornwall

The town has a phantom coach drawn by headless horses that appears in the days before Christmas. Tradition has it that eyes should be turned away from the sight lest the spectral coachman

Okehampton Castle

bear the onlooker away. St Gluvias's church is haunted by the spirit of Captain Martin, a bell ringer there in the 1880s, who perished when his schooner was wrecked.

Penzance Cornwall 🍺

Chapel Street
The street is haunted by the unlucky Mrs Baines who, attempting to catch out the guard she had set to look after her orchard, was herself shot by him. She is said to have lived at number 18. Like Penryn (see above), Penzance has a deadly coach drawn by headless horses, seen in this part of the town.

Kenegie
The old mansion of Kenegie stands on the edge of the town and is now a hotel. It was a home of the Bolitho family from Victorian times until the 1920s, and the ghost of a former housekeeper still wanders through its rooms – a tall woman in a long black dress with a large bunch of keys hanging from her belt. Voices are often heard coming from empty rooms, and the kitchen sometimes echoes to a girl's high-spirited laughter, but the most unusual presence at Kenegie is the one that enjoys stroking the faces of young women, lightly brushing their cheeks with the back of an unseen hand.

Plympton Devon

4 miles E of Plymouth

In the 1970s several lorry drivers travelling at night on the A38 near the village complained of a large pair of hairy hands clawing at their windscreens. (See also Postbridge, below.)

Poole Dorset 🍺

Museums

A museum now occupies an early-Tudor house known as Scaplens Court, which is haunted by the ghost of Agnes Bear. She was maidservant to the mistress of the house, and both women were murdered here in 1598 during the course of a robbery. Another museum in the town, the former Guildhall, has the spectre of a clerk who hanged himself here in Victorian times.

The Crown Hotel

Various manifestations have been reported from the hotel. There is ghostly piano playing, the sinister noise of a body being dragged across the floor, and the sounds of the rushing feet of children and their panic-stricken screams. It is said that a previous landlord of the Crown locked away his two deformed children in a secret room above the stables. They were never seen again.

Porlock Somerset 🐃

The famous hill is haunted by grey horses, presumably the shades of a runaway team that came to grief on the steep gradient. Three sailors, one of whom is black and another a boy, haunt the beach at Porlock Weir. Their bodies were washed up here and buried in Marsh Field, close by.

Portland Dorset 🐕

The Isle of Portland has a shaggy spectral hound known as the Tow Dog ('Tow' rhymes with 'cow'), which has the usual blazing eyes as big as saucers but does no harm to people other than blocking their way.

Postbridge Devon 💀

8 miles SW of Moretonhampstead

The road to Two Bridges has a manifestation called the Hairy Hands. This malevolent spirit was held to be responsible for a fatal accident in 1921, when the Dartmoor Prison doctor was killed. He was riding a motorbike when he swerved off the road and broke his neck. Shortly after this another motorcyclist survived when he managed to resist two hairy hands that gripped his own and tried to force him off the road. The Hairy Hands have also plagued car drivers, and once appeared at the window of a caravan that had parked nearby for the night. (See also Plympton, above.)

Poundstock Cornwall ✠

Penfound Manor dates back to Saxon times and a stream flows through the house between the kitchen and the Great Hall. (There

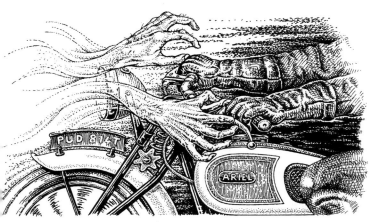

Postbridge

is a good view of the house from the public footpath which passes close by.) The Penfound family always seem to have followed losing causes and they lost Penfound when they supported the Jacobites in 1745. Earlier they had been Royalists and the haunting originated when young Kate Penfound fell in love with a neighbour's son whose father favoured Parliament. The only course left to them was to elope, but tragically they disturbed Kate's father who killed them both. The anniversary of the elopement falls on 26 April, and at midnight of this date Kate's ghost used to appear. Sometimes the killing was re-enacted as well. Although nothing has been seen since 1914, there are still enough inexplicable noises heard at the manor to keep alive stories of its ghosts. Penfound belongs to the parish of Poundstock, where another member of the family, William, haunts the church. He opposed powerful barons who were plundering the district and was cut down by them as he was assisting at Mass on the feast of St John on 27 December 1357.

Powderham Devon ✠

4 miles S of Exeter

There were several reports of St Clement's churchyard being haunted shortly after the outbreak of the Second World War. The ghost wore a grey cloak and passed through the gate into the churchyard.

Princetown Devon

Childe's Tomb lies in desolate boggy country 3 miles to the south-west of the town, near the old tin mine at Whiteworks. Childe was a hunter who, during the reign of Edward III, got lost in a snowstorm. He killed his horse and sheltered in the carcass, but nevertheless died of exposure. He left a note saying that whoever buried him could have his lands, and the monks of Tavistock hurried to carry out the bequest. Ghostly monks have been seen carrying a body.

Purse Caundle Dorset 🐾

4 miles E of Sherborne

The bowling green of the medieval manor house sees the gathering of King John's Hounds, a spectral pack controlled by the horn of a ghostly huntsman, which haunts on New Year's Eve and Midsummer's Eve. The evocative sound of plainsong is also heard at the manor, for no obvious reason, and an apparition used to appear on the staircase until it was removed in 1874.

Quantock Hills Somerset 💀

Beware of the Quantock's Wild Rider – if you hear him you will have misfortune, if you see him you will die. The northern hills, near West Quantoxhead, are haunted by the Woman of the Mist, an old woman bearing a bundle of sticks.

St Blazey Cornwall 🐾

4 miles E of St Austell

The road through the village is reputed to be haunted by an unnatural animal that looks like a bear but sounds like a horse.

St Ives Cornwall ⚓

A White Lady bears a lantern around the bay on particularly stormy nights to forewarn of shipwreck. A phantom ship has also been seen off St Ives Head. It may be the *Neptune*, a vessel which sank here after the appearance of a spectral ship in distress. The ghost ship vanished as rescuers were about to throw a line aboard, but soon afterwards an identical and only too real ship appeared. This was the unfortunate *Neptune*, which went down with all hands.

St Just Cornwall

6 miles W of Penzance

Kenidjack Castle, a prehistoric fort, is frequented by spectral witches led by Old Moll. Pixies are also active here and can lead the unwary to spend eternity in their other-worldly haunts.

Sandford Orcas Manor House Dorset �

5 miles NE of Yeovil

The beautiful Tudor building (open to the public) has altered little over the 350 years of its existence. Its former reputation as one of the most haunted houses in England was damaged when many of its ghosts were found to be the inventions of a tenant who left in 1975. The most enduring story is that of a ghostly spinet, which is heard playing near the gatehouse, and there is also the figure of a man in a white smock who frequently walks past the kitchen window. This is the ghost of a farmer who hanged himself here.

Sedgemoor Somerset ✕ ☠

2 miles E of Bridgwater

This was the scene of the rout of the Duke of Monmouth's peasant army by the forces of James II on 3 July 1685. Monmouth's ghost appears annually on this date, escaping from the battlefield. There are also sad groups of soldiers to be seen, clutching staves and pikes, who shout, 'Come on over!' at the King's Sedgemoor Drain. One of the Duke's men captured here was made to run a race against a horse. He was promised that his life would be spared if he won the race. He did but was killed nevertheless. The sound of galloping hoofs and the soldier's laboured breathing have been heard, and the ghost of his sweetheart, who drowned herself in the Drain after his death, has been seen.

Sennen Cornwall

8 miles SW of Penzance

The Irish Lady is one of the rocks offshore. It took its name from the sole survivor of an Irish vessel wrecked on the rock, who clung

Sennen

to its slippery surface for some hours before dropping into the stormy sea. Now her ghost clings to the rock. Sennen is also a favourite haunt of mermaids.

Shaftesbury Dorset 👑 🍺

Picturesque Gold Hill is haunted by the cortège of King Edward the Martyr, who was killed at Corfe Castle in 978.

The Grosvenor Hotel has a Grey Lady and a ghostly monk (another appears in the ruins of the abbey).

Shebbear Devon 🍺

7 miles NE of Holsworthy

Each year on 5 November the Devil's Stone, which stands just outside the churchyard, is turned by the bell ringers, who have previously rung a clamorous peal in order to frighten the Devil away from the stone. If the stone remains unturned, it is said, the Devil will hide beneath the huge lump of conglomerate (which is alien to the geology of the district) and bring disaster to the village. Shebbear's pub takes its name from the stone and is haunted by a little girl of about seven accompanied by a man with a grey beard. The latter is the ghost of a man murdered at the inn, and the little girl his daughter who was with him at the time.

Shepton Mallet Somerset

At a fiveways junction one mile to the south of the town is Cannard's Grave Inn, which is named after a villainous innkeeper. Not content with highway robbery and smuggling, he took to forgery as well. When he realised that he had been found out he hanged himself and was buried at the crossroads, where his ghost still prowls to surprise the late traveller.

Sherborne Dorset 🕐

Sir Walter Raleigh was granted the Manor of Sherborne by Queen Elizabeth I in 1592 and he built the New Castle here – the heart of the present mansion. His ghost is supposed to appear at midnight on the eve of Michaelmas Day (29 September), sitting on a stone seat close to the ruins of the Old Castle (open to the public). The New Castle has a haunted chamber which Lady Chatterton once occupied when she was a child. In her memoirs, published in 1878, she wrote of the experience she had in this room of seeing a battle re-enacted in front of the bed hangings.

Shute Devon

3 miles W of Axminster

Uniquely, the coachman who haunts this village appears without his coach. His mistress was so annoyed by his driving that she struck and killed him at Shute Pillars.

Sixpenny Handley Dorset

11 miles NE of Blandford

If you are driving on the A354 look out for a ghostly Bronze Age horseman, wearing a flowing cloak and waving a sword, where the Cranborne road crosses at Bottlebush Down. One of the best substantiated of Dorset ghosts, it was graphically described by the archaeologist R.C. Clay after he witnessed its appearance in 1924.

South Cadbury Somerset ♛

4 miles SW of Wincanton

On Midsummer's Eve King Arthur and his knights are supposed to rise from their graves to ride together down the hill from the Iron Age fort. The hill is a legendary burial-place of King Arthur.

Stogumber Somerset

12 miles W of Bridgwater

Heddon Oak lies a mile to the west of the A358 at a crossroads and was used to hang two of Monmouth's men sentenced by Judge Jeffreys. The sounds of the men's execution are still occasionally heard at the spot, while some complain of a difficulty in breathing as they pass it. Stogumber village is occasionally visited by the Wild Hunt, but on hearing it no one dares look out of the window to see it, because it is on its way to claim the soul of someone who has just died after living an evil life.

Just to the west of Stogumber is the village of Combe Sydenham, the home of Sir Francis Drake's father-in-law, Sir George Sydenham. His pallid ghost rides a headless grey horse northwards up the B3188. Drake was betrothed to Sydenham's daughter for eight years, until Sydenham lost patience and arranged a marriage to a more reliable suitor. Legend has it that when Drake, a wizard, heard of this, he fired a cannon from his ship hundreds of miles away. The cannonball hit Stogumber church as the bride walked up the aisle, causing the wedding to be abandoned. In fact the church was struck by a meteorite a little larger than a cricket ball, which was for many years preserved at Combe Sydenham. (See also Buckland Abbey, above.)

Stowford Devon 🐇

6 miles E of Launceston

Haine House, to the west of the village, has three haunted locations, each marked by a stone. The first marks the spot where a pageboy was buried under a beech tree – he was murdered by the butler and his wife. The second is where a huntsman was eaten by his own hounds, and the third marks the grave of John Cator, but no clues are offered as to why he deserved a stone. Haine House also has its own spectral Black Dog, while the terrace is haunted by a headless man, and the King Charles Room by an old lady.

Stratton Cornwall 🐇

2 miles E of Bude

Little remains of Binhamy Castle except its dry moat, which is haunted by a white hare and by the ghost of Sir Ralph de Blanc-Minster who lived at Binhamy. He went on a Crusade and was killed in the Holy Land in 1270. His sinister faceless effigy may be seen in Stratton church.

Studland Dorset 🐇 🕐

The ghost of a white donkey appears on the heath each year on 22 December or thereabouts. Its owner was waylaid and robbed of his money and the spirits the donkey was carrying by a deserter from the navy, who then killed the owner. The donkey was allowed to gallop away, but returns on the anniversary of the crime in search of its long-dead owner.

Tarrant Gunville Dorset

5 miles NE of Blandford

Eastbury House was built by Vanbrugh, but today only the north wing survives. A headless coachman with headless horses pulling a spectral coach races down the drive to the house to collect William Doggett's ghost. Doggett was the villainous steward of a former owner of the house, Lord Temple. He committed suicide when his misdeeds were about to be discovered. In spite of this, Doggett was buried in Tarrant Gunville church. When the church was rebuilt, the grave was opened and his body was found to be as fresh and rosy-cheeked as it had been when he was inhumed a century before. Thus Doggett was suspected of being a vampire as well as a ghost.

Taunton Somerset 🏨 🍺

The County Museum is housed in the castle, which was the scene of the worst of Judge Jeffreys's 'bloody assizes'. The savage judge is supposed to haunt the museum, as does a blonde woman who appears wearing seventeenth-century dress. A former curator felt himself clutched by a pair of ghostly hands.

Jeffreys also haunts the Tudor Tavern where he stayed during the assize and, possibly, the Castle Hotel, which has the Fiddler's Room where ethereal violin music is heard.

Tavistock Devon 🍺

Betsy Grimbal's Tower

This tower was the gatehouse of the great abbey that once dominated the town. Betsy was killed by a soldier on the spiral staircase of the tower and her ghost is supposed to be glimpsed at the windows. A national disaster usually follows – a policeman saw her in 1966 just before the Aberfan accident.

Kilworthy House

Now a residential school, Kilworthy House was once the home of the Glanville family, and was then much larger – it lost its top floor in a fire long ago. Its White Lady is the ghost of one of the Glanvilles, who murdered her husband. The woman's own father, a judge, sentenced her to death. There is also a Green Lady and a ghost which plays classical music on the piano downstairs.

Tetcott Devon

7 miles N of Launceston

Squire John Arscott died here in 1788. He was a famous eccentric who employed a jester, Black John, and kept a pet toad called 'Old Dawty' which fed at his table. Locals believed it to be his familiar, but it came to an unhappy end when it was eaten by another of his bizarre pets, a tame raven. Squire John took a jar filled with flies to church and fed them to spiders when the service became tedious to him. His ghost rides the countryside around the village, mounted on his favourite horse, Blackbird. An earlier member of the same family – the Wicked Arscott – was lynched from an oak in the park, an incident which is supernaturally re-enacted on occasion.

Torquay Devon ✠ 🍺 🏨

St John's Church

The church used to have a haunted organ that would sometimes play by itself. This phenomenon began in 1883 when the organist, Henry Ditton Newman, died. Before the funeral his body lay in the church, with one of the congregation keeping watch, when suddenly the organ began its uncanny recital. The same thing happened on other occasions, until 1956 when the instrument was replaced. Montpellier House, the former choir school and later the vicarage, also claims the ghost of Henry Ditton Newman.

The Palace Hotel

For some years this was the home of Dr Henry Philpotts who, as Bishop of Exeter, was so unpopular that he preferred to live in Torquay. Later he built himself a villa next to the hotel which was eventually incorporated into it. The parts of the hotel used by the bishop are haunted by his ghost, which has been seen by chambermaids, porters and guests. He wears full ecclesiastical dress including, presumably, a mitre.

Torre Abbey

The abbey (open to the public) is haunted by the spectre of a Spanish girl. She was imprisoned in the tithe barn with 396 other Spaniards taken from a galleon at the time of the Armada in 1588. The terrible conditions in the barn caused many deaths, including the girl's. The ghost of Lady Cary is driven down the avenue from the abbey in a brightly lit coach. She is smiling and dressed in finery as though for a ball. The uncanny thing is that she travels in silence, no sound of hoofs or wheels being heard on the drive.

Torrington Devon 🐾 ✗

This small town lies at the heart of North Devon's 'Black Dog' country. The spectral hound here is especially fond of the villages to the south-east along the Torridge valley. A ghostly soldier haunts Castle Hill, a psychic echo of the Battle of Torrington in 1646.

Trent Dorset

2 miles NE of Yeovil

Trent Barrow has a pool which is one of several places where Excalibur, King Arthur's sword, is supposed to have been thrown (see also Dozmary Pool, above). This pool is haunted by the sound of galloping hoofs and screaming voices, reminders of a stagecoach accident when all the occupants were drowned here.

Uplyme Dorset 🏠 🐾

The Black Dog pub is on the Devon side of the village, its name celebrating a widespread haunting in the West Country (more than fifty sightings of spectral Black Dogs have been reported from Devon alone). This particular phantom hound befriended a local farmer, living quietly with him but taking neither food nor water and hurting neither man nor beast. In spite of this the farmer lost patience with him one day and chased the dog with a poker. The animal escaped by leaping at the ceiling, vanishing through it in a cloud of falling plaster. This was followed by a shower of gold coins which the farmer used to establish an inn. The dog kept away from the farmer after this, but continues to haunt the neighbourhood. As a bringer of good fortune he makes a welcome change from other Black Dogs, which usually attract disaster and death.

The Duke of Monmouth began his planned invasion of England by landing at Lyme Regis from the Low Counties on 11 June 1685, and he led his troops along the road from Uplyme to Yawl. His ghostly force still haunts this stretch of road.

Washford Somerset 🚂

2 miles SW of Watchet

A ghost train haunts the mineral line which climbed up the valley to Roadwater and was closed in 1917. Although the track was taken up when the railway was closed, a train has since been heard here, probably due to a fatal accident on the line in 1857 when two trains collided.

Weare Giffard Devon

3 miles S of Bideford

The ghost of Sir Walter Giffard, who died in 1243, walks from the gatehouse of the hall to the church, eternally seeking his wife. There is also a churlish ghost that says to those who see him, 'Get ye gone,' or words to that effect.

Wedmore Somerset 🍺

7 miles NW of Glastonbury

The George Inn has the ghost of a lady wearing an Edwardian-style grey dress. She is harmless, but there is also an ill-tempered spirit here, said to hold down people in their beds, giving them a fearful sense of paralysis.

Wellington Somerset

In the 1950s and the 1970s there were persistent reports of a phantom hitch-hiker haunting the road between Wellington and Taunton. The ghost was said to have been responsible for several accidents and usually appeared late on nights of very wet weather, flashing a torch and throwing himself towards passing traffic. On one occasion a lorry driver gave the hitch-hiker a lift and put him down four miles later. The hitch-hiker's figure reappeared some miles further up the road, yet no one had overtaken the lorry.

Widecombe-in-the-Moor Devon 🍺

9 miles NW of Newton Abbot

The Old Inn harbours the ghost of Old Harry, who potters about the place and is seen in odd corners, and the unearthly sobs of a child, which may be heard from an empty bedroom. It is suggested that the sobs are caused by Mary Jay, a poor orphan who committed suicide about two hundred years ago when she found herself pregnant. She was buried on a lonely spot on the moor, where her grave always has fresh flowers.

Wistman's Wood Devon 🐗

2 miles N of Two Bridges – the centre point of Dartmoor – and reached by a moorland footpath

The stunted oaks here are the only substantial remnants of the trees that once covered most of Dartmoor. It is a lonely place full of foreboding, a favourite haunt of the whisht hounds from whom it takes its name. A funeral procession of monks in white robes has been seen here. On the way to Wistman's Wood, look right to Crockern Tor for the chance of seeing Old Crockern's ghost riding a skeleton horse.

Withycombe Somerset

5 miles E of Minehead

The tombstone of Joan Carn stands by the south door of the church. She was a notorious witch who murdered three husbands and was eventually killed in 1612 by being thrown into a pond at Sandhill Farm, about half a mile from Withycombe. Her ghost was exorcised from Sandhill, but it is supposed to be returning to Withycombe at the rate of a cockstride a year.

Wolfeton House Dorset

3 miles NW of Dorchester

The gatehouse is haunted by Cornelius, an Irish Catholic priest who refused to recant and was imprisoned at Wolfeton House (now open to the public) in 1594. He was taken to Dorchester where he was hanged, drawn and quartered. A ghostly carriage may be seen being driven up the staircase of the house – this seems to be the re-enactment of a wager on such a feat won by a member of the Trenchard family. There is also a headless Grey Lady, the spirit of a Lady Trenchard who killed herself after a dinner party. Before her suicide her spectre was seen at the dinner table by a judge. The ghost stood behind Lady Trenchard holding her head beneath her arm in classic style.

Wool Dorset

5 miles west of Wareham

Woolbridge Manor was the home of the Turberville family and it is only those with Turberville blood who see the phantom coach which, on Christmas Eve, careers across the heath to another Turberville home, the manor house at Bere Regis.

Worbarrow Bay Dorset

10 miles E of Weymouth

A smuggler was cornered here by revenue men who stoned him to death. His anguished cries may still be heard on nights when the moon is waning.

Zennor Cornwall 🍺

4 miles SW of St Ives

This lovely village is famous for its mermaid, a legend graphically commemorated in the carving of a pew-end in the church. The Tinners' Arms has a poltergeist which is active before electrical storms, while the lane up to Foage Farm (a public footpath for most of its length) is haunted by a cyclist with a blood-spattered face, wearing a Victorian workman's clothes. It has been suggested that he was a miner at Rosevale who was a victim of an underground explosion.

Southern England

ΕΠΙ ΚΥΡΙΟΝ
ΜΝΑΝ ΣΟΥ

Avebury Manor Wiltshire

Wiltshire, Hampshire, Berkshire, Surrey, Sussex, Kent and Isle of Wight

Littlecote House in Wiltshire, with its twenty ghosts, must be the most haunted site in the region. William Darrell, who owned the property in the sixteenth century, was a notorious libertine supposed to have thrown a new-born baby (his bastard child) into the fire. Although subsequently tried for murder, he bribed the judge, was acquitted and lived for another fourteen years. He was killed by a fall from his horse which is supposed to have shied when it saw the baby's ghost.

The most frightening apparition is perhaps that seen by a member of a ghosthunting group organised by Rudyard Kipling in Gladwysh Wood near his home at Burwash in Sussex. Kipling's friend was confronted by a macabre figure whose hands were clasped around the decaying flesh of his throat and who made terrible sounds as he choked.

Those who seek royal ghosts should visit Windsor Castle, haunted by three of this country's monarchs, while the ghost of King William Rufus may be seen in lonely parts of the New Forest near Cadnam, where he was murdered on 2 August 1100.

Alton Hampshire ✠ 🐕 🍺

St Lawrence's church was the scene of a bloody battle during the
Civil War when Royalists were besieged here, their colonel making
a heroic last stand in the pulpit and putting six or seven
Roundheads to the sword before falling himself, with sixty of his
own troops around him. This savagery is sometimes re-enacted in
the church, though the conflict is heard rather than seen.

The Crown Hotel is haunted by a dog who was mistreated by his
owner and finally killed when he smashed it against the hearth. In
the 1960s building work revealed the bones of a dog in a false wall
by the chimneybreast. The whimpers and scratching of the poor
beast are still heard.

Angmering West Sussex

5 miles W of Worthing

The shade of a giant monk haunts the countryside around
Ecclesden Manor, to the north-east of the village.

Arborfield Berkshire ✠ 🕐

2 miles S of Reading

If you are in the churchyard of St Bartholomew's at midnight on
New Year's Eve you may see the ghost of a young bride standing by
the yew tree next to the church. She is the spirit of a girl who was
about to marry the gardener at the hall (demolished soon after the
Second World War) when she was murdered by a jealous butler.

Arundel West Sussex ✠

Hiorne's Tower in the park is haunted by the spirit of a young girl
who threw herself from the top when her suitor deserted her, while
the castle (open to the public) has the ghost of a humble scullion in
the kitchen and a Blue Man, a Cavalier, in the library.

Doubt has been cast on the authenticity of a photograph taken in
1940 purporting to show ghosts at the altar of St Nicholas's
church. However, many people are uneasy at the atmosphere both
here and in the adjoining Fitzalan chapel.

Avebury Wiltshire 🍺

The village is built within the stone circle, encompassing
28 acres, which dates from Neolithic times but was in use
for a thousand years, well into the Bronze Age. The pagan
rituals enacted here could have generated the ghosts – small
figures are said to play among the stones on nights when there is a
full moon. Lights and music have been seen and heard coming from
among the stones – possibly the supernatural memorial to Avebury
Fair which was held in the village until Victorian times.

Avebury Manor (open to the public) is a lovely Tudor house which
has a White Lady whose lover was a Cavalier killed in the Civil War.
Grieving at his death, she killed herself by jumping from a window.
Another Royalist haunts the Crimson Room (now called the
Cavalier Room) leaving a strong smell of roses. He may be the

ghost of Sir John Stawell who loved the manor but forfeited it for his support of the King.

Balcombe West Sussex 🚂

8 miles E of Horsham

The railway tunnel is haunted by four soldiers killed by a train during the First World War.

Battle Abbey East Sussex 👑 ✕

The abbey (open to the public) was founded by William I as a thanksgiving for his victory and was built around the spot where King Harold fell when the arrow pierced his eye. Harold's ghost appears in the ruined abbey with the fatal arrow still embedded in its skull. Another manifestation is a fountain of blood that occasionally springs from the earth.

Bayham Abbey Kent 🏺

4 miles SE of Tunbridge Wells

The beautiful ruins (open to the public) are haunted by a procession of monks wearing white robes. The sounds of chanting and of bells are heard.

Bearsted Kent

1 mile E of Maidstone

The ghost of a rider with wide-brimmed hat and silver spurs haunts the lane that leads from the village to the Pilgrim's Way.

Beaulieu Hampshire 🏺

7 miles SW of Southampton

Ghostly lay brothers wearing brown habits are the most frequently seen phantoms at Beaulieu Abbey (open to the public). Little remains of the great Cistercian monastery apart from the gatehouse, which was incorporated into the palace built by Sir Thomas Wriothesley. The smell of incense often drifts through the palace and the sound of Gregorian chant is heard, usually before a death in the village. The Blue Lady of Beaulieu is said to be the ghost of the Countess Isabella who was cheated of her inheritance. The only malevolent ghosts are those of a butler who murdered a maidservant (he lurks at the top

Beaulieu

37

of the stairs) and a Royalist soldier who was killed in a small room above a secret staircase.

Billingham Manor Isle of Wight ♛

4 miles S of Newport

The house was once rented by a famous ghosthunter, Sir Shane Leslie, who found it 'very haunted'. A scent of Madonna lilies accompanies the appearance of the ghost whose earthly life ended when he was killed in a duel concerning a Miss Legh. Leslie also wrote of a secret panel in the dining room which, when he pushed it open, revealed the severed head of Charles I, an apparition that slowly faded away. Charles was held captive at Carisbrooke Castle and the Worsleys who owned Billingham at the time devised a plot to free him. Before the abolition of capital punishment, islanders believed that the king's head appeared at the manor on the eve of an execution at Parkhurst Prison.

Bisham Berkshire

5 miles S of High Wycombe

Lady Hoby, who died in 1609 at the age of 81, haunts the abbey because of her cruelty to William, the son of her second marriage, whom she eventually killed because of his smudged copybooks. Her portrait dominates the Great Hall and she is said to step from its frame to walk the house. She was last seen to leave the frame in 1910 by Admiral Vansittart who had been playing chess with his brother within sight of the painting. Bisham Abbey is now the National Sports Centre.

Bluebell Hill Kent

4 miles N of Maidstone

A fast stretch of dual carriageway now takes the Chatham to Maidstone road up Bluebell Hill but on 19 November 1965 the road was unimproved and passed the Lower Bell pub. At the crossroads here, close to the picnic site, the crash took place that laid the foundation of one of the most celebrated of phantom-hitch-hiker stories. At about eleven in the evening a Ford Cortina and a Jaguar collided. Three of the girls in the Ford died, one of whom was going to be married at Gillingham on the following day. She is the ghost on Bluebell Hill that flags down cars, gets in and chats to the driver in an excited way about her imminent wedding, then vanishes before the destination is reached. In 1974 a motorist experienced a variation on the hitch-hiker theme. In this instance, after midnight on a wet July night, he was distressed by hitting a figure that seemed to appear from nowhere. He stopped and found the unconscious figure of a girl about ten years old lying in the road. Having failed to stop passing traffic, he wrapped her in a blanket by the roadside and went to contact the police. When they arrived at the scene the blanket was there but the girl had gone, and was never found in spite of an exhaustive search. Many people believe that this incident proves that Bluebell Hill has a second ghost.

Box Wiltshire 🚂

6 miles NE of Bath

The famous railway tunnel was built in 1841 by Brunel and is 300 feet deep for some of its mile-and-three-quarter length. Railway trackmen dislike working inside its portals and say that a phantom steam train which never materialises can sometimes be heard rushing towards them.

Bracknell Berkshire

The road to Ascot (A329) is haunted by the figure of a policeman who has a hideously mutilated face.

Bradford on Avon Wiltshire ✛

Tiny St Lawrence's church dates from the tenth century and for several centuries until 1856 served as a cottage. The ghosts of a group of people in medieval clothing have been seen by a priest serving communion, a haunting confirmed by an American medium in 1932 who thought the group might have been lepers.

Bramber Castle West Sussex

8 miles NW of Brighton

This bleak and crumbling pile of masonry was the home of William de Braose who signed the Magna Carta and thus fell out with King John. In retribution the king imprisoned William, his wife and four of his children at Windsor where they were starved to death. However, it is at Bramber that the pitiful cries of the children are heard, usually in the month of December.

Bramshill Hampshire

8 miles NE of Basingstoke

Bramshill House was originally the home of the Cope family but is now a police staff college. It has a dozen or so ghosts of which the Grey Lady is the most commonly seen. She is usually encountered early in the morning and leaves a distinctive fragrance of lilies of the valley in her wake. The White Lady is the ghost of a young bride who hid herself in the Mistletoe Bough chest that is in the reception area at Bramshill. She closed the lid of the Italian chest and kept quiet as a Christmas game of hide-and-seek went on around her. Probably she fell asleep in her hiding place and suffocated, for her body was found later with a sprig of mistletoe in her hands. Some say that these events took place in Italy and the ghost is that of Genevre Orsini who died in this way in 1727. The fifth baron Cope brought the chest, they say, and the poor girl's ghost, back with him after his Grand Tour. Similar stories are told at Marwell, Hampshire, and Minster Lovell, Oxfordshire.

The only unpleasant ghost at Bramshill is that of a gardener who drowned in the lake. His presence brings a feeling of threatening evil. The little green man seen only by children may be the shade of Henry Cope, a notable eccentric and friend of George III, who would consume only green food, wear only green clothes, and had

his rooms, horses and carriage decorated in green. He became
insane and after an unsuccessful suicide attempt at Brighton in
1806 was committed permanently to an asylum in 'a straight
waistcoat'. Other ghosts are a deerkeeper who was carelessly shot
by an archbishop; a nun and a woman in Stuart-style clothes in the
chapel; an old man with a long beard, and a tennis player from the
1930s, said to be the young son of Lord Brocket, the last private
owner of Bramshill, who died after falling from a train at Surbiton.

Bramshott Hampshire ✠

8 miles S of Farnham

The village has more ghosts than any other village in Hampshire,
though their reasons for lingering here are mainly unknown. St
Mary's churchyard has an appealing little girl in a Victorian bonnet
as well as a terrifying apparition in a white shroud. Boris Karloff
used to live at Bramshott.

Breamore House Hampshire

7 miles S of Salisbury

The house (open to the public) has the portrait of Christian
Dodington, the wife of William Dodington who finished building the
mansion in 1583. No mortal hand is allowed to touch this painting
or death will strike that person on the same day – thus the painting
has remained in the Great Hall, fading and undusted, for almost
four hundred years. The son of William and Christian, another
William, murdered his wife at Breamore in 1629, and her ghost
haunts the Blue Bedroom. Fortunately she is seldom seen, for an
appearance heralds the death of the owner of Breamore.

Brighton West Sussex ⚓

John Beal's is a long-established stationer's shop in East Street
which was troubled in 1950 by a dark spectral figure wearing a
cowl. Present-day staff did not know of the ghost. The Lanes have
the ghost of a medieval nun wearing a grey habit, and the Pavilion
(open to the public) has one of a short, stout old lady who may once
have been housekeeper, though one witness identified her as
Martha Gunn the Brighton Bather, a pioneer of sea-bathing.

A spectral tenth-century galley has been seen off the beach. This
is the *Nicholas*, which sank with all hands (and her pilgrim
passengers) on her return from a voyage to Constantinople.

Brimpton Berkshire

6 miles E of Newbury

About two hundred years ago, on Brimpton Lane, a carriage taking
revellers to the Hunt Ball plunged into the river at Abel Bridge.
Late-night travellers who pause at this spot in January may still
hear psychic echoes of the tragedy – the screams of the passengers
and the snorts and whinnies of the horses. They may even catch a
glimpse of the doomed carriage and pair.

Burwash East Sussex

10 miles SE of Tunbridge Wells

Kipling, who felt himself to be psychically gifted, lived at Bateman's just outside the village. He felt nearby Gladwysh Wood to be particularly evil and he organised a ghosthunt there. One of the hunters, separated from the rest of the party, was suddenly confronted by a fearsome figure. It was that of a man whose flesh was rotting from the bones and who clasped his own throat in an apparent attempt at self-strangulation. He emitted terrible sounds as he choked. It was later suggested that this might have been the ghoul of David Leary, executed for the murder of a fellow labourer whose body was found in the wood. On the scaffold Leary swore that he was innocent, and that he would prove this by returning 'to haunt those people who have hounded me to my death'.

Buxted East Sussex

1 mile NE of Uckfield

In 1661 Nan Tuck, a half-witted young girl, was accused of witchcraft and suffered the ordeal of trial by water. She managed to escape from the ducking chair but was pursued by villagers and eventually found hanging from a tree. It seems likely that she was lynched and that is why she returns to haunt Tuck's Wood (where she died) and Nan Tuck's Lane.

Cadnam Hampshire ♛

8 miles W of Southampton

The Rufus Stone (a mile and a half south-west of Cadnam) marks the spot in the New Forest where William Rufus was murdered on 2 August 1100 (though some say that the correct date for this anniversary would be 22 July and that the killing was a pagan ritual intended to renew the potency of the kingdom). The monarch's ghost follows the trackway to Winchester where his body was taken for burial in a humble cart.

Canterbury Kent ✠ ◗ ☠

The martyred St Thomas à Becket is said to haunt many places in England but not the cathedral where he was slain. Another archbishop, Simon of Sudbury, is supposed to haunt the city for the reason that his body was buried in two pieces – the head at Sudbury (see Eastern England), the rest at Canterbury. He built the Westgate, the grandest city gate surviving in Britain, but in 1381, the year following its completion, he was murdered and decapitated in London by Wat Tyler's peasants.

An entrance into the King's School is named Dark Entry and the story of its ghost was told in *The Ingoldsby Legends*. Nell Cook was a servant of a canon whom she caught in misdemeanour with a girl he claimed to be his niece. For this she unaccountably murdered them both and her ghost appears every Friday night in Dark Entry, but beware – seeing it is said to bring death within the year.

Chanctonbury Ring West Sussex

6 miles N of Worthing

The beech trees that managed to survive the 1987 hurricane give the prehistoric hillfort a unique character. They were planted in the 1760s and are said to be uncountable, though if anyone is lucky enough to find the right number he will wake the ghosts of Julius Caesar and his army. Other hauntings here include an old man with a white beard, and the uncanny sound of galloping horses which never appear.

Chapmanslade Wiltshire 🐇 💀

3 miles E of Frome

Black Dog Woods to the north-west of the village are the haunt of a large dog with fiery eyes and to see him means death before Christmas. The story is of a highwayman who trained his dog to spring on coachmen as they gingerly descended the steep hill. He was easily able to rob the coach in the ensuing confusion. The coachmen soon became wise to the ploy and the highwayman was shot by a guard's blunderbuss. The Black Dogs of Wiltshire often drag chains and may be headless.

Chatham Kent

Nelson's connections with the dockyard at Chatham are less apparent than his associations with Portsmouth or Great Yarmouth, but it is here that his ghost appears, with eyes and arms intact. There is also a supernatural presence lurking in the ropewalk, and a supervisor who died four years ago returns as a ghost to haunt the flag loft, digging workers in the ribs (and not just once but several times) to make sure that they are getting on with their work. She is also glimpsed as a 'corner of the eye' apparition (an image that might be real or imaginary), in which case she desists from rib-digging.

Chilham Kent 🍺

5 miles SW of Canterbury

The White Horse pub used to be the vicarage, which is why Reverend Sampson Hievar, who died in 1677, is supposed to be the ghostly figure that enjoys sitting in the inglenook. The castle has a Grey Lady.

Cobham Surrey 🐇

4 miles NW of Leatherhead

Among the ghosts in this well-haunted village is that of a blue donkey, once seen by a party of bell ringers at St Andrew's church.

Combe Berkshire

9 miles SW of Newbury

Combe Gibbet stands at the summit of Inkpen Hill (979 feet). The bones of many a felon mouldered at this lonely spot, among them a mother and father who drowned their offspring in the dew pond close by (known as Murderers' Pool). The bodies of a carrier and his lady love also hung here for many years. They drowned the carrier's wife in the pool but their plotting was overheard by the carrier's youngest son, who betrayed them. Their unquiet spirits, with many others, linger at the top of the hill.

The manor, formerly a priory, enjoys the other-worldly sound of nuns chanting plainsong and, predictably since this is another place where Charles II enjoyed a sojourn with Nell Gwyn, figures dressed in clothes of the period have been seen in the garden.

Corsham Wiltshire ✛

The churchyard is haunted by a malevolent ghost called an elemental, an ugly dwarf about thirty inches high supposed to be the spirit of an evil monk.

Crondall Hampshire ✛ ✗ 🐑

3 miles NW of Farnham

All Saints' church was fortified and used as a Roundhead stronghold during the Civil War. The avenue of lime trees leading to the church is haunted by a man on horseback wearing armour and a foot-soldier in thigh boots and breastplate who walks into the church, kneels at the altar, and then vanishes. These soldiers may have been among those involved in a skirmish at Crondall on 27 January 1645 when six Roundheads, who had surrendered, were put to death. Crondall also has a ghostly flock of sheep and Alma Lane is haunted by the sound of running footsteps, those of the shade of a military messenger who was murdered by footpads while carrying the news of the victory at Waterloo from Portsmouth to Aldershot.

Cuckfield West Sussex 🍺

Geranium Jane is the resident ghost at the King's Head, so called because she was killed when a pot of geraniums fell on her head. Rumour had it that this was no accident and that she was carrying the child of the proprietor at the time. In support of this thesis is the occasion of her appearances: to male members of the staff indulging in extra-marital adventures.

Cuckfield

Datchet Berkshire 🍺

2 miles E of Windsor

At the Royal Stag pub a strange fingerprint sometimes appears on a window (it was photographed in 1979 and

1984). It is a remembrance of an occasion when a young boy was left outside in a blizzard while his father caroused within. There is a tombstone in the cellar (commemorating William Herbert) that always returns here if taken away from the pub.

Devizes Wiltshire ✕ 🦐

The Battle of Roundway Hill on 13 July 1643 was a famous Royalist victory for their commander, Lord Wilmott. Parliamentary forces under General Waller were besieging the town when the Royalists counterattacked and separated Waller's cavalry from his main force. Waller's cavalry was driven down a precipitous slope near Oliver's Camp, 'where never horse went down nor up before'. Eight hundred men died in what became known as Bloody Ditch, but it is ghostly horses that are seen here, and not soldiers.

Dover Kent

The castle has the ghost of a headless drummer-boy killed by robbers who were after the garrison's payroll, and those of a Roman soldier and a black monk have also been reported.

Dunnose Point Isle of Wight ⚓

1 mile E of Ventnor

On 24 March 1878 the three-masted training ship HMS *Eurydice* foundered off the Point when she was caught by a sudden violent squall with all sails set and her gun-ports open. There were only two survivors, while more than three hundred drowned. The *Eurydice* sails on as a ghost ship off Dunnose Point.

East Cowes Isle of Wight 🛩

A headless airman has been seen parachuting down to earth, a psychic memory of a wartime tragedy.

East Wellow Hampshire ✟ 🌑

8 miles NW of Southampton

Florence Nightingale is buried in St Margaret's churchyard and it is probably her ghost that is seen here and inside the church which she attended for many years. A spectral coach-and-four drives from Embley Park to the church. Midnight on New Year's Eve is the time for seeing this. Colonel William Morton, one of those who signed the death warrant of Charles I, was a native of the village and his ghost walks from the site of the old manor to the churchyard.

Eastbourne East Sussex

The shoreline midway between the town and Pevensey is known as the Crumbles (now dominated by a modern shopping centre of the same name). It used to be haunted by two murder victims, Irene Munro who was killed in 1920, and Emily Kaye who died, savagely mutilated, four years later.

The Devonshire Park Theatre is haunted by the ghost of a violinist wearing evening dress, while the Royal Hippodrome has that of a stage manager who fell from the fly door and was killed.

Eastwell Kent 🍺

1 mile N of Ashford

Eastwell Park has a phantom horseman who, on Midsummer's Eve, rides up to the house (now a hotel) from the Pilgrim's Way. He then directs his steed to the lake, where he vanishes into the water.

Eton Berkshire

The Grey Lady of the College is the wraith of Jane Shore, mistress of Edward IV, who persuaded him not to dissolve the school founded by his Lancastrian foe, Henry VI. When Jane lost royal favour, she was imprisoned. The provost and fellows gained her release and gave her quarters in Lupton's Tower facing the school yard. She died in 1526 and haunts the tower and the cloisters.

Faringdon Wiltshire ✠

The north side of the churchyard is haunted by the headless phantom of Sir Robert Pye. He was a supporter of Cromwell and besieged his father (who was on the Royalist side) in Faringdon House.

Farnham Surrey ✠

St Andrew's church has seen ghostly re-enactments of a pre-Reformation Mass.

Faversham Kent 🍺

The Shipwright's Arms at Hollowshore is remote and difficult to reach, at the end of a rough track by the side of an inlet of the Swale. Its haunting derives from an incident one Christmas Eve when the landlord was disturbed in bed by someone banging on the door of the pub. Thinking it was one of the locals he had just turned out he shouted that he would not stir for man or devil and returned to sleep. The next morning he found the body of a shipwrecked sailor on the doorstep, dead from exposure. It is the ghost of this unfortunate that haunts the pub, leaving a smell of decay in its wake. The haunting last occurred on the night of the great hurricane in October 1987.

Gatcombe Isle of Wight ✠

2 miles S of Newport

An oak effigy of a crusader rests in the sanctuary of St Olave's church, a toy dog at his feet (this is reanimated every hundred years to dance on its hind legs on Midsummer's Eve). The crusader represents Edward Estur. He belonged to the family who founded the church in 1290, and the story is that some hundreds of years later Lucy Lightfoot, a farmer's daughter, became obsessed with love for the effigy and the man it represented. She visited the church every day to spend time with her medieval lover, and was with him on 13 June 1831 when a terrible storm hit the island, followed by a total eclipse of the sun. Later that day a local farmer passed the church and found Lucy's horse tethered outside, sweating and distressed, but Lucy had vanished and was never found. The jewel and lodestone set in the hilt of the crusader's iron dagger had also disappeared. More than thirty years later a remarkable coincidence was discovered – Edward Estur had fought in the Holy Land in the fourteenth century and had been accompanied by Lucy Lightfoot of Carisbrooke. The story seems to suggest that some form of reincarnation in reverse took place, a time warp triggered by the storm and eclipse.

Golden Hill Fort Isle of Wight 🎬

1 mile N of Freshwater

The vast hexagonal fort was built to guard against Napoleonic invasion: today it is used by craftsmen and small industry. Many people have seen ghosts here, among the ghosts a sailor who enjoys watching others work and smiles as he does so, and that of a soldier dressed in First World War uniform.

Goodwin Sands Kent ⚓

4 miles offshore from Deal

The treacherous Goodwin Sands have claimed the lives of many thousands of seafarers over the years. There have been several accounts of phantom ships in these waters – the *Violet*, for example, a steam packet that sank in 1857, and the *Lady Lovibund*, a schooner that went down on 13 February 1748 with a wedding party on board. The *Lovibund* appears every fifty years, on the anniversary of the tragedy, smashing through pounding breakers. There is also a spectral galleon, a Canadian liner named the *Montrose*, and the *Shrewsbury*, a man-of-war that survived the Great Storm of 1703 when four other vessels of her squadron perished, but nonetheless returns to haunt the hazardous waters.

Gosport Hampshire

The body of Jack the Painter swung from the gibbet on Blockhouse Point for many years and the eerie squeaking of his chains is a supernatural memory of this. He was executed in 1777 for setting fire to the ropeworks in Portsmouth dockyard.

Great Shefford Berkshire

5 miles NE of Hungerford

This was the village to which Wild Darrell sent for the midwife who later testified against him (see Littlecote, below) and his ghost (with the head hanging grotesquely showing the way he died) is seen in the woodland just to the north of where the Hungerford road crosses the motorway.

Guildford Surrey 🍺

The Angel Hotel is haunted by a ghost wearing a uniform like that of a Polish army officer in the early 1900s.

Hastings East Sussex

Little remains today of the castle dating from 1069, but on occasion it is reincarnated and appears floating in the sky above the sea, 'young and bright, with standards fluttering in the breeze'.

Havant Hampshire

Gypsies' Clump is a part of Havant Forest just to the north of the town. It is haunted by the spectre of a hard-drinking poacher called Charlie Pearce who lived at Rowlands Castle. One night he drank too freely from the kettle of gin he carried with him and was swept off his horse by an overhanging bough that ruptured his windpipe. His ghost is easily identified by the weals seen on his throat.

Herstmonceux East Sussex ☞

9 miles W of Hastings

The castle has many ghosts and even more reasons for their presence there. The phantom drummer may be the ghost of the elderly, reclusive Lord Dacre who was said to beat a drum to scare prospective lovers away from his young wife. However, the giant figure on the battlements, glowing with fluorescence and beating sparks from his drum, is more likely to have been a device invented by smugglers to keep the curious away from the abandoned castle at the end of the eighteenth century. The Grey Lady is the ghost of a girl starved to death by her governess, while a White Lady is that of a girl who drowned herself in the moat rather than suffer at the hands of the wicked baron. Herstmonceux's most unusual ghosts are those of a sleepwalking man and a woman on a white ass.

Hever Castle Kent ♛

7 miles W of Tonbridge

Anne Boleyn's family home was Hever Castle (open to the public) where Henry VIII came to court her. The ghost of the ill-fated queen – she lost her head at the age of twenty-one – may be seen on the bridge over the River Eden on Christmas Eve.

Highworth Wiltshire ✠

6 miles N of Swindon

A ghost haunting St Michael's church has been described as having no features on its face except sunken dark shadows where the eyes should be. This is often a daytime ghost and has been seen both inside and outside the church.

Hinton Ampner Hampshire

7 miles E of Winchester

The old manor was so badly haunted that its owners, after years of sleepless nights caused by noisy spirits, pulled it down. The haunting was put down to the alliance of Lord Stawell with his sister-in-law Honoria, with whom he lived after the death of his wife in 1740. Village gossip had it that a child was born of this union and then disappeared. However, both Lord Stawell and Honoria lived on happily at Hinton Ampner until Honoria died in 1754, his lordship dying a year later. In death the couple abandoned the apparent equanimity of their earthly life and rowed continually. This, with slamming doors, heavy overhead footsteps, and the occasional apparition, caused the abandonment of the house and its eventual demolition in 1793. Significantly, a child's skull was found when the fabric was being pulled down. Only the stables and walled garden of the old house now remain and a new house, the present National Trust property (open to the public), was built about fifty yards away. This proved to be ghost-free, though some sensitive souls report feelings of disquiet in the magnolia garden, where the walls of the old manor used to stand.

Icklesham East Sussex 🍺

4 miles SW of Rye

Icklesham

The Queen's Head is haunted by the ghost of a landlord named Gutsell who enjoyed the party held at his wake so much (his coffin was brought into the bar) that he proved reluctant to leave the premises. His shadowy figure is often seen by the fireplace chewing a stub of straw.

Ightham Mote Kent

4 miles E of Sevenoaks

Dame Dorothy Selby gave a warning to Lord Monteagle to stay away from Parliament on 5 November 1605, and this led not only to the discovery of the Gunpowder Plot but also to Dame Dorothy's death, it is said, at the hands of Guy Fawkes, who had her immured in a secret room here. The beautiful house (open to the public) is haunted by her ghost.

Kemsing Kent ✠ 🌑

3 miles NE of Sevenoaks

A spectral knight in armour gallops up to the church at Kemsing on the night of 29 December and, having tied up his horse, walks down the church to the altar and kneels in prayer for a moment before disappearing. This is supposed to be the ghost of one of the four knights who murdered Thomas à Becket at Canterbury Cathedral in 1170.

Kilmington Wiltshire ✠ 🐎

7 miles S of Frome

The churchyard is haunted by Lord Stourton who, with a villainous gang that also appears, murdered William Hartgill, his father's steward. Stourton was hanged at Salisbury in 1557 (see also Salisbury, below). The victim haunts the church itself and the village also has the ghost of a headless horse seen in Bull Lane.

Leatherhead Surrey

A spectral anchorite – a hermit-like monk confined to a small room within a church – haunts the parish church of Ss Mary & Nicholas.

Leeds Castle Kent 🐾

5 miles E of Maidstone

The Black Dog of Leeds is generally considered to be a harbinger of misfortune to those who live in the castle (open to the public), though on one occasion its appearance seems to have been instrumental in saving the life of a resident. This lady was sitting in one of the Tudor window bays overhanging the moat when the Black Dog appeared. Thinking it was real she moved from her seat to pet it only to see it walk past her to disappear through the wall. At the same moment the alcove where she had been seated broke away from the surrounding masonry and crashed into the moat. It has been suggested that the animal is the ghost of a familiar of the Duchess of Gloucester, imprisoned here for witchcraft in the fifteenth century.

Lewes East Sussex 🌑

Anne of Cleves' House contains a museum of domestic artefacts as well as the famous Knights Table that once belonged to the deanery at South Malling. Legend has it that Thomas à Becket's killers came to the deanery after the murder and threw their cloaks and accoutrements on the table. Repeatedly the table, made of a slab of Petworth marble, threw its burden to the ground, and on 29 December each year the table is supposed to whirl itself round and speak the words, 'Remember poor Thomas!' Many people find the atmosphere at Anne of Cleves' House psychically oppressive with the Tapestry Room noted for its cold spots. An apparition of an old lady is often seen and there is another of a young woman who hangs on a rope from a beam.

Liphook Hampshire 🍺

The Royal Anchor is haunted by the ghost of a highwayman, Captain Jack or Jacques, cornered and shot in one of the bedrooms.

Littlecote House Wiltshire

2 miles W of Hungerford

There are more than twenty ghosts at this great, sprawling old house, the home of Peter de Savary (and open to the public), making it one of the top five haunted houses of Britain. In 1575 Littlecote belonged to William Darrell, whose family had lived here since 1415. One of the great scandals of the Elizabethan age began when Darrell sent for a midwife from a nearby village. At the dead of night she was blindfolded and then driven off to a house where she was taken to an upstairs room and the blindfold was removed. In the room a woman was in labour, a nobleman with her. When the baby was born the man snatched it from the midwife's arms and threw it to the back of the blazing fire. He then gave the midwife a purse of money and ordered that she be blindfolded again and driven home. However, she had torn off a piece of the bedcovering and hidden it in her clothes, and as she was lead downstairs she counted them. This gave her evidence to offer the magistrate to whom she told her story the next day. The squire of Littlecote already had the nickname 'Wild Darrell' because of his debauchery and it came as little surprise when the clues offered by the midwife identified Littlecote as the house to which she had been taken. Darrell was arrested, but bribed the judge to acquit him, and lived on for fourteen more years before being killed by a fall from his horse (popularly supposed to have been caused by an appearance of the babe's ghost).

Littlecote House

John Aubrey wrote of the episode a century later in *Brief Lives* and stated that it was believed that the child's mother was Darrell's wife's maid. However, it was said locally that the mother was Darrell's sister, which gave a stronger reason for his drastic behaviour. This naturally spawned a host of ghost stories. Wild William appears at the stile where he was killed, sometimes on horseback and accompanied by phantom hounds, but in a coach when an heir to Littlecote is about to die. A sad-faced woman walks in the room where the murder was committed, holding a baby.

Another ghostly woman, this time seen in the garden, is connected with a second story of a baby's death. Soon after Peter de Savary bought Littlecote in 1985, a sale of effects of the previous owner was held after the house had been turned out. On the morning of the sale, de Savary, walking in the grounds, was confronted by a lady dressed in a tweed skirt and fashionable sweater, 'just like a lady you would find in Hungerford doing her shopping', he told *Hello!* magazine in October 1993. He greeted her and was about to walk on when she stopped him, saying that he was a wicked man and, with his family, would suffer for what he had done. Extremely puzzled, he enquired how he had upset her.

'You have taken my baby's things,' she replied, and he answered that if any of his staff had indeed moved anything then he would immediately see that it was restored to her. 'No, I cannot have them,' she replied, and then went on to explain where the clothes were, and the rightful place they belonged.

De Savary said that he understood her instructions and would see that they were carried out immediately. With that assurance given the ghost smiled, said: 'You and your family will be blessed in this house for ever,' and vanished.

Remarkably the missing clothes were found, with a sketch of a baby's face and below it the words: 'Early in the morning of Friday,

June 21st, 1861. Calm & cold – oh so beautiful.' Another note, still kept at the house, has slits to hold the stems of flowers and the inscription: 'Gathered at Baby's Grave, July 23rd 1861.' All these items were replaced as the ghost had instructed.

In the chapel at Littlecote there is a charming cast of a sleeping baby, the memorial to the child which its mother later drew, calm and cold and beautiful.

Littlecote's remaining ghosts come as something of an anti-climax after these. On a dark, wet night in the summer of 1993, a stunt-rider appearing in a tournament encountered a figure beckoning to her. The figure was faceless, wore a robe and cowl and was 'blacker than black'. A legion of Roman soldiers marches through the park, and the ghost of Gerald Lee Bevin, who was a tenant of Littlecote in the 1920s when he served seven years for a famous City swindle, also haunts the place.

Perhaps it is not surprising to hear that Peter de Savary and his family have learned to come to terms with their ghosts, though there are areas of the house best left alone at night. 'There's a kind of aura, a mutual respect, a territorial respect. We imagine they are saying: "That's fine, you de Savarys can enjoy that part of the house, but please don't come and disturb us in the other parts." So we don't go to those parts after dark. We've made a deal.'

Longleat House Wiltshire

3 miles SW of Frome

The Green Lady of Longleat House (which is open to the public) is the spirit of Lady Louisa Carteret, the unhappy wife of the second Viscount Weymouth who came to his title in 1714. He must have been an unpleasant man to live with, arrogant and ill-tempered, and perhaps it was because of this that his wife took a footman as a lover. When the viscount discovered her infidelity he threw the servant from the top of the stairs to the flagstones far below. The body was buried beneath these flags and sure enough a skeleton was found under them in 1915. Lady Louisa died in childbirth on Christmas Day 1736 and still roams the corridors of Longleat, looking either for happiness or for her long-dead lover.

Loseley House Surrey

2 miles SW of Guildford

The house (open to the public) dates from the sixteenth century and is haunted by a Brown Lady whose portrait hangs here. There is also a Grey Lady; she may be the ghost of a woman who murdered her stepson so that her own son might inherit the house.

Lydiard Millicent Wiltshire 🕐

3 miles W of Swindon

Lady Blunt appears in the garden of the manor each year on 30 October. This is the anniversary of a murder she witnessed two hundred years ago. She was betrothed to a curate and tragically saw him murdered at the Rectory. She subsequently married Sir Ferdinando Blunt.

Lymington Hampshire 🍺

The Angel Hotel has the ghosts of a coachman who appears early in the morning, a phantom sailor, and a blonde girl dressed in white who haunts the second floor.

Lympne Kent

7 miles W of Folkestone

At night footsteps ascend the main tower of Lympne Castle (open to the public) but are never heard to come down. They are supposed to come from the spirit of a Roman soldier killed by a fall from the tower. The ghosts of six Saxon villagers, killed by their Norman overlords in reprisal for their raids on baggage trains, haunt the countryside around.

Margate Kent

The Theatre Royal is a venue for two ghosts, most often seen in January – the shade of an early impresario, Sarah Thorne, and that of an actor who threw himself to his death from one of the boxes.

Meopham Kent

9 miles NW of Maidstone

A lady dressed in orange is said to walk Steel Lane. She was a French woman who followed her soldier-lover to England after the French wars and, having been rejected by him, hanged herself. A headless figure also walks in the village, from the inn to the church.

Michelham Priory East Sussex 👑 🐎

6 miles N of Eastbourne

The Grey Lady gazes sadly into the moat where she drowned, while the apparition of King Harold wanders off in the vague direction of Battle Abbey (see above), where he also appears. There is also a spectral monk, a Blue Lady, and a ghostly white stallion which in days gone by would frighten the horses in the stables.

Netley Hampshire 🕐

3 miles SE of Southampton

Only the chapel remains of the Royal Victoria Military Hospital which abounded in ghosts up to, and during, its demolition in 1966. The most unwelcome was the Grey Lady who often appeared to a patient about to die.

Visit Netley Abbey on Hallowe'en night and you may see Blind Peter, a ghostly Cistercian monk who guards the abbey's hidden treasure. This is said to be concealed at the end of a long tunnel, once explored by a man named Slown who was frightened literally to death by what he found.

North Tidworth Wiltshire

4 miles N of Andover

The sprawling army camp is haunted by a soldier, who is either a Highlander in a kilt or a Roman soldier. Evidence for the latter is based on a Roman pavement being found here in 1836. The neighbouring village of South Tidworth was the scene of famous poltergeist activity in the seventeenth century caused by a demon drummer. An itinerant drummer was arrested by a local magistrate who confiscated his drum and committed him to Gloucester gaol. This triggered disturbances at the magistrates house in South Tidworth which went on for twenty years.

Penshurst Place Kent

5 miles SW of Tonbridge

A woman in Elizabethan dress climbs the stairs of Penshurst Place (open to the public) and she may be the same ghost as that haunting the lime avenue. Sir Philip Sidney's ghost is also supposed to walk here, though this has been denied by the owner of Penshurst, Viscount de l'Isle.

Petworth West Sussex 🍺

The Angel Hotel is haunted by an old lady who once sat by the inglenook waiting for her friend to come downstairs. Unhappily, on her way downstairs the awaited lady slipped and was killed in the fall. Overcome by shock the old lady herself died two days later and her ghost returns to sit in the same chair she occupied when the accident occurred.

Pevensey Castle East Sussex ✕

4 miles north east of Eastbourne

The ruins of the Roman stronghold (open to the public) are the haunt of Lady Pelham who died in the fourteenth century and whose ghost glides over the ramparts. She bravely resisted a besieging army while her husband was absent from the castle. There are also reports of a great army, seen by moonlight as it winds its way across the surrounding marshes, and the sounds of battle, ringing out from below the castle's ancient walls.

Pluckley Kent

5 miles W of Ashford

Some writers claim this to be the most haunted village in England. Its fourteen ghosts are: a White Lady at the site of the old Manor House; another White Lady in the churchyard where there is also a Red Lady who seeks her unshriven child; a white dog in the church itself; a Cavalier put to death by Roundheads in the village; a smiling monk who sometimes accompanies a lady ghost from Rose Court; a phantom schoolmaster in Dicky Buss Lane who committed suicide; a miller's ghost at the old mill, where there is also the shade of a gypsy woman who fell asleep with her pipe alight and so caused a fire in which she was burned to death; a highwayman who was cornered at Fright Corner, run through with a sword and left pinned to a tree to die a lingering death; a spectral colonel who walks Park Wood; a phantom coach-and-four that travels the road to Smarden, and a brickmaker who fell into the clay pit and smothered – this last haunts Brick Walk.

Polesden Lacey Surrey

4 miles SW of Leatherhead

This National Trust property (open to the public) has two ghosts. The first is a conventional figure who wears a brown garment with a hood and is seen on the bridge that takes the drive over a sunken right of way, and the second is a strange sonic manifestation described as being like a whistling whirlwind, most often heard on the Nun's Walk in the wood near the terrace.

Portsmouth Hampshire 🍺

The White Swan in Guildhall Walk has the spectre of a Victorian barmaid who was murdered by her sailor husband. Next door is the Theatre Royal where a dressing room is haunted by the actor who slit his throat here in the 1880s.

Pyecombe West Sussex

5 miles N of Brighton

The old road past the village was haunted by a young girl killed in a road accident. Whether this ghost remains active on the new road is unknown. November 23 used to see the celebration of the successful exorcism of the village smithy, once a haunt of witches.

Quarr Abbey Isle of Wight 👑

2 miles W of Ryde

The ruins of the original monastery are situated half a mile from the modern Benedictine abbey and are haunted by the ghost of Eleanor of Aquitaine, wife of Henry II and mother of Richard I and John. She was banished to Quarr for some years by her husband, but died in France in 1204. Legend says she was buried here in a coffin of gold.

Reculver Kent ⊕

7 miles W of Margate

The place has a Saxon church built on the site of a Roman fort. Babies' skeletons were found here during an archaeological dig, perhaps explaining accounts of ghostly cries having been heard.

A fight between an exciseman named Gill (who was killed) and a smuggler is re-enacted on the cliff edge.

Richborough Castle Kent

2 miles N of Sandwich

The impressive Roman fort (open to the public) is haunted by ghostly legionaries.

Rochester Kent 🌐

Charles Dickens loved the city and wished to be buried in the old graveyard by the west door of the cathedral. His fame, however, meant a final resting place in Westminster Abbey, but his ghost haunts here. His ghost is also supposed to be seen on Christmas Eve outside the Corn Exchange, where he sets the hands of his watch as the time approaches midnight. The castle (open to the public) has a White Lady who appears on Good Friday, the anniversary of her death in 1264. She is the shade of Lady Blanche de Warenne, who was accidentally killed by an arrow in the heart shot by Ralph de Capo (her betrothed) when the castle was besieged by Simon de Montfort.

Rodbourne Cheney Wiltshire

1 mile N of Swindon

The ghost of a Mrs Dyer, hanged in 1896, walks from her cottage to the churchyard carrying a baby.

Romsey Hampshire 🍺

The upper floors of the Palmerston restaurant, which faces the statue of the statesman in the marketplace, are haunted by the ghost of a white-haired old man who has been named Charlie by staff. Close by is the Swan Inn where, during the Civil War, two Roundheads were hanged from the sign bracket. Their agonised death-throes have been heard.

Rye East Sussex 🍺 🕐

The Mermaid, one of Britain's oldest and most famous hostelries, has the supernatural re-enactment of a duel in which one antagonist is eventually run through by the other's rapier. The body of the dead swordsman is then dragged to a corner of the room and lowered through a trapdoor. These events are supposed to take place each year on 29 October. In the town hall a gibbet cage still contains a fragment of the skull of John Breeds, hanged for a botched murder in 1743. He killed the brother-in-law of his intended victim, who returns to haunt the scene of the crime, Lamb House (open to the public). Rye also has phantom monks who were responsible for immuring one of their brethren. The walled-up monk cursed them before he went mad (making gobbling sounds like a turkey) and died. The monks walk near the chapel of the Austin Friars on Conduit Hill, while the strange noises made by their dying colleague are still heard in Turkey Cock Lane.

Salisbury Wiltshire 🐰 ⊕

White birds are said to gather around the spire of the cathedral when the bishop is about to die. This phenomenon was first recorded in 1414 as 'the great sign of the birds', and was noted too in 1885 and 1911. Within the cathedral St Ormond's tomb is remarkable for containing the body of a murderer as well as saintly remains. Lord Stourton was executed in Salisbury marketplace on 16 March 1557, the hangman using a silken noose as a concession to the peer. However, it was a wire noose that was hung above the tomb as a reminder of Stourton's fate. Although this was removed in 1780 its fluorescent outline has been seen since on several occasions floating above the tomb (see also Kilmington, above).

Scotney Castle Kent

6 miles SE of Tunbridge Wells

The Darrell family owned the castle in the eighteenth century. One of them, involved in smuggling, killed a revenue man and threw his body into the moat. It is the dripping figure of the revenue man that haunts the ruins (open to the public).

Selborne Hampshire 🐎

3 miles SW of Alton

The ghost of the great naturalist Gilbert White has been seen in the garden of the cottage he inhabited. (However, since there are believed to be no surviving likenesses of White, it may not be him at all.) Ghostly monks, and a phantom hound, haunt the environs of the priory. The hound is the shade of a dog that was the inseparable companion of a racehorse trained at Selborne a century ago. The dog was killed in an accident at the farm near the priory and now haunts the priory looking for its former friend.

Semley Wiltshire

5 miles E of Shaftesbury

Pyt House (open to the public) was the home of the Bennett Stanford family. The skeleton preserved here belonged to Molly, a housemaid who was hanged for the fatal scalding of her daughter, born out of wedlock but whose father was said to be 'one of the family'. Betty's bones have been allowed to leave the house on only three occasions. On the first a wing of the mansion caught fire; on the second the son and heir died; and on the third the only daughter died, so that the branch of the family died out.

Sissinghurst Castle Kent

3 miles NE of Cranbrook

Sir Harold Nicholson, whose wife Vita Sackville-West created the famous garden (open to the public), often spoke of meeting a revenant priest walking its fragrant paths. The gentle priest may have been one of the victims of Bloody Baker, Sir John Baker who built the castle and was accused of torturing and killing hundreds of Protestants during the reign of Queen Mary.

Southampton Hampshire

Ghostly Roman soldiers haunt the area around Bitterne Manor close to the new Northam Bridge across the River Itchen.

Stanton St Bernard Wiltshire

4 miles E of Devizes

In the early years of the nineteenth century the wife of the farmer who lived in the manor died. Before dying she asked that she be buried wearing all her fine rings. The sexton heard of this, and after the funeral went to the vault and opened up the coffin. He tried to remove the rings from the fingers, but when this proved difficult began severing the fingers with a knife. At this the 'corpse' awoke, rose from her coffin and, taking his lantern, made her way back to the manor where she made a sensational reappearance, blood dripping from the stumps of her fingers, in the doorway of the dining room. This scene is re-enacted on the anniversary of the premature funeral.

Stonehenge Wiltshire 🔖

Quite close to the stones there is a monument to Captain B. Lorraine and Staff Sergeant R. Wilson who died here in 1912 when their aircraft crashed. They were the first members of the Royal Flying Corps to lose their lives. Just before D-Day Sir Michael Bruce drove past Stonehenge with several companions. They all saw a plane crash into a small wood but when they searched the area all they found was the memorial. Coincidentally, the aviation pioneer Colonel F.S. Cody also died after crashing close by.

Sunninghill Berkshire 🍺

5 miles S of Windsor

The prestigious Berystede Hotel incorporates the country mansion built for the Standish family after a fire in 1886 destroyed the original house. Eliza Kleininger, Mrs Standish's French maid, died in the blaze and her ghost haunts the modern hotel.

Thames Ditton Surrey

2 miles SW of Kingston-upon-Thames

The Home of Compassion is a nursing home for the elderly, formerly run by Benedictine nuns. There have been many reports of ghostly nuns in grey robes (usually in the area of the chapel) as well as sightings of ghostly dogs and children.

Tidmarsh Berkshire

5 miles W of Reading

In June when there is a clear full moon the ghost of a boy who was drowned in the little River Pang may be seen rising from its waters near the rectory.

Totton Hampshire 🐾

3 miles W of Southampton

Testwood House is now offices but was once a hunting lodge used by Henry VIII. It is well haunted, having a spectral dog and the sounds of a spirit-driven coach as well as more random ghosts such as faces peering from windows and the inexplicable rattling of doors. There is a tradition that the cook was murdered by another member of staff at the house and that her ghost haunts here, but the apparition of a male figure has also been seen.

Trottiscliffe Kent 🐾

4 miles W of Maidstone

The Pilgrims' Way is haunted hereabouts by a gigantic dog. Note that the village is pronounced 'Trosley'.

Uppark West Sussex

5 miles SE of Petersfield

The house is now immaculately restored (by the National Trust; now open to the public) after the terrible fire in 1989. Whether this affected the activities of its ghost is so far unknown, for Uppark was previously haunted by the benign presence of Sir Harry Fetherstonhaugh. He 'discovered' the fifteen-year-old beauty who later became Lady Hamilton, and was a great friend himself of the Prince Regent. In his seventies he married a dairymaid from the estate. He died in 1846 aged ninety-two and, before the place caught fire, his ghost frequented the Red Room.

Verdley Castle
West Sussex 🐾

3 miles NE of Midhurst

Little remains of the castle here, which has the ghost of the last wild bear to be killed in England.

Vernham Dean
Hampshire

7 miles NW of Andover

The village is haunted by the ghost of a vicar who deserted his parishioners when the Plague struck in 1665. His spirit is the shadowy bent figure seen struggling up Conholt Hill, where the villagers fled after the first deaths.

Verdley Castle

Warblington Hampshire

1 mile SE of Havant

The headless shade of Margaret Pole, Countess of Salisbury, the old lady who led the executioner such a dance at the Tower of London (see Greater London; and St Leonards, South Midlands), haunts the ruins of the castle and the churchyard. The castle is also visited by a smuggler's ghost. The Old Rectory in Pook Lane, once Spook Lane, stands on the site of the parsonage famously haunted by a whistling ghost in 1695. The culprit was supposed to be a wicked former parson who had fathered bastard children on his maid and then murdered them.

Wardour Castle Wiltshire

5 miles NE of Shaftesbury

Blanche, Lady Arundel, is the ghostly figure who may be seen walking from the ruined castle (open to the public) to the lake at dusk. The redoubtable sixty-year-old lead the defence of the castle when it was besieged for five days by 1300 Roundheads. At this point, threatened by mines and petards, a truce was agreed. The arrangement was betrayed by Cromwell's troops and Lady Blanche, with her small garrison of twenty-five men, was brutally put to the sword.

Warlingham Surrey

6 miles SE of Croydon

Slines Green pond is haunted by the ghosts of passengers on a stagecoach whose horses, frightened by a highwayman, bolted, taking the coach into the pond and drowning its occupants.

Waterlooville Hampshire

6 miles N of Portsmouth

Hopfield House is a large, Victorian Gothic house which had the reputation of being dangerously haunted. Its first owner resented the idea of anyone living here apart from his descendants and it seems that his malevolent spirit made life intolerable for occupiers of the house after his family left, causing two of them to commit suicide. There have been no recent reports of a malevolent spirit and the house is now divided into flats. The area of Ferndale in Waterlooville is haunted by the ghost of an old drover who hanged himself from an oak tree about a hundred and fifty years ago. He appears as a brooding, besmocked figure smoking a pipe, and when he disappears the smell of his tobacco lingers on.

Waverley Abbey Surrey

2 miles SE of Farnham

The tranquil grounds (open to the public) are frequented by a ghostly monk who was hanged, drawn and quartered – locals believe he is looking for his missing entrails.

West Clandon Surrey

3 miles NE of Guildford

The grand house (open to the public) was built by Leoni for the second Lord Onslow. He got his fortune from his wife, Elisabeth Knight, who died before the house was completed. Her ghost walks here, a dark lady dressed in cream satin.

West Kennett Wiltshire ● ➴

4 miles W of Marlborough

The long barrow here, a Neolithic tomb, is one of the finest to be seen in Britain and is close to Avebury stone circle as well as Silbury Hill (the largest manmade mound in Europe). A ghostly priest enters the tomb at sunrise on Midsummer Day accompanied by a white dog which, uniquely, has red ears.

West Malling Kent ⛏

5 miles W of Maidstone

The airfield was often bombed during the Second World War and many people died. A phantom airman haunts the site, wearing full

Battle of Britain flying gear. In *Ghost Stations*, the first of Bruce Halpenny's series of books on haunted airfields, he writes of the strange 'ghostly brick' which often hit security vehicles in the middle of the airfield where no intruder could hide. Halpenny suggests it may reflect an incident when a Spitfire pilot made an emergency landing. The landing was successful but as the plane came to a halt it scraped a wall. A brick was thrown through the windscreen, killing the pilot.

West Stoke West Sussex

3 miles NW of Chichester

About a mile to the north of the village is Kingley Vale, the finest yew forest in Europe and also one of the most sinister of places. The trees are said to be memorials at the graves of warriors who fell in a battle between Saxons and Vikings in 894. It is easy to feel that their ghosts haunt the gloomy woods.

Weybridge Surrey

The site of Brooklands, the famous prewar racing track, is haunted by a figure in helmet and goggles who may be the ghost of Percy Lambert, killed at the end of the railway straight when a tyre burst during a record-breaking attempt.

Willingdon East Sussex

2 miles NE of Eastbourne

The London road goes through this village on the outskirts of Eastbourne. The road is haunted by a lady wearing the coat and veil of an Edwardian motorist. She attempts to stop motorists to warn them of the accident in which she, with two male companions, was killed. Another version maintains that she was a golfer killed in a car crash in the 1920s.

Winchelsea East Sussex ✠

A black man in a red uniform haunts the churchyard, where the ghosts of two highwaymen hanged at Tyburn in 1782, the Weston brothers, have also been reported.

Winchester Hampshire 🍺 ✠

Dame Alice Lisle sheltered two rebels from Monmouth's defeated army at her house, Moyles Court, near Ringwood. When they were discovered the old lady was brought before Judge Jeffreys and condemned to be dragged through the streets on a hurdle before being burned at the stake. Public outcry led to the sentence being reduced to simple decapitation, and she stepped out to the scaffold from the window of the Eclipse Inn at Winchester on 2 September 1685. She haunts both the Eclipse and Moyles Court, always with her head still on her shoulders.

The cathedral close is haunted by a monk who limps, and a remarkable photograph taken in the cathedral in 1957 showed thirteen spectral figures standing in front of the altar. The Theatre Royal is haunted by John Simpkins who, with his brother James, founded the theatre in 1913. The cells below Castle Hall house a figure in a frock coat and tricorn hat who vanishes through walls.

Windsor Berkshire ♛

Windsor Castle

Herne the Hunter is reputed to roam the royal golf course. Herne was a keeper wounded while rescuing Richard II from an enraged stag. Driven insane by the pain of his injuries, the keeper killed the animal and tore off its antlers, holding them above his head as he ran about the forest. Eventually he hanged himself from an oak tree close to the castle. This tree was cut down in 1796, after which hauntings ceased until Edward VII planted a replacement. Ainsworth (in *The Romance of Windsor Castle*) gave the ghost a blue phosphoric light and a red-eyed owl perching on its arm. Henry VIII is supposed to have seen the ghost, while twentieth-century sightings speak of Herne as a galloping horseman who appears on the eve of national disaster (he was seen just before war broke out in 1939 and before the death of George VI in 1952). In 1976 a young guardsman posted on the east terrace of Windsor Castle to guard the royal apartments was found unconscious. When he came to he swore that he had seen a statue grow horns and come to life.

The castle (open to the public) is haunted by Elizabeth I (in the Library), George III (his face is seen at the window of the locked room where he spent the years of his insanity), and Henry VIII (the sounds of a lame man painfully walking in the cloisters are heard near the deanery). The deanery itself is visited by the ghost of a young boy who cries, 'I don't want to go riding today.'

Theatre Royal

The original theatre burned down in 1908 and a girl in the gallery named Charlotte died in the blaze. She is the ghost that haunts the rebuilt theatre.

Worthing West Sussex 🎺

The Connaught Theatre is walked by a Grey Lady wearing Elizabethan costume and ghostly piano music has also been heard.

Yattendon Berkshire

7 miles north east of Newbury

Hippisley Coxe in *Haunted Britain* wrote that the happy spirit haunting the Old Rectory was the most charming ghost in Britain. Sometimes she wore grey silk, sometimes black, but she enjoyed parties and she helped the household by finding concealed hens' nests and performing other chores where psychic gifts were an advantage. Unaccountably she was exorcised from the house and her cheerful presence ended.

Greater London

Anne Boleyn

There is an amazing diversity to the ghosts of London. They range from the phantom omnibus which roamed the streets of Kensington to the ghostly featherless chicken of Highgate, the result of an early experiment in food preservation carried out by Francis Bacon, Lord Chancellor of England.

The Tower of London must rank at the head of any list of haunted locations. As well as an array of royal and noble ghosts it has the spectre of a bear, a reminder that not only was the cruel sport of bear-baiting carried out here, but that monarchs often had their own private zoos at their palaces. Shades of royalty also walk at Hampton Court. At Lambeth Palace Anne Boleyn is seen embarking on the skiff that took her downriver to her execution at the Tower (where her ghost also haunts the Chapel Royal).

London's more humble ghosts include the pathetic phantom of Sarah Whitehead at the Bank of England. Her brother, an employee of the bank, was executed for forgery in 1811. Sarah refused to accept that he was dead and visited the bank each day for the next twenty-five years asking after him. After her own death her ghost, dressed in a dark Regency silk dress, continued the quest and is still seen in the environs of the Bank.

Acton W3 ✠ ✟

Although built only in 1870, St Dunstan's church is haunted by ghostly monks.

Addington 🍴

4 miles SE of Croydon

Addington Palace, the home of the Royal School of Church Music, is haunted by Archbishop Edward Benson, while the more modern part of the village has the ghost of a German pilot who was killed when he bailed out of his aircraft during the Second World War.

'Digger Harry' haunts Beare's Wood, now a scouts' campsite. About two hundred years ago he lived in a delapidated cottage here with his wife. When she died of old age Harry said nothing, but buried her where she would still be close to him. When her disappearance was noticed, Harry was brought to trial for murder and, though found guilty, served only six months in gaol because of his great age. When he returned to Beare's Wood, Harry found that he had forgotten where he had buried his wife, and died of a broken heart. Digger Harry's ghost was first reported in 1932. The scouts' liking for ghostly yarns told in the light of the campfire mean that the legend will probably endure, and that Digger Harry will continue its search for the lost grave for some time to come.

Baker Street NW1 🍺

The Volunteer pub at the northern end of the street stands on the site of a medieval manor house owned by the Nevill family. The entire family perished when their house burned down in 1654 and the spirit of Rupert Nevill lingers to haunt the pub, lurking in the dark recesses of the cellar dressed in surcoat, breeches and fancy stockings. At 228 Baker Street (228B was Sherlock Holmes's address), the London Transport electrical sub-station is haunted by the shade of Sarah Siddons, the great actress, whose home once stood on the site (see also Lancaster, North West England).

Bank of England EC2

The small enclosed garden at the centre of the building is haunted by the ghost of Sarah Whitehead who died in 1836. Her brother was a bank employee who was convicted and hanged for forgery in 1811. Sarah could not accept this and she visited the bank each day for the next twenty-five years asking after him. There is also the gigantic ghost of a cashier who was nearly eight feet tall. He was morbidly terrified of his body being taken by resurrectionists after his death and persuaded the governors to allow him to be buried within the bank precincts. During alterations a lead coffin nearly eight feet long and bound with an iron chain was found.

Bellingham SE6

Alice Grant was knocked off her bicycle by a brewery dray on
2 September 1898 and her distinctive ghost haunts the spot.
She wears a white blouse with leg-of-mutton sleeves and a long
black skirt.

Berkeley Square W1

Number 50 is one of the most famous haunted houses in Britain. It
has been occupied by Maggs Brothers, the antiquarian booksellers,
for many years and little has been heard of its ghost in the present
century, though tales used to abound. The house seems to have
acquired its reputation in 1859 when a Mr Myers took the lease. He
was jilted by his bride-to-be and spent the next twenty years as a
recluse occupying just one room. In 1879 it was said that the house
had a room that was supernaturally fatal to mind and body and
articles were written for popular magazines detailing the horrible
deaths various tenants had suffered at the hands of the evil spirit.
However, many of these stories seem to have been inspired by
Bulwer-Lytton's chilling story *The House and the Brain*, published
in 1859 when Mr Myers first came to the house.

Bexley

Hall Place, the headquarters of the local library, is the ancient
manor house dating from 1537. Its ghosts pre-date this, however,
one of them being the Black Prince who appears at dusk in shiny
black armour (fortunately only rarely) to foretell death and
destruction. His wife Joan (the Fair Maid of Kent) came from the
neighbourhood and he is supposed to have stayed at the medieval
manor before embarking for Crécy. Lady Limerick, who lived here
from 1917 to 1943, saw the Prince's ghost on four occasions and
each portended a family sorrow or a defeat for the British army.
Hall Place also has a White Lady, a wraith who saw her husband
killed whilst stag hunting, and the ghost of an unhappy
maidservant in an attic.

Biggin Hill ●

6 miles SE of Croydon

A Spitfire is the other-worldly manifestation at the airfield here.
The sound of its engine is heard as it makes an approach, usually
on 19 January, though it was on a summer's day in 1987 when
Patrick Muirhead, a London radio presenter, saw the ghostly
aircraft. He was piloting a light aircraft on one of his first solo
flights and thought that the Spitfire was a real one. However, when
he returned and mentioned the incident to his instructor he was
told that no Spitfires had been aloft that day and that the machine
he saw could only have been the ghost.

Blackheath SE3, SE9

Hare and Billet Road
The shade of a darkly dressed Victorian lady waits for her lover here and may be seen on misty autumnal evenings. When he failed to make the rendezvous she hanged herself from the branch of a great elm tree by the road.

St John's Park
The public library is housed in the former vicarage which, in 1874, was the home of Elsie Marshall when her father became the incumbent. She grew up to be a missionary and was killed by bandits in China in 1895. Her spirit returned to her home in Blackheath where she had been so happy as a child and the librarians know it is her spirit that they can feel brushing past them as they replace the books in the stacks.

Shooters Hill
A White Lady haunts the junction with Well Hall Road. Her skeleton was found nearby in 1844 and the savage wound that had matted the golden hair at the back of her head proved that she had been murdered.

Bow Road E3 🍺

The original Black Swan pub was destroyed in 1916 in one of the first Zeppelin raids on London. Four people were killed including Cissie and Sylvia Reynolds, the pretty daughters of the landlord. Their ghosts haunt the present Black Swan and are held responsible when anything goes wrong there.

British Museum WC1 💀

Exhibit 22542 is an Egyptian mummy-case of a singer to the priesthood of Amen-Ra and from the time of its discovery in the 1880s it steadily built up a horrendous reputation. By the time it reached the museum its evil influence was reckoned to have caused thirteen deaths, one of them a photographer. Once on display here its malevolence continued – another photographer died on seeing his photographs of the case, and attendants were reluctant to stay in the gallery with it. It was said that the body inside the case had been shipped to America and caused the sinking of the *Empress of Ireland* in the St Lawrence. Sir Ernest Budge, Keeper of Egyptian Antiquities, was on record as saying that the mummy case had an influence on the outbreak of war in 1914. In 1921 the exhibit was exorcised by two young men famous for their psychic power and they persuaded the familiar spirit, which had been attached to the case as a protection, to leave. This entity was like a jellyfish with a flat face, and the story might well have inspired *Ghostbusters*.

A similar story comes from a time when, many years ago, I was helping a colleague take photographs in the museum for an encyclopedia of art. One of the objects to be photographed was an African mask made of wood and dried grass. As my colleague placed this in front of the camera his hand began to bleed profusely from a deep gash. We examined the mask closely and could find no sharp edge that could have caused the wound. The grass itself was too dry and old to cut so deeply into flesh. We both assumed that a curse had been placed on the object and feared that more deadly consequences might follow. Fortunately the cut hand healed normally, but the mystery remains one of the most intriguing I have experienced.

British Museum

Bruce Castle N17

The castle, at Tottenham, is really a Tudor mansion now serving as a museum. Its ghost is that of Constantia, the lovely wife of Lord Coleraine, who jumped from the balustrade above the entrance porch with her baby in her arms. This tragic event took place on 3 November 1680 and Constantia's death scream was often heard again on that date, though not since an informal service of exorcism early in this century. However, there have been modern reports of figures in eighteenth-century dress who just fade away when approached.

Buckingham Palace SW1

The ghost of a monk who died in a punishment cell of the priory that occupied the site before the Dissolution appears on the Great Terrace on Christmas Day. On the first floor of the palace itself (open to the public), the sound of a gunshot occasionally echoes through the corridors and must seriously worry those responsible for security. However, it is but a supernatural reminder of a tragedy from the early years of the century when Major John Gwynne, private secretary to Edward VII, shot himself with his own revolver.

Buckingham Street WC2

William Etty, the Victorian painter of sensuous nudes, lived at number 14 and it may be one of his models that haunts the building. She is always described as being a happy ghost, as is that at number 12, the spirit of Samuel Pepys, the Jacobean diarist, who once lived at this address.

Camberwell SE5

Churchyard Passage by St Giles church is haunted by the shadowy figure of an old-time clergyman that seems to be growing fainter as the years pass.

Canonbury N1 🍺 🕐

The Old Queen's Head at the top of Essex Road is not the original pub used by Sir Water Raleigh and Queen Elizabeth – this was pulled down in 1829. Nevertheless the present building is haunted by a lady in Tudor dress as well as by a sad little girl, and on the first Sunday of the month doors are opened and closed by unseen hands and disembodied footsteps sound on the stairs. Legend says that the Virgin Queen had a tunnel built from the Queen's Head to Canonbury Tower so that she could secretly meet her lover, the Earl of Essex.

Charlton House SE7

The house (open to the public) was designed by Inigo Jones and its most famous ghost is that of Sir William Langhorne, a wealthy merchant, who died in 1714 at the age of eighty-five. Although he was twice married he failed to beget an heir and this may be the reason why he pesters female residents and visitors to the house – he was once even accused of rape. A serving girl holding a baby in her arms is a wraith that appears in the grounds. After the north wing of the house was bombed, a baby's corpse was found concealed in a chimney, mummified by the smoke and heat.

Chelsea SW3 🐾

Cheyne Walk
The fashionable riverside here is haunted by the ghost of a bear (see also the Tower of London, below). In the sixteenth century bear-baiting took place in a pit in this district.

Elystan Street
There is a postwar house here on the site of a tombstone-maker's yard that was bombed in the war. The house is haunted by an ephemeral mob, which gathered to watch a policeman being lynched in the 1820s.

Chiswick W4

Both Walpole House, in Chiswick Mall, and Chiswick House itself (which is open to the public) are haunted by the ponderous ghost of the Duchess of Cleveland, a mistress of Charles II before he met Nell Gwynne. She died of dropsy at Walpole House, where her

THE GOOD GHOST GUIDE

spirit walks with a heavy tread. Her spirit also peers through the windows of Chiswick House – strange, since it was built fifty years after her death.

Cleopatra's Needle WC2

The riverfront here at Victoria Embankment is a favourite venue for suicides and the tall, naked figure that jumps from the parapet by the Needle might be taken for one of these – except that there is never a splash as he hits the water. Pain-racked moans and mocking laughter are associated with this haunting.

Clerkenwell WC1

29 Doughty Street was one of the many homes of Charles Dickens (see also Rochester, Southern England) and his ghost has been seen outside the house, a short dapper figure in dark clothes and a stovepipe hat.

Cockfosters

The spectre of Geoffrey de Mandeville, Earl of Essex, haunts the Cockfosters and East Barnet district, its territory including Trent Park, home of the Middlesex Polytechnic at Cockfosters. Here the ghost appears at Christmas (usually in six-year cycles, thus he is scheduled to visit again in 1998). The ancient warrior is dressed in full armour, a red cloak, and wears a scarlet plume in his helmet. In life the earl was a renegade who, outlawed by the king, fled to the fens and gathered considerable wealth by banditry. He was killed at Mildenhall, Suffolk, in 1144.

Colindale NW9 🐾 💀

The Hyde is haunted by an ephemeral donkey that dazzles the beholder with a myriad of colours as it passes, and the ghost of a haymaker who was killed by his workmate with a pitchfork. The haymaker is a dangerous ghost, and those encountering it run the risk of being pitchforked themselves.

Croydon Airport ✈

1 mile SW of Croydon

The central tower of London's first airport still stands by Purley Way and as early as the 1930s it had a ghost. This was the presence of a Dutch pilot killed in a crash caused by fog. Two weeks after his death an Imperial Airways pilot was preparing his flight plan when a voice behind him told him not to leave, saying, 'The weather is just the same as when I took off.' As he turned he caught a glimpse of a figure wearing flying kit. It faded as he focused on it but nevertheless he recognised the Dutch airman. Sure enough, although the skies were clear at the time, fog descended on the airport shortly afterwards. The spectres of three nuns also appear occasionally. They were among twelve passengers burned to death after a crash in a snowstorm in January 1947. The sound of an other-worldly choir may derive from communal singing in a factory shelter. During the first air-raid on London in 1940 a perfume

factory was hit and sixty
people died.

The Roundshaw estate
now covers much of the
former airport and there
have been reports of a
wartime pilot's ghost here
who rides a motorbike. He
may be the same phantom
that features in an account
held in the files of the
Society for Psychical
Research. This tells of a
pilot in combat uniform who
regularly appeared in a
house on the estate. The
householder complained
that it would not be so bad
except the ghost was so
clumsy – he always made a

Croydon Airport

point of knocking over a tailor's dummy dressed in Nazi uniform.

Crystal Palace SE19

The headless ghost of a platelayer wanders through the tunnel
between Crystal Palace and Gipsy Hill. He was decapitated while
working on this length of track. There are also stories of an
abandoned tunnel beneath Crystal Palace Park which contains
the bricked-up remains of a train. However, though there were
accounts of a ghost train complete with skeleton passengers
being discovered when a girl fell down a shaft in 1978, the buried
train is really an experimental one that was driven by compressed
air. It proved to be a failure, and was indeed bricked up and
forgotten.

Docklands E14

The ghost of Lord Nelson has been identified at the old pub in
Coldharbour, the Gun Inn, where he had clandestine meetings
with Lady Hamilton.

Drury Lane WC2

A theatre has stood on the site of the Theatre Royal on Drury
Lane for more than three centuries, the present building dating
from 1812. Its Man in Grey is probably the most celebrated of all
theatrical ghosts. He walks at the back of the upper circle,
crossing from one side to the other, and usually haunts at
daytime. His appearance is welcomed by the management for it
usually signifies that the current production will be a hit. A fire-
watcher saw him during the blitz as bombs fell all around. About
a hundred years ago a skeleton with a dagger between its ribs
was found concealed in a wall close to where the ghost begins its
walk. This went some way towards confirming the old story that

the Man in Grey is the ghost of a young man up from the country who fell in love with an actress and was killed by a rival.

The shade of Dan Leno, a great comic performer who died in 1904, is a gentle spirit that seems to welcome actors into his old dressing room, while the ghost of Charles Macklin is a grim and fearsome figure that strides across the stage just before curtain-up. He was an Irish actor who, in 1735, during a dispute with a colleague about a wig, struck him in the eye with a stick. The fellow actor died of the injury.

Enfield

A remarkable haunting occurs in Bell Lane when the phantom stagecoach known as the Enfield Flyer dashes along the road – but six feet above it. The coach is black and two ladies wearing large hats sit inside as it travels towards the reservoir, once the valley of the River Lea. It is thought that the coach may have come to grief attempting to ford the river.

Gower Street WC1

A ghost named Lizzie always appears at the University College Hospital in Gower Street when a nurse is about to administer morphine. Lizzie herself was a nurse who accidentally killed her fiancé when he was a patient by giving him an overdose of the drug. Opposite the hospital is University College itself which keeps the preserved body of one of its founders in a glass case. This is Jeremy Bentham, who died in 1832, and was a philosopher who preached the presently unfashionable doctrine of promoting the greatest happiness to the greatest number. Bentham's ghost wanders down the corridors to the library, his walking stick (which he called Dapple) tapping the floor as he walks.

Greenwich SE10

Blackwall Tunnel Approach
A motorcyclist clad in leathers is the ghost seen roaring towards the tunnel. He was killed in an accident here in 1972.

Royal Naval College
The Queen Anne Block is haunted by the 'filmy' ghost of Admiral Byng who was imprisoned here before being unjustly executed for treason in 1757.

Ham House ☞

2 miles SW of Richmond

Dating from 1610, the magnificent house (administered by the Victoria & Albert Museum and open to the public) is haunted by an evil old lady usually believed to be the ghost of the Duchess of Lauderdale who, with her equally unpleasant husband, restored and enlarged the house in the 1670s. Her ghost is heard wandering through the rooms, her cane tapping the floorboards. The ghostly sound of 'Greensleeves' being played on the virginals has been reported recently.

Hammersmith W6 ✠

Over the centuries Hammersmith has suffered greatly from
hoaxers who enjoyed frightening the villagers by pretending to be
ghosts. In 1804 one unfortunate plasterer was shot because a
vigilante thought he had found the troublesome phantom. St
Paul's churchyard has a ghost that appears every fifty years at an
appointed hour when the moon is full. In 1955 a crowd of four
hundred people waited in the churchyard to witness the haunting.
Most left when the time came and went without a ghost
appearing, but those who took British Summer Time into account
and waited an extra hour were rewarded by the sight of a spectre
floating from the porch of the church to a tomb and disappearing
inside.

Hampstead NW3 🍺

Church Row

The red-haired housemaid who furtively leaves one of the houses
at dawn is the ghost of a girl who murdered a child left in her
care. The ghost carries a large carpetbag containing the victim's
corpse.

Spaniards Inn

The notorious highwayman, Dick Turpin, mounted on his famous
black horse, is supposed to be the ghostly rider that gallops
across the Heath up to this famous pub, which once served as his
London headquarters.

William IV

A dentist's surgery once stood opposite this Heath Street pub and
this was where a girl committed suicide. Her ghost stares in at
the pub's customers who can see that her hair is plaited and that
she wears a white shift like a shroud.

Hampton Court 👑 ✠

A galaxy of ghosts haunts this royal palace (open to the public).
Its builder, Cardinal Wolsey, has been seen in spectral form only
once, at a *son et lumière* performance in 1966, but two of Henry
VIII's wives are regular ghostly presences at the palace.
Catherine Howard, the fifth wife, found the king repulsive and
took her favours elsewhere. Condemned for this she ran through
the palace, pursued by guards, seeking Henry's pardon. He
ignored her, continuing with his prayers in the chapel, and
Catherine went to the scaffold still demented, having to be held
down beneath the fall of the axe. Her desperate cries still echo in
the corridors and her fists beat on the door of the chapel. (This
scene is very similar to Anne Boleyn's pleas for mercy at Lambeth
Palace, see below.) The White Lady who walks up the stairs and
through the Silver Stick Gallery is the wraith of Jane Seymour
who was queen for just a year before dying in childbirth.

Mrs Sibell Penn was the devoted nurse to the sickly King
Edward VI who died at the age of sixteen in 1553. Mrs Penn lived

on another nine years before dying of smallpox and being buried in the old church at Hampton. When this building was pulled down in 1821 and her tomb moved to the porch of the present church, her ghost began to walk. This is the most commonly seen phantom at Hampton Court, and it may also be heard as the distinctive click-clack noise made by an ancient spinning wheel, which comes from the wall of a room in the south-west wing.

Haymarket SW1

The Haymarket Theatre is London's second oldest theatre and, like the Man in Grey at the Theatre Royal on Drury Lane (see above), the ghost of John Buckstone is seen only if the production is doing well. Buckstone performed as a comedian here and was the theatre's manager for twenty-five years. He died in 1879 and the following year he was seen watching from the Royal Box. His ghost is harmless but seems to find enjoyment in startling people.

Highgate N6, N19 📫 🐾

Cemetery

The wraith of an old madwoman makes a dolorous search among the tombs for the children she once murdered, a ghost with bony fingers waits at the main entrance, and a tall gaunt man in a black hat melts into the walls of the cemetery at Swain's Lane.

Highgate Hill

Ye Olde Gate House is an ancient pub: its first licence was issued in 1310 and it was the final stopover for drovers bringing their herds to London before they descended to Smithfield the next day. Its ghost is Mother Marnes, an old lady killed here for her money. She is seen wearing a black dress, but never when children or animals are on the premises.

Pond Square

There can be few more improbable ghosts than that of a featherless chicken but just such a creature has haunted Pond Square since 1626. The story is told in Aubrey's *Anecdotes* and concerns Francis Bacon, the Lord Chancellor of England, who had interest in science as well as law. As he descended Highgate Hill on a snowy day the idea occurred to him that snow might preserve flesh just as well as salt and so left his coach at the bottom of the hill to buy a hen, had the farmer's wife exenterate it (remove its innards), and then stuffed its body with snow. Bacon's brainwave was successful but the chill that he caught proved fatal and he died within three days. The carcass of the unfortunate hen began haunting the district soon afterwards, and continued to do so after the houses were built around Highgate Pond in Georgian times. However, appearances of the squawking ghost with its stumpy wings seem to have died out in modern times.

Ickenham 🚋

2 miles NE of Uxbridge

A middle-aged woman wearing a red scarf haunts the station. She is the wraith of a woman who was electrocuted when she fell from the platform on to the rails.

Kenley

3 miles S of Croydon

The village is haunted by a Grey Lady who cradles a baby in her arms. She seems to emanate from the site of the lost village of Watendone and has been seen in many locations in Kenley.

Kensington W8, W11 👑

Kensington Palace

The palace (open to the public) was the birthplace of Queen Victoria and remains a royal residence. George II made it his favourite home and died there in 1760, waiting in vain for news from his native Germany. His fretful words in broken English ('Vhy tondt dey com?') and his wan face at a window make up this haunting. He died just before the messengers arrived with the long-overdue dispatches.

St Mark's Road

The phantom bus that haunts North Kensington between the Cambridge Gardens and Chesterton Road junctions just to the north of the Westway flyover is one of the most intriguing of London's hauntings. It was first reported in June 1934 following the death of a young motorist whose car swerved off the road and burst into flames early one morning, allegedly to avoid colliding with a number 7 bus. After this account was publicised many other people came forward to tell how they had been forced off the road by a similar apparition, but the vehicle had always vanished just as a collision seemed inevitable. There have been no recent reports of the ghost bus being seen and no reasons have ever been put forward why it should appear in St Mark's Road.

Kentish Town N7

Dr Hawley Harvey Crippen lived at Hilldrop Crescent and was hanged on 23 November 1910 for murdering his wife, whose head was never found. On the night of his execution his ghost was seen carrying a strangely shaped parcel which he took to the murky old ponds that were then a dismal feature of the neighbourhood.

Lambeth Palace SE1 👑

This is another place haunted by the busy ghost of Anne Boleyn, who was tried at the palace for adultery before being taken for execution to the Tower. Her ghost is seen embarking on the boat that took her on this last journey and her sobbing, pleading voice is heard by the door to the Undercroft where the trial was held before Archbishop Cramner. Lollards Prison in the palace is haunted by the souls of those who were kept here before being burned to death for their beliefs. A haunted door locks and unlocks itself.

Langham Place W1 🍺

The Langham is now re-established as a hotel after having been used by the BBC for many years. It was built in Edwardian times and its ghost is that of a German officer who jumped to his death from a room on the fourth floor just before the First World War. The main BBC building on the other side of Langham Place has a phantom butler who makes stately progress along the corridors bearing a tray of drinks. His decorum is spoiled, however, by the holes in his socks.

Limehouse E14

In the old days when Limehouse was the roughest district of the docks, the vicar of Ratcliff Cross ran a refuge for sailors and became notorious for murdering those with money and dumping their bodies in the river at Ratcliff Cross Stairs. This was the basis for a hoax haunting in 1971 which, unknown to its author, was already established in fact and had been known to locals for generations. They say the ghost of the old vicar is usually seen in the dusk of summer evenings.

London Bridge SE1 🍺

Crucifix Lane is just to the east of the station and the Horns pub is hidden beneath the arches of the railway. One of its two ghosts, that of an unhappy little girl seeking her mother, has been exorcised, but the other, that of a harmless old lady, remains.

Newgate EC1

The only part of the old prison that remains is the wall to be seen at the back of Amen Court. The infamous Black Dog of Newgate is reputed to crawl along the top of this. The Black Dog is the diabolic reincarnation of a prisoner who was eaten by his fellows when famine struck during the reign of Henry III. The passageway to the execution dock was floored with an iron grating which gave it the name Birdcage Walk. The last man to be executed at Newgate was lame and his irregular tread can still occasionally be heard in Newgate, sounding on the grating that disappeared long ago.

Newgate Street EC1 ✠

Greyfriars' churchyard on Newgate Street close to St Paul's is a quiet oasis from the bustling City. Queen Isabella was buried here with the heart of the husband she had murdered on her breast. Hers is one ghost in the churchyard. Her rival is another murderess, Lady Alice Hungerford, who poisoned her second husband and was hanged at Tyburn in 1523. When both of these phantoms appear at once there is an unholy row in the churchyard between them. The third ghost takes no part in this. In life she was Elizabeth Barton, a deranged serving girl prone to fits. Opponents of Henry VIII cleverly interpreted these as being divine messages opposing the monarch's divorce plans, which resulted in the Maid of Kent, as she was known, being executed at Tyburn.

Norwood

St Joseph's College was built as a private house and in 1864 was occupied by a Mr Prior who bred racing horses. His senior groom, Daniel Philpot, bet his life savings on one of the stables' horses which lost, whereupon he hanged himself. His ghost haunts the Oak Room and appears every five years (1998 will be the year of his next visitation).

Piccadilly W1

Naval and Military Club

The ghost of an officer killed in an air-raid in 1941 haunts the Naval and Military Club and usually appears in the Egremont Room. The apparition, which wears a distinctive ankle-length greatcoat, has been identified as the ghost of Major Henry Bradell, nicknamed Perky because of his cheerful nature. The other ghost belonging to the club is less benevolent and seems to take delight in terrifying people. It is supposed to be that of a man who went berserk and died after a visit to the 'In and Out' (the club takes this nickname from the prominent letters on its lantern-topped gates).

Vine Street Police Station

The sound of old-fashioned hobnailed boots is occasionally heard in the corridors of Vine Street Police Station, probably Britain's most famous 'nick', situated a few paces to the west of the statue of Eros. The sound of the boots comes from the ghost of a sergeant who committed suicide in the early years of this century.

Red Lion Square WC1

A trio of Roundhead leaders are the phantoms here, the ghosts of Cromwell, Ireton and John Bradshaw, whose bodies were disinterred after the Restoration and tried for treason at Westminster Hall. Having been found guilty the corpses were dragged to Tyburn for a macabre form of execution. The three ghosts walk across the small Bloomsbury square diagonally, ignoring the paths, deep in conversation. The bodies (though not the heads) were buried here on completion of the macabre rites.

St Magnus the Martyr EC3 ✠

This Wren church on Fish Street Hill close to the Monument has a monkish ghost with an aura of extreme sadness. Since he is most often seen near the tomb of Bishop Coverdale of Exeter, who made the first translation of the Bible into English, he is usually taken to be the shade of the bishop.

St Paul's Cathedral EC1 ✠

All Soul's Chapel at the western end of the cathedral is the haunt of an old, shadowy clergyman who wanders listlessly about, whistling tunelessly and in a high key.

Shepherd's Bush W12

The tiny Bush Theatre was once a BBC rehearsal room situated on an upper floor of the former Shepherd's Bush Hotel. Dylan Thomas's ghost has been seen here, standing at the back of the auditorium. The hotel was a favourite drinking ground of Thomas when he worked at the BBC.

Smithfield EC1 ✥ 🕐

The priory church of St Bartholomew the Great is walked by the ghost of its founder, Rahere, who established the monastery and neighbouring hospital in 1123. Some believe he always appears on 1 July at seven in the morning.

Stanmore NW9 ✕ ✥

A great battle is supposed to have taken place close to the present Honeypot Lane soon after the Roman invasion and this might account for the terrifying 'thing' that rushes past people on dark evenings with a sound like a tornado. Old Church Farm, nearer the centre of Stanmore, was once the rectory and its grounds were haunted by a ghoul that rose from its grave in the churchyard to visit the farm. The spirit, which may have been that of an old parson, also liked to visit villagers on their deathbeds.

Strand WC2 🚋

Adelphi Theatre

The theatre has the ghost of William Terriss, a leading actor of his day, who was killed by a minor-role player overcome with jealousy. His ghost is clad in a grey suit and appears from a cloud of greenish light. It has also been reported from Covent Garden underground station.

Coutts Bank

The fourth Duke of Norfolk was beheaded on the site of what is now Coutts Bank for treason against Elizabeth I on 2 June 1572. His moaning, headless ghost has proved so persistent at the bank over the years that a service was held in 1993 to 'put his tormented soul to rest'. Those who have seen the apparition have not explained how a headless spectre manages to moan.

Somerset House

The Admiralty was originally housed here and so, predictably, the haunting is by Nelson. His ghost favours bright spring mornings for its appearances – the sharply defined figure is that of a frail man with an empty sleeve. What makes the haunting unique is the aura above the ghost's head, a sort of wispy cloud.

Temple EC4

The quiet courtyards and passageways of the inns of court are the haunt of the shade of Sir Henry Hawkins (1817–1907) who earned his soubriquet of 'Hanging Hawkins' because he was the judge of so many murder trials and not because he was particularly vindictive. He is seen at midnight in all his finery, carrying a bundle of papers.

Thamesmead SE28

In September 1878 a tragic accident took place in Barking Reach, the stretch of the Thames opposite Thamesmead. The pleasure-steamer *Princess Alice* was rammed by a collier and sank immediately, killing 640 day-trippers. Many of them might have survived but the accident happened close to the point where London's sewage was released, untreated, into the river and its toxicity prevented them from keeping afloat for any length of time. The victims' cries can be heard on the anniversary of the accident.

Tower Hill EC3

This, the landscaped approach to the Tower of London, was once the place of execution for prisoners being held in the Tower. During the Second World War a sentry saw a strange procession pass him here. Priests and law officers in medieval costume walked by a stretcher on which lay a corpse, its head lying in the crook of an arm. The onlooker was able to describe the clothes of the men bearing the stretcher in detail and an expert later confirmed that these would have been the uniforms of the Sheriff of London's guards in medieval times.

Tower of London EC3 ♛ 🐾 🕐

This is the most haunted site in the kingdom (and is open to the public). It is so haunted that a book has been written on its ghosts, and a selection follows here.

Traitors' Gate was the watergate entrance for prisoners condemned at Westminster. A brown-robed monk is the ethereal presence here and may be the ghost of Thomas à Becket. Attempts at constructing the gate ended in failure until an oratory was incorporated into the structure and dedicated to the martyr saint. During the Second World War traitors faced the firing squad close to the gate and the ghost of one of these unfortunates has also been seen, dressed in a drab utility suit of the 1940s.

The Wakefield Tower has the ghost of Henry VI who was stabbed to death here (probably by Richard, Duke of York, later Richard III) on 21 May 1471. The king's dolorous ghost appears at the hour before midnight on the anniversary of the murder.

The headsman's scaffold was situated on Tower Green and a host of psychic memories linger at the site. Queen Anne Boleyn was beheaded here in 1536 and her spirit haunts it, though she appears in more spectacular fashion in the Chapel Royal walking in a grand procession of ghosts. Some say that the lady on the green is not Anne Boleyn but Margaret Pole, the Countess of Salisbury, who was executed here five years later (see also Warblington, Southern England). She was more than seventy when she was vindictively condemned by Henry VIII, who really wanted the death of her son, Cardinal Pole. She refused to lay her head on the block and the headsman was forced to chase her around the scaffold, swinging his axe wildly until she fell at last, hideously wounded. This awful event generates the sinister shadow of an axe that sometimes passes across Tower Green, finally becoming sharply defined against the wall of the White Tower.

The Martin Tower is particularly feared by the sentries for the persistence and malevolence of its ghosts. The upper rooms were those used by George Boleyn, Anne's brother, before his execution – he was hanged, drawn and quartered – and his ghost walks here. Thomas Percy was imprisoned in this tower for sixteen years for his part in the Gunpowder Plot. His spirit is an active one, sometimes trying to push visitors down the stairs. In 1817 a sentry guarding the Jewel Room in this tower was confronted by the enormous ghost of a bear. He attempted to spear it with his bayonet before fainting from fright. He was able to give an account of his nightmarish ordeal on the next day but died soon after. Bears suffered great cruelty through the years when bear-baiting was practised at the Tower.

Twickenham ✠

Alexander Pope was buried in St Margaret's churchyard and his body rested peacefully in its grave until the skull was stolen in 1830. This generated an outbreak of psychic fury, with the hunch-backed apparition of the satirist hobbling about the church and churchyard, talking to itself between frenzied coughing. Although the ghost has not been seen recently, the uneven sound of a cripple's footsteps has been heard inside the church.

Vauxhall SE1 🚋

When the tunnel beneath the Thames was being excavated in 1965 to accommodate the Victoria Line, the workmen encountered the Quare Fellow, a menacing phantom who came towards them with arms outstretched. They thought it was a spirit disturbed from its rest when they dug through an old plague pit of 1665.

Wandsworth Prison SW18

The dolorous ghost of a Victorian lady inmate named Annie haunts the prison in a shabby grey institutional dress.

Wanstead E11 ✠

The churchyard has the unnerving ghost of a skeleton that wheels a coffin cart. As it approaches an ornate tomb, a White Lady emerges and embraces the bony figure, assumed to be her husband.

West Drayton ✠ 🐾

3 miles S of Uxbridge

The church is haunted by a spectral black bird, larger than a raven, which lurks in the vaults and perches on the coffins. Its flutterings

are occasionally heard but there have been no sightings since
1869. It is said to be the spirit of a murderer.

Westminster Abbey SW1 ✛ 🖾

The Cloisters are the favourite walk of Father Benedictus who
usually appears between five and six in the evening. Perhaps 'walk'
is misleading here as his feet are seen an inch or so above the
flagstones, representing the settlement and wear that has
occurred since the Middle Ages. (A similar phenomenon occurs
with the ghost of Archbishop Laud at St John's College, Oxford; see
South Midlands.) Benedictus is believed to have been killed by
robbers while defending the relics and treasures in the Chapel of
the Pyx at the time of the Dissolution. Another ghost is seen in the
nave by the grave of the Unknown Warrior. Dressed in the uniform
of an infantryman of the First World War, he may be the ghost of
the warrior himself.

Whitechapel E1

A huddled figure surrounded by a halo of ghostly light may be seen
lying in the gutter in Durward Street behind Whitechapel station. It
is the ghost of Polly Nicholls, the first victim of Jack the Ripper.

Wilton Row SW1

Acclaimed as the most famous haunted pub in the world, the Grenadier on Wilton Row makes a big thing of its ghost, which usually makes its presence felt in the month of September. In the early nineteenth century a young guards officer was caught cheating at cards and in the scuffle that followed fell downstairs and was killed. The apparition appears as a shapeless blob (ectoplasm), may also manifest itself as a poltergeist, and can even generate puffs of cigarette smoke that feel hot.

Eastern England

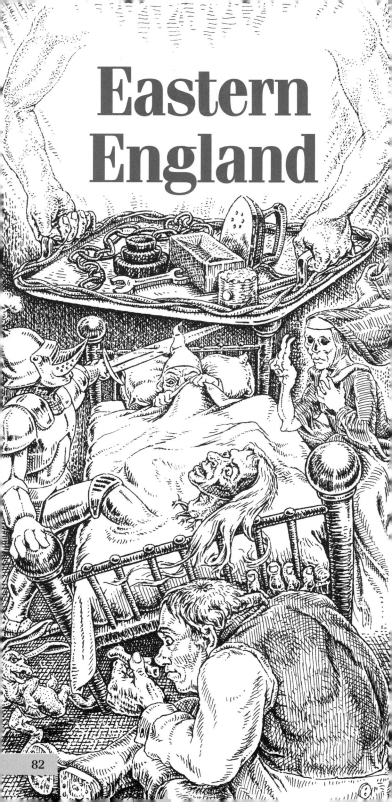

Woodcroft Castle, Combe.

Lincolnshire, Cambridgeshire, Norfolk, Suffolk, Essex, Hertfordshire and Bedfordshire

Black Shuck is the East Anglian version of the black dog and here he has yellow eyes as big as saucers. Sight of him brings the usual death within the year. Shuck's Lane is a common streetname in north Norfolk where his presence is taken particularly seriously, while in Suffolk he was blamed for causing death and chaos in 1577 when ball lightning hit Bungay church and tore through the congregation.

Barnwell Abbey House on the eastern outskirts of Cambridge was once regarded as the most haunted house in England. It has at least six bizarre ghosts including those of Jacob Butler, the Giant Squire, who looks for his lost dog; a man in armour, and a woman's disembodied head.

The ghost of Oliver Cromwell, a celebrated East Anglian, haunts Sidney Sussex College at Cambridge where his head was laid to rest in 1960, more than three hundred years after his death. At the restoration of the monarchy in 1660, his body had been exhumed and the head severed from it in a ghoulish mock execution.

A political opponent of Cromwell, Dr Michael Hudson, is the ghost of Woodcroft Castle near Peterborough. He is a ghost without hands. Pursued to the castle battlements, he clung to the masonry high above the moat until a Roundhead soldier discovered him and slashed at his wrists, causing him to fall to his death.

Abbot's Langley Hertfordshire ✛

5 miles SW of St Albans

The church and vicarage are still (despite exorcism) haunted by the ghost of a maidservant who was cruelly treated by the vicar's wife.

Ashwell Hertfordshire ✛

4 miles NE of Baldock

The churchyard is haunted by a headless figure dressed in black.

Aspley Guise Bedfordshire

13 miles NW of Luton

The old manor house is to the north of the village. Weathercock Lane leads to it and is haunted by the ghost of Dick Turpin who is said to have used the manor house as a hideout .

Aylmerton Norfolk

3 miles SW of Cromer

The Shrieking Pits are haunted by a grief-stricken White Lady looking for the body of her child. She and her child were killed by her husband in a fit of rage. The pits themselves are probably medieval iron-workings.

Ayot St Lawrence Hertfordshire 🍺

6 miles NW of Hatfield

George Bernard Shaw's ghost has been seen at the house (Shaw's Corner, open to the public) where he lived from 1906 until his death in 1950. The ghost of Lawrence of Arabia, a friend of Shaw's and frequent visitor here, has also been rumoured to haunt the house.

   The Brocket Arms has the ghost of an elderly monk. Sometimes only his face is seen, hazily, as though through smoke.

Balsham Cambridgeshire 🐾

11 miles SE of Cambridge

The phantom black dog which may be encountered on the Wratting road is a shuck-monkey. It has a monkey's face.

Beccles Suffolk

A ghostly coach-and-four with headless coachman drives up to Roos Hall on Christmas Eve.

Beeleigh Abbey Essex 🕐

1 mile W of Maldon

The eerie wailing heard each year on 11 August is an echo of the grief of Sir John Gate who, on that date in 1553, was awaiting execution on the block. He was beheaded eleven days later at Tower Hill in London.

Bircham Newton Norfolk

9 miles W of Fakenham

The wartime airfield (owned by the Construction Industry Training Board) has a phantom sports car, full of laughing airmen, which races across the base to crash into the back of a hangar. The

Bircham Newton

squash court is haunted by the ghosts of three keen players killed when their Avro Anson bomber crashed close by. Another two phantom sportsmen have been seen engaged in a fencing contest.

Bishop's Stortford Hertfordshire

A Grey Lady is resident at The George and is seen veiled by a swirling mist. The George was once a coaching inn and has a tradition that a woman was stabbed to death in Room 27.

Blickling Hall Norfolk

12 miles NW of Norwich

EDITOR'S CHOICE In the sixteenth century Blickling belonged to the Boleyn family and Anne Boleyn spent her childhood at the hall (open to the public). Her father, Sir Thomas, enjoyed a poor reputation locally and his decapitated body is condemned to make a ghostly circuit of this part of Norfolk in a coach drawn by headless horses, passing over twelve bridges including those at Aylsham, Coltishall and Wroxham. This event takes place on the anniversary of his daughter's execution, 19 May, and there are some who believe that it is Anne in the coach and not Sir Thomas.

Since a glimpse of the passenger can prove fatal to the beholder, it is an argument unlikely to be resolved.

Blythburgh Suffolk ✛

4 miles W of Southwold

A black dog intruded into the church here on the same day – 4 August 1577 – as at Bungay (see below), which is only seven miles away. At Blythburgh he caused injury and left deep score-marks in the church door which may still be seen.

Toby's Walks, a recreational area on the A12 just to the south-west of the village, takes its name from a sad crime of passion which took place in 1754. A black dragoon, a drummer named Toby Gill ('Black Toby'), murdered a girl from Westleton on the heath here and was executed nearby. His body was left to swing on a roadside gibbet. Although his ghost haunts the locality, Black Toby does not strike his drum.

Borley Essex ✛ ☛

2 miles NW of Sudbury

The rectory was reputed to be the most haunted house in England before it was demolished in 1944 (it had at least twelve ghosts). Psychic attention has been transferred to Borley church, which has also acquired the reputation of being haunted. Ghostly music has been heard inside and a phantom nun seen in the churchyard.

Boston Lincolnshire ✛

The ghostly re-enactment of a young woman's death leap with her infant child from the top of Boston Stump, the 272-foot-high octagonal tower of St Botolph's church, occasionally takes place on autumnal evenings.

Bovingdon Hertfordshire ✛

3 miles SW of Hemel Hempstead

The churchyard was once desecrated by a murder and because of this the spirits of those buried near where the crime was committed are restless. A 'gleaming presence' haunts Box Lane.

Bradwell-on-Sea Essex

16 miles NE of Southend-on-Sea

A Roman on horseback haunts the neighbourhood of Othona, the Roman castle.

Breckles Hall Norfolk ☠

9 miles NE of Thetford

A spectral coach occasionally draws up at the entrance to the hall, a beautiful Tudor house which was the home of the Catholic Woodhouse family until, financially ruined by the fines imposed on them because of their religion, they sold the estate in 1599. Anyone who witnesses the arrival of the coach is doomed, being either taken off in it to disappear forever, or left lifeless on the drive, with no mark on the body to account for mortality.

Bungay Suffolk ✚

A weathercock featuring a black dog adorns a lamp-post near the town centre. This commemorates a remarkable event that occurred in St Mary's church during a service on 4 August 1577. A fiery black dog tore through the congregation and killed two of them, leaving another alive but shrivelled 'like a drawn purse'. Naturally Black Shuck was blamed for this – hereabouts he is said to be the demon spirit of the wicked Hugh Bigod, which also haunts Bungay castle – but the violent events in the church are likely to have been caused by ball lightning since a storm raged at the time. (See also Blythburgh, above.)

Burgh Castle Norfolk

3 miles SW of Great Yarmouth

A mystery surrounds the identity of the ghostly figure who plunges, draped in a white flag, from the ramparts of this Roman stronghold (open to the public). Once the sea came up to its walls but the walls now face lonely marshes.

Bury St Edmunds Suffolk ✚

The precincts of the cathedral as well as the ruins of the abbey and its gateway are all visited by ghostly monks.

Caistor Lincolnshire ✚ 🎷

11 miles SW of Grimsby

The church is haunted by a phantom monk playing the organ.

Cambridge Cambridgeshire 🐇

Barnwell

The Abbey House stands at the eastern exit from the city, close to the remains of the twelfth-century priory. It has at least six formidable ghosts, which once gave it a reputation as the most haunted house in England. There is a spectral animal about the size of a hare which goes about on its hind legs; a Black Nun; a ghostly man in armour; a bad-tempered spirit that wakes sleepers up by pressing on their chests with a heavy tray; the disembodied and ghastly white head of a woman that also brought sleepers an unpleasant awakening, and finally the ghost of Jacob Butler, the Giant Squire, who lived at Abbey House in the eighteenth century. Although in life he was a rumbustious and generous character, he appears as a sad ghost, for ever seeking a dog which he loved so much that he died soon after losing it.

Corpus Christi College

Rooms in Old Court were seriously haunted by the Corpus Ghost in the early years of the twentieth century. Sir Shane Leslie, then an undergraduate, led an attempt to exorcise the ghost, which materialised as a figure that seemed to be cut off at the knees, and had a dark mark on the throat. In *Ghosts of the Cambridge Colleges*, Geoff Yeates suggests that this supports the theory that the ghost was the spirit of Dr Henry Butts, master of the college, who committed suicide on Easter Day, 1 April 1632: he strangled himself with his garters, tying them to a portal so low that his knees almost touched the floor.

Christ's College
The Fellows' Garden is haunted by the ghost of a clergyman and college member named Christopher Round, a tall, stout figure wearing an old-fashioned swallow-tailed coat and a beaver hat. He had set himself up in rivalry with a medical fellow of Christ's who was involved in early experiments into anaesthesia. Academic rivalry became inflamed when Round began to believe that the doctor was courting the woman he loved. In fact the rival was attending the woman for a serious illness which could only be cured by an operation under anaesthetic. He often experimented on himself, and would return to the college in a state resembling intoxication. One night he returned in this condition and Round took the opportunity to murder him, thus bringing an early death to the woman he loved and causing his remorseful ghost to walk in the Fellows' Garden.

Sidney Sussex College
The head of Oliver Cromwell was finally laid to rest in the ante-chapel of the college in 1960 and may be the cause of the strange haunting here. In 1967 the rooms of two undergraduates in the south wing of Chapel Court were haunted by a terrifying entity described on one occasion as being a floating, pale yellow head which seemed to be lacking its ears. The following day another undergraduate, who had not heard of the previous day's haunting, encountered a large pale blue and purple eye in a room above the one where the ghost had been seen before. The subsequent over-active attention of the Cambridge University Psychical Research Society seems to have put an end to the haunting.

Girton College
The ghost of a Roman centurion was seen by two early women undergraduates when college buildings were being erected. Parts of Girton are situated on an Anglo-Saxon cemetery, which suggests that the undergraduates may have been mistaken in the identity of the soldier.

Sherratt and Hughes, Trinity Street
This is claimed to be the oldest bookshop in Britain, founded on these premises in 1581. It has two ghosts – a White Lady and that of a gentleman in Victorian evening dress – but there are no obvious reasons for their materialisation.

Cammeringham Lincolnshire
7 miles N of Lincoln
The Cammeringham Light is an apparition that appears out of a cloud of mist. It looks like a woman driving a chariot (the Roman Ermine Street is only a mile east of the village) and some people believe it to be the ghost of Queen Boadicea.

Canewdon Essex

6 miles N of Southend-on-Sea

The village has maintained its reputation as 'the witchcraft capital of Essex' to the present day, and its last self-confessed wizard or warlock, George Pickingale, survived into the twentieth century, dying in 1909. Thus it is hardly surprising that a 'Ghost Witch' haunts Canewdon – a creature that rises from its grave in the churchyard, has 'paralysing eyes' and, because it often appears near the village pond, is thought to be the lost soul of a witch who was executed here by drowning.

Canvey Island Essex

An old Dutchman who wears buckled shoes and has rosettes on his knee breeches haunts the quieter places of the island. He carries a mysterious bundle on his shoulder.

Castle Rising Norfolk A:

5 miles NE of Kings Lynn

Queen Isabella (see Nottingham Castle, North Midlands) was confined here at the castle (open to the public) by her son, Edward III. Altogether she spent twenty-seven years in relatively comfortable imprisonment, though in the years before her death in 1358 she suffered from dementia. Her crazy laughter still echoes through the Norman castle on stormy nights.

Caxton Gibbet Cambridgeshire

10 miles W of Cambridge

The gibbet still stands close to the crossroads here, where the Cambridge to Bedford road crosses Ermine Street. The inn opposite the gibbet, often untenanted in recent years and once called the Caxton Gibbet, is haunted by the spectre of the son of one of its landlords. The son murdered three guests in Room 5 and disposed of the bodies in the well that was situated at the bottom of the present staircase. The murderer's body is supposed to be the last one to swing from the sinister gibbet. There are also reports of a phantom hitch-hiker between here and Graveley.

Clacton-on-Sea Essex

The site of the old ballroom at the former Butlin's holiday camp, opposite the Martello Tower, is haunted by the ghost of a soldier killed in a fight there.

Colchester Essex 🍺

Castle

James Parnell, the first Quaker martyr, died in a dungeon at the castle (open to the public) in May 1656. Already an invalid, he was made to climb a rope from his cell to obtain meagre rations. He fell from the rope and suffered fatal injuries.

Red Lion Hotel

The three-star hotel has the ghost of Alice Mellor, murdered there in 1633. There was also a room so badly haunted that it was sealed up and forgotten, only to be re-discovered in 1972. It was then incorporated into the modernised hotel and has caused no difficulties since.

Conington Cambridgeshire 🚂

8 miles S of Peterborough

In 1948 road users had to open the gates across the busy East Coast railway line themselves and on 16 October that year Colonel A.H. Mellows was killed when, his companion having opened the gates, he drove his black Chrysler into the path of the four o'clock London express. Signalmen at the Conington box used to witness re-enactments of this tragedy, but the signal box is now closed and there have been no recent reports. Today the crossing is controlled from Holme, where a remote-control television camera keeps a vigil of the proceedings there.

Cromer Norfolk 🐾💀

The resort is at the centre of Norfolk's 'Black Shuck' coast. Shuck's Lane runs past the landward side of the town from Runton to Overstrand. The phantom black dog is the size of a calf with (if he is not headless) eyes like yellow saucers. Meeting Shuck means death within the year to anyone unwise enough to look at his terrible features.

Crowland Lincolnshire 🍺

8 miles NE of Peterborough

The Abbey Hotel is haunted by Henry Girdlestone, a local farmer who, in 1844 after a session at the bar, wagered that he could walk a thousand miles in a thousand hours. By the time he stumbled back to the Abbey Hotel he had covered more than 1025 miles in 1176 hours and thus narrowly lost the bet. The sound of his stumbling footsteps is sometimes heard emanating from an attic.

Dedham Essex 🍺

6 miles NE of Colchester

An employee of the Sun Hotel, a maidservant named Elsa, was the last unfortunate to be burned at the stake in Essex for witchcraft. She was executed within sight of the building and has haunted the upper floor of the hotel and its staircase ever since, often sitting on the stairs with her head in her hands, quietly weeping.

Doddington Hall Lincolnshire

5 miles W of Lincoln

The hall (open to the public) has a Brown Lady, seen by the brides of the house. There is also the story of the screaming girl, a wraith which throws itself off the roof to avoid the attentions of the dastardly squire.

Dunwich Suffolk ☕

4 miles SW of Southwold

In Norman times Dunwich had nine churches and a population of five thousand. Most of the city vanished beneath the waves in January 1326 when a storm threw up a shingle bar across the harbour entrance. The ruins of Greyfriars still stand at Dunwich, the last of its monastic houses, and the ghosts of Franciscan monks walk in procession here chanting ancient verses. The bells of the lost churches of Dunwich are heard ringing on stormy nights.

East Kirkby Lincolnshire ✈

7 miles SE of Horncastle

The airfield is now the Aviation Heritage Centre which includes a reconstruction of an operational Second World War bomber station. Visitors may see the ghost of a pilot who died when a B17 crashed. He walks towards the control tower, his open parachute dragging along the ground behind him.

East Raynham Norfolk

4 miles SW of Fakenham

Raynham Hall, the seat of the Marquess of Townshend, is not open to the public but can be seen well from a public footpath. It is famous for its Brown Lady, photographed in 1936 descending the staircase. Captain Marryat, author of *The Children of the New Forest* and *Masterman Ready*, once saw the ghost and fired his pistol at her, whereupon she vanished. In 1849 the staff at Raynham were so frightened by the Brown Lady that they walked out en masse. She is supposed to be the spirit of Dorothy Townshend who had six children in thirteen years and then died of smallpox. There is also a Pink Lady, who appears to herald the death of the head of the family, and a Red Cavalier (the human variety, not the one with wheels).

Eynesbury Cambridgeshire

1 mile S of St Neots

Nanny Izzard, a witch expelled from Great Paxton, haunts the village on certain nights, whizzing around on her broomstick in traditional style. Ghostly noises disturb the Old Rectory.

Felbrigg Hall Norfolk

2 miles SW of Cromer

The library at the hall (open to the public) is haunted by the reclusive, scholarly ghost of William Windham who loved his books at Felbrigg and died in London in 1810 attempting to rescue a friend's books from a blazing library.

Fillingham Lincolnshire

9 miles N of Lincoln

The grounds of the castle are haunted by a man on a big white horse (possibly someone who committed suicide here in the past) and a Green Lady seeking a long-lost lover.

Grantchester Cambridgeshire

2 miles S of Cambridge

The Old Vicarage, with its vivid associations with Rupert Brooke, is now the home of Jeffrey and Mary Archer. Its top floor has a presence, a restless spirit that often moves books.

Grayingham Lincolnshire 🐃

8 miles NE of Gainsborough

Beware of exploring the countryside between this village and Hemswell, 3 miles south, for this district is infamous for its Black Dogs, some as big as tables.

Gunby Hall Lincolnshire

7 miles W of Skegness

Ghost Walk, a path in the park, is haunted by the daughter of Sir William Massingberd and her lover, the postilion. Sir William, who built the hall (open to the public) in 1700, shot the postilion when he tried to elope with the girl.

Happisburgh Norfolk

12 miles SE of Cromer

The place is pronounced 'Hazebrugh' and is at the centre of a part of the coastline that was lonely and remote and thus popular with smugglers two hundred years ago. Its ghosts may have been invented to deter the curious from investigating strange sights and sounds. There is one phantom smuggler who carries a headless, legless torso in his arms (such a body was once recovered from the old well at Well Corner), while another (which might be the same one) looks as though he is carrying something on his back. Only when he gets really close is it apparent that his burden is his own almost-severed head, held on by a flap of skin at the back. Smugglers used to tie lanterns to the backs of donkeys to imitate Black Shuck here (the lanterns might also have served to entice ships to sail too close to the shore).

Hatfield House Hertfordshire 👑

The house (open to the public) has a spectral coach-and-four which drives into the entrance hall and up the stairs. There is also the phantom of a veiled lady, while the ghost of Elizabeth I haunts the Old Hall where she learned of the death of her half-sister, Queen Mary, and her accession to the throne.

Hatfield Peverel Essex

6 miles NE of Chelmsford

Shane's Shaggy Dog is the spectral hound that once walked between the two entrance gates of the house named Crix on the Chelmsford side of the village. It was a harmless ghost unless tormented, and a carter who struck it with his whip was immediately struck himself by a bolt of lightning. The dog made a spectacular final appearance: when it caught sight of its first motor vehicle, it ignited spontaneously and was not seen again.

Haverholme Priory Lincolnshire

3 miles NE of Sleaford

Much of the romantic building was dismantled in 1927 but enough remains to make it clear why Dickens modelled Chesney Wold in *Bleak House* on it. Lord Halifax described its haunting in his *Ghost Book*, while the bridge in the grounds is troubled by a strange manifestation – a violent whizzing noise that terrifies dogs.

Hickling Broad Norfolk

11 miles NW of Great Yarmouth

A skating drummer-boy who fell through the ice when he was on his way to visit his sweetheart haunts this broad. His drum is heard beating on frosty nights in February.

Hintlesham Suffolk

5 miles W of Ipswich

The façade of the hall is in Queen Anne style and this disguises the Elizabethan building that lies behind. The estate was bought by the Lloyd family in 1747 and the son of Richard Savage Lloyd was starved to death by his stepmother soon afterwards. Her remorseful ghost is seen in the library and on the stairs.

Hinxworth Hertfordshire

4 miles SE of Biggleswade

Hinxworth Place is disturbed by inexplicable noises (including the crying of a child) on stormy evenings in autumn. The story is of a young boy dressed convincingly as a ghost who so startled his nurse that she attacked the 'spectre', causing the boy to fall down the stairs and be killed.

Hitchin Hertfordshire

The priory has a Grey Lady, and every year on 15 June the ghost of a headless Cavalier rides the three miles from Highdown to the west of the town.

Holme Hale Norfolk

4 miles E of Swaffham

The Elizabethan Bury's Hall is one of the most haunted mansions in the county. The Green Room seems to be at the centre of the disturbances, which in recent years have been heard rather than seen and most often occur when there have been alterations to the house or a change of owners. About a hundred years ago the figures of a priest and a young girl were often seen walking in the garden, nearly always during Lent and Easter. The priest is said to be the ghost of Father Moreau, a Frenchman who was chaplain to the Bedingfield family and had his throat cut by Cromwellian soldiers on Good Friday.

Holywell Cambridgeshire 📕 🕔

6 miles E of Huntingdon

The gravestone in the bar of the riverside pub Ye Olde Ferryboat is that of Juliet Tewsley who killed herself when her love went unrequited. Her body was buried close to the spot where she died and later the pub was built on top. She appears as a White Lady on the anniversary of her death, 17 March, walking to the slab and pointing to it, then drifting out of the pub to vanish down the river.

Houghton Hall Norfolk

8 miles W of Fakenham

The hall (open to the public) is haunted by a Brown Lady who may be the same ghost that haunts East Raynham (see above). She so disturbed the Prince Regent when he slept in the State Bedroom that he vowed not to spend another hour in the house, saying, 'I have seen what I hope to God I may never see again.'

Huntingdon Cambridgeshire

Nun's Bridge is haunted by the phantom of a nun who was killed with her lover, a monk. There are also reports of a ghostly nurse.

Irby Dale Wood Lincolnshire

6 miles SW of Grimsby

The Irby Boggle is the ghost of Rosamund Guy who was killed here by her fiancé on 1 November 1455. Irby Dale Wood is in Lincolnshire but the village, Irby upon Humber, is in Humberside.

Kensworth Bedfordshire

2 miles SE of Dunstable

'The path over Bury Hill to the church is said to be haunted by a witch and a headless milkmaid,' say Janet and Colin Bord in *Atlas of Magical Britain*.

Kessingland Suffolk

4 miles S of Lowestoft

Rider Haggard (author of *King Solomon's Mines*) was one of a number of people who saw a sea monster here. His account dates from 1912, though other sightings were reported fifty years earlier, as well as in 1923 and in 1978. Haggard wrote that the beast was around 60 feet long and had about thirty pointed blobs along its back, which dwindled in size as they neared its tail. He made it sound very much like the Loch Ness monster.

Kimbolton Castle Cambridgeshire ♛

Catherine of Aragon, first wife of Henry VIII, was held prisoner at the castle (open to the public) during the final two years of her life when she was in constant dread of being poisoned. She haunts the Queen's Chamber where she was confined. The ghost of a small child flung to its death from the battlements is also supposed to haunt the castle.

Knebworth House Hertfordshire

1 mile W of Stevenage

Edward Bulwer-Lytton, a friend of Dickens, was a celebrated novelist in Victorian times with a keen interest in the occult. His ghost story *The House and the Brain* is one of the most chilling ever written, so it is fitting that his spirit remains at the house he loved. Visitors to Knebworth House (open to the public) will find it a place fit to be haunted with its Gothic towers and grotesque gargoyles, which Lytton believed fended off evil. The façade conceals the Tudor part of the house, and Jenny, the ghostly spinner who is occasionally heard working in a room at the top of the east tower, is probably of this era. This haunting is usually a forewarning of a death in the house.

Knebworth House

Lakenheath Suffolk 🖌

9 miles W of Thetford

RAF Lakenheath, still an important NATO base operated by the USAF, has persistent stories of a ghost that is particularly active in the area close to the Brandon road. It may be the spirit of one of the Australian pilots who flew Stirling bombers out of Lakenheath during the Second World War.

Layer Marney Essex

6 miles SW of Colchester

The terrifying apparition that rides down a staircase of the spectacular tower (open to the public) is that of Lord Marney, who died in 1523 without seeing the rest of the house completed.

Lincoln Lincolnshire 🍺

Greestone Steps

A ghostly cleric in seventeenth-century garb haunts the steep steps that lead up to the cathedral.

White Hart

The White Hart Inn in Bailgate is one of the most haunted hotels in the Forte group. There is the shade of a mobcapped maid on the first floor, victim of a murderous rat-catcher; another called the Faceless Highwayman because he was hideously disfigured when a flaming brand was thrust into his face, and a smartly turned-out gentleman ghost in smoking jacket and cravat, who is a comparatively recent manifestation.

Little Gaddesden Hertfordshire

6 miles NW of Hemel Hempstead

A benign spectre haunting the village pond and the manor house is that of Jarman, who killed himself when he was rejected by Lord Bridgewater's daughter. He is supposed to have the remarkable talent of making any light (oil, candle, gas or electric) go dim on one night of the year. It cannot be a very effective means of haunting as no one in the village knows which night is benighted.

Long Melford Suffolk 🍺

3 miles N of Sudbury

The Bull, once a coaching inn, is now a hotel. Its ghost dates back to 1648 when Richard Evered was murdered here by Roger Greene. The strange thing about the crime was the disappearance of the victim's body, which was laid out at the hotel and then vanished overnight. It is Evered's ghost that walks here.

Long Melford Hall (open to the public) is haunted by the ghost of Countess Rivers, a Royalist supporter turned out of her home by an unruly mob from Colchester.

Louth Lincolnshire

The gardens and the road outside Thorpe Hall are haunted by a Green Lady. She is the revenant of Donna Leonora Oviedo whom the first owner of Thorpe Hall, John Bolle, met when he was with Raleigh at the Siege of Cadiz in 1596. He refused to compromise himself with the Spanish aristocrat but she insisted that he took her portrait (in which she wears a green dress) home with him. On his part, Bolle began the tradition of laying a place for Donna Leonora at the dinner table, a custom that survived here until the 1920s. Some say Leonora eventually came to England and, finding Bolle still unresponsive, killed herself in Thorpe Hall's gardens.

Ludham Norfolk

10 miles NE of Norwich

St Benet's Abbey occupies a remote site on the marshes opposite the confluence of the rivers Bure and Thurne. The ruins of the abbey are haunted by the ghost of a monk who betrayed the abbey to the Normans.

Madingley Cambridgeshire

3 miles W of Cambridge

The path between the church and the hall is haunted by Lady Ursula Hyde, who disapproved of her husband's sacrilegious habit of installing furniture ransacked from churches and monasteries at the new house he had begun in 1543. A young man in Elizabethan clothes with a green face and an expression of loathing is a ghost haunting the upper terrace of the hall.

Manningtree Essex

Seafield Bay is in Suffolk, across the river from Manningtree, and its lonely shore is haunted by a crippled witch named Elizabeth Clarke, one of many witches executed here by Hopkins, the Witchfinder General.

Markyate Hertfordshire

4 miles SW of Luton

Markyate Cell is an ancient house standing on Watling Street, a haunt of highwaymen. In fact, it was used in the seventeenth century by a highwaywoman, Lady Ferrers, who mugged travellers by dropping on them from an overhanging bough. However, she was eventually shot, and since then her ghost has ridden recklessly about the countryside.

Mersea Island Essex 🕐

6 miles S of Colchester

The spectre of a Roman soldier patrols the shoreline facing the mainland and is most likely to be seen by moonlight at the time of the autumn equinox (23 September). A caller on a radio phone-in on ghosts said that he had been in a taxi coming away from a pub in West Mersea when they had encountered a group of Roman soldiers in the middle of the road. The driver drove his vehicle straight at the soldiers and it passed through them without hitting any. When they looked back the Romans had vanished.

Metheringham Lincolnshire 🏍️

8 miles SE of Lincoln

Public roads have been restored across the site of the wartime bomber base, and those using them may be flagged down by a girl wearing a green coat. If she wears an RAF badge on the lapel she is the ghost of a WRAF who was killed when her fiancé crashed his motorcycle, on which she was the pillion passenger. She appears to be solid enough when she asks for assistance and she has a fragrance of lavender, but when the apparition vanishes it leaves a smell of putridity.

Minsden Chapel Hertfordshire 🕐

3 miles S of Hitchin

A spectral monk appeared in a photograph of the ruined chapel taken in 1907 and may be the same one that appears on Hallowe'en, ghostly bells heralding its arrival.

Mistley Essex 🍺

8 miles NE of Colchester

The evil Witchfinder General, Matthew Hopkins, met his end in this village and is buried here. One story is that he was seized by a mob and made to take the swimming test that had destroyed so many of his victims. This took place in Mistley Pond in August 1647 and after his death by drowning his spirit returned to haunt the village to this day.

The stables of the Thorn Hotel are haunted by the spirit of a young lad who was fighting with another boy, fell beneath a horse, and was kicked to death. Inside the hotel there is the ghost of a latterday serving wench.

Morley Norfolk

13 miles SW of Norwich

Morley Old Hall attracted considerable attention in 1965 when its ghost appeared on television during an interview about a haunting here. A small bearded monk was seen by twenty-three people, who wrote to Anglia Television asking about the identity of this figure.

Mundesley Norfolk 🕐

6 miles SE of Cromer

The reason why the Long Coastguardsman haunts the coast from this village to Bacton is unknown. He may be seen on any night at midnight as long as there is no moon, and he enjoys shouting and laughing on a stormy night.

Murrow Cambridgeshire

9 miles NE of Peterborough

Oliver Cromwell's ghost haunts the pimple known as Ghost Hill in this flat fenland.

Newmarket Suffolk

The ghost of the famous jockey Fred Archer, who died in 1886, haunts the racecourse and has been known to make race horses shy during a race.

North Benfleet Essex

8 miles W of Southend-on-Sea

On the north side of the A13, near Fanton Hall, is Screeching Boy's Wood, said to take its name from the noise made by the ghost of a ploughboy killed by his master in 1734. An alternative version has it that the boy had his head cut off by a woodsman and thus haunts the place as a headless ghost. But if the poor lad is headless, how does he screech?

Norwich Norfolk 🍺

Adam and Eve pub

The fourteenth century inn is situated near the modern law courts on St Martin's Plain where, on 1 August 1549, an army of peasants under Robert Kett engaged a royal detachment led by Lord Sheffield. At the height of the fighting, Lord Sheffield unwisely removed his helmet and waved it in the air to show himself to be a noble. A local butcher named Fulke took the opportunity to strike a telling blow and Lord Sheffield was taken to die at the inn where his ghost, affectionately called 'Sam', now haunts. Fulke himself came to grief soon afterwards: he was executed after the defeat of Kett's rebels at the Battle of Dussindale, where three thousand peasants were slaughtered.

Bridge House Inn

The cellars of the pub opposite Bishop's Bridge were used as dungeons in the sixteenth century. Hundreds of Wycliffe's followers were imprisoned here for their beliefs, then burned alive in Lollards Pit close by. Not surprisingly, the ghost of one of these unfortunates haunts the pub.

Castle

The official journal of the county gaol, which once occupied much of the castle (open to the public), carries an interesting entry in 1820. It relates how three young men held here before being transported were terrified out of their wits by a supernatural entity they were unable to describe. Their obvious distress impressed the hard-bitten gaoler enough for him to mention it in the official record that was inspected by the magistrates. Norwich Castle dates from 1067 and the last of its public executions took place here eight hundred years later. It now houses a museum and attendants speak of seeing a floating skull and the wraith of an old lady in black Victorian dress. She is believed to be the ghost of Mrs Bulwer, an early benefactor of the museum.

Maddermarket Theatre

The theatre served as a Roman Catholic church for some years at the end of the eighteenth century. It is haunted by a black-robed priest who returns in ghostly form to celebrate mass.

Magdalen Street

Number 19 is now occupied by a Save the Children charity shop but in 1873 was a disreputable pub (at that time Norwich had a pub for every day of the year and a church for every week). A woman was murdered in a bedroom and her ghost caused considerable trouble in the 1970s when the premises were leased to Oxfam. The woman's ghost appeared at the top of the stairs and a typewriter often operated by itself. The Save the Children staff are wary of going upstairs by themselves.

Offord Cluny Cambridgeshire

3 miles S of Huntingdon

The Manor House has an unusual and charming form of haunting. The ghost of a little old lady has appeared to at least four generations of new wives soon after their arrival at the house.

Oulton Broad Suffolk

2 miles W of Lowestoft

George Borrow lived in a cottage here and did much of his writing in a summer house overlooking the Broad. He believed in ghosts, so it is appropriate that he is one now, seen wearing a long cloak and distinctive wide-brimmed hat.

Owmby Lincolnshire

10 miles N of Lincoln

The cars (wetlands) of North Lincolnshire surrounding this village were drained by Vermuyden's Dutch engineers in the seventeenth century. Local people resented this interference with nature and killed many of the Dutchmen. For the deaths they blamed the Tiddy Mun, a sinister creature of the marshes who was the size of a toddler but had the wizened appearance of an old man. He was a helpful spirit if appeased with the offering of a basin of water at the time of the new moon.

Ranworth Norfolk ◑

9 miles NE of Norwich

Charles Sampson, a Harley Street doctor, published *Ghosts of the Broads* in 1931 and it has proved an enduring work, enjoyed by thousands of visitors to the unique district. However, many of his stories are tongue-in-cheek inventions, and this may be so in the case of the ghost of Colonel Thomas Sidney who Sampson says returns to Ranworth Broad on 31 December each year. The hard-drinking squire challenged a neighbour to a race on horseback, and when the latter strode ahead the colonel drew his pistol and shot his rival's horse. The rider broke his neck in the fall, and that night the Devil came with his Wild Hunt to claim Colonel Sidney's soul, galloping away with him across the Broad, steam rising from where the hooves touched the water. This is the spectacular sight which, says Sampson, the patient watcher will see here on the last night of the year.

Ravensden Bedfordshire

3 miles NE of Bedford

The lane from the village to Buckden is frequented by an evil-looking woman who trails black garments. This ghost has been reported in daylight.

St Albans Hertfordshire ✦ ◕ ☞

Abbey

Ethereal singing may be heard in the nave of the abbey (cathedral) if you are fortunate enough to be there at 2 a.m. The music has been identified as the Albanus Mass, composed by Dr Fayrfax who died in 1521 and is buried in the crypt. The shade of an extra bishop appears behind the new one when he is being enthroned.

Mallinson House

A figure wearing a powdered wig and silver-buttoned tunic has been seen in an upstairs window of the beautiful mansion in St Peter's Street. It is the ghost of a butler who committed suicide after being caught drinking his master's brandy. In 1872 a crowd of two hundred gathered outside the house hoping for a glimpse of the ghost, but it did not appear again until 1977.

St Ives Cambridgeshire ☞

Room 13 of the Golden Lion Hotel has the supernatural presence of a Green Lady who, not content with being an apparition, activates poltergeist activity too, pulling bedclothes off the bed and opening locked doors.

St Osyth's Priory Essex ✦

2 miles W of Clacton

The headless ghost of the priory's founder, St Osyth, daughter of the first Christian king of East Anglia, walks once a year at the scene of her martyrdom, a holy well in Nun's Wood. The shade of a brown monk walks the grounds of the priory itself (which is open to the public).

Salisbury Hall Hertfordshire

4 miles SE of St Albans

The Tudor and Jacobean moated mansion has been converted into offices. Charles II installed Nell Gwyn in the house soon after meeting her, and she is supposed to have persuaded the king to bestow the dukedom of St Albans on their bastard child by dangling the baby over the moat and threatening to drop him. Nell's ghost wears a blue fichu (three-cornered shawl) and is often heard laughing. The hall also has the phantom of a Cavalier wounded in a skirmish at South Mimms who sheltered here and took his own life rather than be captured. He impaled himself on his sword, and the ghost appears with a sword through its torso.

Sandringham Norfolk

6 miles NE of Kings Lynn

The royal home (open to the public) is said to have been haunted even before first George V and then his son, George VI, died here. The ghost is active on Christmas Eve when hollow footsteps are heard and things are mysteriously moved about. The ghost of a boy lamplighter has also been described.

Sawston Hall Cambridgeshire 👑 ☕

6 miles S of Cambridge

Queen Mary slept at the hall in 1553 though at the time she did not know that her brother (Edward VI) had died and that she was monarch. Rebels supporting Lady Jane Grey burned down the house on the day following the queen's visit, but Mary promised her host that she would rebuild his home. She kept this promise and her spirit is believed to visit the Tapestry Room, as does that of a Grey Lady which strikes the door three mighty blows at the beginning of her manifestation. Weird spinet music is also heard, though there is no such instrument in the house.

Scampton Lincolnshire 🐾 🗡

5 miles N of Lincoln

The RAF base (the home of the Red Arrows) has been haunted by a black dog different to most others encountered in these pages. This is the ghost of Nigger, the black labrador owned by the wartime hero Guy Gibson who led the dambuster raid on Germany on 16 May 1943. Nigger was killed on the main road outside the camp hours before his master took off on the raid. Gibson feared that this might be a bad omen and kept the dog's death secret from his team, but the operation was a success. However, Gibson was killed over Germany the following year. Nigger's ghost has been seen both during the day and at night; his grave may be seen at Scampton.

Scole Norfolk 🍺

2 miles E of Diss

The Scole Inn dates from 1655 and has the ghost of a White Lady who haunts the staircase and a room on the first floor. She was killed by her jealous husband who suspected her of having an affair with a highwayman. The highwayman used a room at the hotel as a refuge, sleeping here with his horse.

Soham Cambridgeshire

6 miles SE of Ely

Before the fens were drained, Soham Mere was a vast area of wetland criss-crossed with dykes and with many dangerous bogs. Joseph Hempsall farmed land on the edge of this wilderness and often crossed the fen to meet with drinking friends at Wicken. One night at Wicken an impenetrable fog descended and Joseph's friends begged him not to try to cross the Big Bog in such conditions. Hempsall shrugged off their advice saying he knew the fen inside out and would come to no harm. His confidence was misplaced for he never reached home. It was left to his ghost to guide the friends to the spot where his body floated in the Big Dyke. The ghost also instructed that the corpse be taken to Wicken for burial but this was ignored and Hempsall was interred at Soham instead. Ever since, Joseph Hempsall's spirit has been restless and haunts the fenland between the two villages. He will continue to do so until he is buried at Wicken.

Southwold Suffolk

Cannons still stand on Gun Hill at the centre of this lovely town, and the ghost of a headless gunner has been seen here. He literally lost his head when a cannon he was firing exploded.

Southwold

Stanbridge Bedfordshire

4 miles NW of Dunstable

A well-publicised phantom hitch-hiker appeared in Station Road on 12 October 1979.

Stiffkey Norfolk

9 miles NE of Fakenham

The hoarse, panic-stricken woman's voice that can be heard calling out from Blacknock on foggy nights is that of a cockle-gatherer's ghost, drowned on the sandbank two hundred years ago.

Stock Essex 🍺

6 miles S of Chelmsford

The Bear Inn has the ghost of Charlie 'Spider' Marshall who was ostler there in the nineteenth century. His party piece was to shin up the chimney in the taproom, wriggle through a narrow passage where bacon was hung for smoking, and emerge from the chimney of the other bar. One Christmas he came to grief and never reappeared after climbing the taproom chimney, at least, not in earthly form.

Stondon Massey Essex ✠

4 miles N of Brentwood

The church and churchyard are haunted by the ghost of Richard Jordan who died in the eighteenth century. Eleven clergy attended his funeral and his body was subsequently found so frequently outside the coffin that in the end it was bound round with chains.

Stow Bardolph Norfolk 🍺

3 miles W of Downham Market

The Hare Arms is haunted by one of its first landlords, a man named Capon, who was given a pie for dinner by his wife. The pie was blamed for making him go mad and kill himself.

Studham Bedfordshire

4 miles S of Dunstable

In 1967 seven boys reported seeing a short blue man with a tall hat and a beard on Studham Common who disappeared in a yellowish-blue mist as they approached but then reappeared at a safe distance. This happened three times and the boys also heard foreign voices. Opinions differ as to whether this was a UFO or a haunting of the fairy variety.

Sudbury Suffolk ✛

The head of Simon of Sudbury, archbishop of Canterbury, is kept at St Gregory's church. He was killed by Wat Tyler's rebels in 1381 and his spiked head was displayed on London Bridge for six days. His ghost haunts St Gregory's as well as Westgate in Canterbury.

Thetford Norfolk 🍺

Bell Hotel

Betty Radcliffe is the ghost of the Bell Hotel whose previous existence was as landlady. She had an affair with an ostler and used Room 10 as a love-nest, where her lover murdered her when she became bothersome to him. The room is haunted by Betty who seldom materialises but causes other manifestations, the most curious being the fingerprints that appear on the inside of the glass protecting a seventeenth-century mural. This phenomenon has occurred as recently as March 1994.

Warren Lodge

The ancient tower-house is situated about two miles out of the town on the Brandon road. It was built in the twelfth century for the Warrener, who supervised the production of rabbits from the surrounding sandy heath for the royal table. Later the small, flint-built structure was used to house lepers and it is probably the ravaged face of one of these that is seen here as a ghost.

Theydon Bois Essex ♛

3 miles S of Epping

Ambersbury Banks is an Iron Age hillfort within Epping Forest said to be haunted by Queen Boadicea and her daughters.

Thurlton Norfolk

5 miles N of Beccles

The gravestone of Joseph Bexfield, wherryman, stands in the churchyard, telling of his death by drowning on 11 August 1809. Locals say that he was led astray by the flickering lights of Jack o' Lanterns (or Will o' the Wisps), fell into a dyke, and was drowned.

Certainly August is a good month for seeing the unnatural light of Jack o' Lanterns, which are pockets of methane gas generated by rotting vegetation and mysteriously ignited, perhaps by lightning. Bexfield's ghost still roams over these lonely marshes.

Tilty Essex

8 miles SE of Saffron Walden

The Cistercian abbey was founded in 1153 and ransacked by King John in 1215. Its monks stoutly resisted the king's soldiers and one of them was beheaded, so it must be his headless figure that haunts the site. In 1942 a skeleton without a head was found, and this confirmed the local tradition.

Tydd St Giles Cambridgeshire

5 miles NW of Wisbech

Hannath Hall has a room haunted by a spirit that may be the ghost of Joseph Hannath's wife. She died about a hundred and fifty years ago and Joseph was so heartbroken that he refused to bury her for six weeks. A maidservant who committed suicide after this incident also haunts the house, as does the ghost of a fair-haired boy who was murdered here.

Walberswick Suffolk ✛ 🐾

1 mile S of Southwold

Few of the ancient buildings here are without some form of haunting. The church, for instance, has the wraith of a Victorian gentleman who may have been a church warden, while the Anchor Inn's poltergeist possibly inspired M.R. James to write his best story – 'Whisper and I'll Come To You'. The Walberswick Whisperer itself is a different entity, a supernatural agency that generates a peculiar noise, half whine, half whistle, which terrifies animals and cannot be explained, while the Suffolk version of Black Shuck (known as the Galleytrot) also haunts the village. The ferryman ignores the figures of an old man and a boy sometimes seen waiting on the landing stage – he knows that they, too, are ghosts.

Wandlebury Cambridgeshire 🐾

4 miles SE of Cambridge

The Gog Magog hills and the Wandlebury hillfort are places redolent of ancient magic. A thirteenth-century account tells how a warrior may challenge a ghostly knight to battle here at dead of moonlit night if he calls, 'Knight to knight, come forth.' It does not tell of the warrior's reward or forfeit, however. It is also a place where phantom Black Dogs are seen.

Wansford Cambridgeshire 🚂 🐾

13 miles W of Peterborough

Yarwell tunnel on the Nene Valley Railway is haunted by a cat called Snowy. His owner, the stationmaster at Wansford, went looking for him inside the tunnel but, being deaf, failed to hear a train approaching from the rear and was struck down by it. Strangely, the cat rather than the owner haunts the tunnel.

Watford Hertfordshire ●

Cassiobury Park, on the west side of the borough, was once the seat of the Earls of Essex. However, the ghost that appears here each year on 9 March is that of Lord Capel and commemorates his execution in 1649 for supporting King against Parliament.

Wicken Cambridgeshire 🐇

6 miles SE of Ely

The fenland variety of Black Shuck runs here, and north-west of the village is Spinney Abbey, a famous haunted site where the chanting of monks is heard and their apparitions occasionally seen. If climatic conditions are favourable, Will o' the Wisps may appear on Wicken Fen.

Wisbech Cambridgeshire 🍺

A ghost nicknamed Charlie haunts the Bowling Green Tap pub in Chase Street. He has been described as resembling the man on the Quaker Oats packet and can be mischievous or even violent on occasions when he indulges in poltergeist activity.

Wittering Cambridgeshire ✈

8 miles W of Peterborough

Although RAF Wittering remains a fighter station (as it was in the Second World War), it is haunted by a bomber which, attempting an emergency landing here early in the war, crashed into the control tower and caused many fatalities. The phantom bomber glides in towards the runway without its engines, making only a swishing noise. The ghost of a Second World War airman has been reported from the control tower.

Woburn Abbey Bedfordshire

10 miles NW of Luton

The house (open to the public) is built on the site of a Cistercian monastery, one of whose abbots was beheaded, which may explain the presence of a figure in a brown habit. A man in a top hat was once seen to walk through a wall in the antique market, while the summer house in the private grounds may be haunted by the Flying Duchess, a famous aviator, who disappeared on a flight in 1937.

Woodcroft Castle Cambridgeshire

5 miles NW of Peterborough

The moated, round-towered castle would not be out of place in Wales and, built in the late thirteenth century, dates from the same era as many of the Welsh strongholds. Charles I's guardian, Dr Michael Hudson, was besieged here in 1648 by Cromwellian soldiers under Colonel Woodhead. Woodhead's brother-in-law led the first, unsuccessful attack and was killed. Enraged, the colonel led the second attack himself and soon succeeded in breaching the defences. Hudson was chased to the battlements where he attempted to hide by climbing over and clinging to the top with his fingertips. He was seen by a Roundhead who chopped off his hands at the wrist, causing him to fall into the moat. He was dragged from the water by soldiers who cut out his tongue. Hudson died soon after and his ghost haunts the scene of his death. Two of the Roundhead soldiers involved in the savagery had unhappy fates. One suffered a terrible death when his gun exploded, while the other, who went around the country for a time exhibiting the torn-out tongue, fell on hard times and died in abject poverty.

Woodham Ferrers Essex

7 miles SE of Chelmsford

The moated Edwin's Hall takes its name from Edwin Sandys, Archbishop of York, who built it in 1619. The ghosts here are those of a Cavalier and a girl who drowned in the moat.

Woolpit Suffolk 🐾

7 miles E of Bury St Edmunds

The village derives its name from wolf-pit, and a phantom wolf has been seen here, coming out of a hole in the ground.

Worstead Norfolk ✠ 🕐

10 miles NE of Norwich

The ghost of a White Lady appears in the church at midnight on Christmas Eve. Once a bell ringer insisted on confronting the ghost alone, intending to give her a Christmas kiss. He was later found rigid with terror in the ringing chamber. 'I've seen her,' he gasped as he died.

South Midlands

Guy's Cliffe

Buckinghamshire, Oxfordshire, Gloucestershire, Hereford & Worcester, West Midlands, Warwickshire and Northants

This region, lying across the middle of the country, is often called the Heart of England. It includes the Chilterns as well as the Cotswolds, and Birmingham, Britain's second city. A multitude of well-haunted locations provides a wide variety of ghosts here. Several bear the warning that sight of them brings death within the year – such as the amorous wraiths at Boughton, adept at persuading susceptible lovers of either sex to meet with them.

Bretforton has a ghost that walks in traditional manner, with head tucked beneath an arm. Edge Hill was the scene of one of the best-documented re-enactments of a battle. A Royal Commission was sent to investigate it and its members recognised many of the protagonists. Hergest Court on the Welsh border has the fearsome ghost of Black Vaughan and his dog. When the master was executed, the faithful dog ran off with the severed head. The dog's phantom is believed to have inspired Conan Doyle with the story of *The Hound of the Baskervilles*.

On the opposite side of the region, at Colnbrook in Buckinghamshire, the Ostrich Inn is haunted. An early, inhospitable landlord had a hinged bed which enabled him to plunge his guests into a cauldron of boiling water in the kitchen below. Either he, or one of his unlucky guests, is still making its presence felt at the inn.

Aconbury Hereford and Worcester ✚ ☠

5 miles S of Hereford

The church is haunted by a dark figure supposed to be the ghost of Sir Roger de Clifford. In an attempt to exorcise him, his spirit was trapped in a bottle and buried beneath his tomb in the wall of the church. The attempt seems to have been unsuccessful. Villagers believe that if touched by the ghost you will die within the year.

Alcester Warwickshire ✚

The Angel Inn, Church Street, ceased to hold a licence about a hundred years ago when it became two private dwellings known as Angel House. It had been a flourishing inn for more than two centuries, its upstairs banqueting hall serving as the town's main venue for civic and public functions. Its ghost is the spirit of a murderer, Captain Richard Hill (see Beoley, below), who mysteriously disappeared from the Angel in 1693. He was probably killed by townspeople angered by his arrogance and dishonesty. The manifestation is usually seen as a phosphorescent shape and was last reported in the 1950s, when the owner's dog was transfixed with fear. The present occupants of the house say it is a friendly and benign place, and they have seen nothing of the Captain's ghost over the twenty years they have lived here. The sound of inexplicable footsteps used to be a common phenomenon but have faded over the years.

The apparition of Sir Fulke Greville (see Warwick, below) has been seen in St Nicholas's church; he is buried there and his effigy enables the ghost to be easily identified.

Alfrick Hereford and Worcester 🐾

8 miles SW of Worcester

This is the most haunted village in old Worcestershire, with a ghostly black dog, a phantom crow, the sound of the hammer of a long-deceased cooper, a wagon and horses, and a couple with their dog who walk from the site of the old forge to the church.

Althorp Northamptonshire

6 miles NW of Northampton

An old household servant visits the bedroom of any guest at the hall (open to the public) who leaves a light burning, just to make sure that there is no danger of fire from lamp or candle.

Amersham Buckinghamshire 🍺

The Chequers Inn is haunted by a white-hooded figure as well as having cold spots and doors that open by themselves. A medium suggested that the ghost was Auden, a man responsible for keeping dissenters locked up before they were burned at the stake. This was the fate of William Tylsworth in 1506 and the Amersham Martyrs in 1521, but the prisoners must have been held in an earlier building on the site, as the Chequers was not yet built.

Ashton-under-Hill Hereford and Worcester

4 miles SW of Evesham

A White Lady runs screaming up the village street and there is also the ghost of a robber-monk named Benedict.

Astley Warwickshire

6 miles NW of Coventry

The castle was the home of the ill-fated Lady Jane Grey, who haunts the ruins with the headless ghost of her father, Henry Grey, Duke of Suffolk. The ghost of the hooded monk in the churchyard is known locally as Willie.

Avenbury Hereford and Worcester ✚ 🐚

1 mile S of Bromyard

The ruined church is famous for its ghostly organ music, said to be played by an organist of the church who was murdered by his ne'er-do-well brother. A service of exorcism was carried out and after this the music continued, 'but the pain had gone out of it'. One of its bells, cast in Worcester in the mid-fifteenth century, now hangs in St Andrew-by-the-Wardrobe, a Wren church in London which is the home of the Redundant Churches Trust. The bell is said to toll of its own accord at the death of a vicar of Avenbury (a tradition that started here and apparently continues in London).

Aylton Hereford and Worcester

3 miles W of Ledbury

Aylton Court has the ghost of a little girl called Emma Foulgar who lived here in the mid-nineteenth century. She was accidentally shot by her brother when he tripped as he entered the house carrying a shotgun. Her body was later taken from its burial place in the churchyard by grave-robbers.

Baddesley Clinton Warwickshire ✚

7 miles NW of Warwick

Nicholas Brome, a man of notoriously violent temper, killed the local priest for chucking Brome's wife under the chin. As penance, Brome was made to endow the church, and was eventually buried at its threshold. His ghost haunts it on every tenth anniversary of his death and his next appearance is due in 1997.

A Black Lady and a priest haunt the manor house (which is owned by the National Trust and open to the public).

Beoley Hereford and Worcester 🌑

2 miles NE of Redditch

Captain Richard Hill fled from London to Moon's Moat at Beoley – described as 'ghoul-haunted woodland' – after murdering an actor, a rival in love. Moon's Moat is possibly Moat House, which is haunted on St Agnes' Eve (20 January) by an apparition of a woman. It is thought that Hill may have committed another murder here, killing the daughter of the house. (See also Alcester, above.)

Bidford on Avon Warwickshire

3 miles S of Alcester

Hillborough, a tiny hamlet between Bidford and Welford, was once a much larger village famous for its ghosts. The 'screaming man' haunts the courtyard of the manor. He enclosed the common land of the village for his sheep and was stoned to death by angry peasants. A ghostly carriage-and-pair haunts the lane, together with a White Lady who is accompanied by a white stag. Another White Lady haunts Hillborough Manor, and it is thought she may be the shade of Anne Whateley, whom Shakespeare abandoned in favour of Anne Hathaway, who was a servant in the house.

Birmingham West Midlands

Alexandra Theatre

The theatre is haunted by the benign presence of Leon Salberg, its second proprietor, who took over in 1911 and died in 1938.

Aston Hall

The beautiful Jacobean mansion (open to the public) was built by Sir Thomas Holte, a violent man alleged to have stabbed his cook in a fit of rage. His cruelty was also reflected in the way he treated his daughter Mary, whom he kept a prisoner in a small tower room at Aston for sixteen years after she attempted to elope. Eventually she went mad and died, and her ghost is seen as grey 'but solid-looking'. There is also the phantom of Mrs Walker, the housekeeper in 1654 (the year of Sir Thomas's death). She walks wearing a green dress with a high collar. Aston's third ghost is that of Dick, an unhappy young servant who hanged himself in 'Dick's Garret', the servants' room at the top of the house.

Warstone Lane Cemetery

A White Lady dressed in crinoline haunts the cemetery and the neighbouring streets. Her appearance is always accompanied by the distinctive smell of pear drops.

Boughton Northamptonshire ✚ ☻ ◕

3 miles N of Northampton

The church has long been in ruins at Boughton Green, which makes the haunting of its churchyard all the more interesting. The manifestation is either of a pretty girl with red hair and blue eyes wearing a white, high-waisted dress, or that of a handsome young man. One of these two appears to a member of the opposite sex on Christmas Eve and arranges a clandestine meeting in the churchyard. When the appointment is kept, the ghost gives a smile and a kiss and then disappears. About two hundred years ago a handsome groom died within hours of being married at the church. His red-headed bride committed suicide in the churchyard soon afterwards. However, be warned – anyone who is approached by the ghost and keeps the tryst usually dies within a month.

Brailes Warwickshire 🕐

3 miles E of Shipston on Stour

The shade of the famous Quaker, George Fox, walks past the old Meeting House, dressed in a cape and tricorn hat. A nun who grieves for a child taken from her to avoid scandal haunts the vicinity of the Roman Catholic church, while the bridge on the Shipston road is frequented by a headless ghost at dusk. The legless ghost of Granny Austin suitably appears on New Year's Eve. She is one of the famous witches of Brailes, whose spirits were greatly feared in the district up to the time of the Second World War, when her ghost was seen by a member of the Home Guard.

Bretforton Hereford and Worcester ✠

3 miles E of Evesham

The churchyard and the fields nearby are haunted by a lady who carries her head tucked underneath her arm. A spectral funeral procession comes here from Weston Subedge and a phantom coach with headless coachman visits from Littleton.

Broadway Hereford and Worcester

The Evesham road out of the village passes the field haunted by Ephraim Rolfe, a boy bird-scarer accidentally shot dead by a farmer who thought he was a poacher. On moonlit nights a skeletal scarecrow may be seen standing in the field where the boy died. There is also the spirit of a kennelman. He unwisely went out in his nightshirt to quieten his hounds and so frightened them (perhaps they thought he was a ghost) that they tore him to pieces. He reappears, of course, in his night attire. (A similar story is told at Besford, twelve miles north-west, and also at Ilmington, see below.) A lady riding side-saddle haunts White Ladies Lane. She is the ghost of an unfortunate rider who fell when hunting.

Burford Oxfordshire ✠ 🔫 🕐

The priory was founded as an Augustinian community but now belongs to a Benedictine order of nuns. It is haunted by a brown-robed monk and a figure who looks like a gamekeeper and carries a barrel-loading gun. The bell at the priory occasionally mysteriously rings itself at 2 a.m., the time the Augustinian monks would have attended the first office of the day.

Burton Dassett Warwickshire

8 miles NW of Banbury

The district was formerly celebrated for its 'Jenny Burn Tails', local name for Will o' the Wisps. In the 1920s these assumed considerable strength, even outshining car headlamps, and were remarkable in that they followed predictable paths, probably in places where rotting vegetation produced a considerable amount of methane gas.

Callow Hereford and Worcester

4 miles S of Hereford

Callow Farm, by the church, was once an inn where travellers were often robbed and murdered, their bodies being taken across two fields to be hidden in a cottage that was pulled down many years ago. This building reappears in ghostly form, and figures carrying a corpse have also been seen, stumbling across the fields.

Callow End Hereford and Worcester

4 miles NE of Great Malvern

Prior's Court has a Grey Lady and a Cavalier who was walled up alive. There is also a butler who continued to welcome visitors for years after his death in the 1920s.

Canley West Midlands 🍺

2 miles SW of Coventry

The local pub, the Phantom Coach, takes its name from an ancient disaster when a coach sank with all hands in the marshes that then surrounded much of Canley. (The marshes have since been drained.) The ghost of the coach has been seen on the road near the pub, which itself suffers from poltergeist activity.

Cheltenham Gloucestershire

A house named St Anne's in Pittville Circus Road was famously haunted between 1882 and 1889 by a tall woman holding a handkerchief to her face.

Childswickham Hereford and Worcester

3 miles W of Broadway

Childswickham House is walked by a Blue Lady whose restless spirit survived a rite of exorcism in the 1870s. Twelve clergymen carried out the service but the exorcism appears to have failed because one of them died within a year and the ghost is still occasionally seen at the windows of the house.

Cirencester Gloucestershire 🍺

Lord Lovelace died in the King's Head in 1688 after being set upon by a party of Stuart supporters in the marketplace. It may be his ghost – described as a Cavalier – that appears at the hotel. The hotel also has a strong poltergeist presence which was particularly active in 1980, when it even shook guests out of their beds. The Black Horse Inn is the town's oldest pub and is famous for the word 'James' mysteriously appearing on a bedroom window at the same time as a medium exorcised the inn's ghost in 1933. The ghost was a stout old lady with an angry expression who wore a fawn dress.

Clifton Hampden Oxfordshire

6 miles S of Oxford

The ghost of Sarah Fletcher haunts the house called the Courtiers and is so appealing that people have fallen in love with her, but if she feels herself ignored she causes a nuisance. Two hundred years ago Sarah's husband, a naval captain, neglected her and was about to marry a wealthy heiress when Sarah presented herself at the church, preventing him from committing bigamy. He took himself off to sea after the terrible row that followed, and Sarah hanged herself from the curtain rail of her four-poster bed.

Colnbrook Buckinghamshire 🍺

4 miles E of Windsor

The Ostrich Inn dates from 1106. In medieval times its landlord was a man named Jarman who introduced a lucrative sideline by building a bed hinged so as to tip its occupants into a cauldron of boiling water in the kitchen below. One guest was lucky enough twice to escape the fate of being robbed and killed, but on the third occasion met his end in the vat. However, it was unlucky for the evil proprietor and his wife. They failed to dispose of the man's horse and this eventually led to the discovery of the hinged bed – which had accounted for sixty victims – and their subsequent execution. Predictably the Ostrich is haunted, but whether it is by Jarman or by one or more of his victims is unknown.

Coughton Court Warwickshire

2 miles N of Alcester

The home of the Catholic Throckmorton family since the early fifteenth century (open to the public), the house is haunted by a Pink Lady who walks from the Tapestry Bedroom through the dining room to descend the main stairs. She may have been a daughter married to one of the Gunpowder Plot conspirators.

Coventry West Midlands ✈

The distinctive sound of piston-engined bombers has been heard above the ruins of the medieval cathedral, which was destroyed in air raids during the Second World War.

Croft Castle Hereford and Worcester

5 miles NW of Leominster

The figure of a giant dressed in leather may be the ghost of Owen Glendower. The spectre of a man in Elizabethan clothes is said to be Sir James Croft, Comptroller of the Royal Household. (The castle is open to the public.)

Cropthorne Hereford and Worcester

3 miles W of Evesham

Holland House is haunted by Mrs Holland, whose ghost is seen in the library. There is also a Grey Lady, and the spirit of a soldier in the dress of the Welsh Regiment which fought in the Battle of Worcester in 1651. Cropthorne Heath has the ghostly cortège of Old Dutton's Funeral – Dutton was an eccentric yeoman farmer who died about two hundred and fifty years ago.

Cumnor Oxfordshire

4 miles W of Oxford

Cumnor Place was the home of Amy Robsart, and her ghost continues to haunt the grounds of the present house, which replaced the Elizabethan one dismantled in 1810. Amy was the wife of Robert Dudley, Earl of Leicester, and she died in mysterious circumstances here in 1560. Her husband was involved in a passionate affair with Queen Elizabeth at the time, and when Amy's ghost was seen on the stairs where her neck was broken in a fall, the public took this as a sign that her death was not accidental.

Curdworth Warwickshire ✠

8 miles NE of Birmingham

A Green Lady haunts the churchyard, which also has a headless ghost said to stand guard over the graves of soldiers killed in the Civil War.

Dudley West Midlands

The castle (open to the public) is haunted by a couple wearing clothing that was fashionable in the 1930s.

Dunsmore Heath Warwickshire

6 miles SE of Coventry

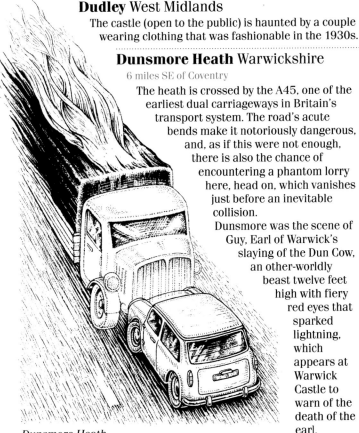

The heath is crossed by the A45, one of the earliest dual carriageways in Britain's transport system. The road's acute bends make it notoriously dangerous, and, as if this were not enough, there is also the chance of encountering a phantom lorry here, head on, which vanishes just before an inevitable collision.

Dunsmore was the scene of Guy, Earl of Warwick's slaying of the Dun Cow, an other-worldly beast twelve feet high with fiery red eyes that sparked lightning, which appears at Warwick Castle to warn of the death of the earl.

Dunsmore Heath

Eardisley Hereford and Worcester 🐾

13 miles NW of Hereford

Parton Cross is haunted by the Dogs of Hell, or the Cwn Annwn as they are known over the Welsh border. They appear when an evil inhabitant of the district is about to die.

Edge Hill Warwickshire ✗

9 miles NW of Banbury

The Battle of Edge Hill took place on 23 October 1642 and was the first major engagement of the Civil War. It was an inconclusive contest, at the end of which more than a thousand lay dead on the battlefield. On Christmas Eve the same year some shepherds and wayfarers found themselves in the middle of a re-enactment of the battle. When they told of the vision more people went to the scene the following night and were rewarded by seeing another supernatural battle. The re-enactments continued, but not every night. Eventually the king heard of the spectacle and sent officers to investigate on his behalf; they also saw the fighting and were able to identify some of those slain. Since then the phenomenon seems to have gradually died away, although the ghosts of Prince Rupert on his white charger and Sir Robert Verney, one hand cut off and the other grasping the royal banner, have been seen on 23 October. The last report of the unreal conflict was in the 1860s.

Erdington West Midlands

3 miles S of Sutton Coldfield

A lady in a pink cardigan haunts a telephone box in Station Road.

Ettington Park Warwickshire 🍺

6 miles SE of Stratford-upon-Avon

The château-like house is now a luxury hotel and has a Grey Lady, the ghost of an Elizabethan servant killed in a fall down the stairs. In the library, which is now the bar, a book propels itself from its shelf across the room and comes to rest on its spine, always open at the same page on which Wordsworth's lines are printed:

> A merry place, 'tis said, in days of yore;
> But something ails it now, – the place is cursed.

However, there is nothing at Ettington to suggest that the house suffers from any malign presence and the ghosts of two children seen playing in the park by the River Stour are certainly harmless. They were drowned in the river and their gravestone is in the ruined church adjacent to the hotel.

Fawsley Park Northamptonshire 🕐 💀

3 miles S of Daventry

The ancient Dower House in the park was last inhabited in 1702. Every New Year's Eve a ghostly huntsman dressed in green appears, but beware of ghostwatching here, for anyone who sets eyes on him will die soon afterwards.

Fotheringhay Northamptonshire

3 miles N of Oundle

Ghostly funeral music is heard in Fotheringhay church, echoes of the music that played after the deaths of Richard, Duke of York, and his son Edmund, killed at the Battle of Wakefield in 1460. Their home was at Fotheringhay Castle, and two years after the battle King Edward IV (Edmund's brother) had the bodies disinterred and reburied at Fotheringhay. Mary, Queen of Scots was executed at the castle in 1587 (see Oundle, below) but, strangely, this is a rare location where her ghost has not been seen.

Gloucester Gloucestershire

Unseen hands help visitors on with their jackets and coats at the Bishop's House.

Goodrich Castle Hereford and Worcester ●

4 miles SW of Ross-on-Wye

In 1646 the castle (open to the public) was besieged by Roundheads under Colonel John Birch. His niece, Alice Birch, was sheltering in the castle, having eloped with her Royalist lover, Charles Clifford. Attempting to escape by horseback, they were both drowned in the River Wye, which was flooded at the time. Their shrieks may still be heard on stormy nights on the anniversary of the tragedy – on or near 14 June – and some have reported seeing the unfortunate couple plunge into the torrent on the back of a white stallion.

Guy's Cliffe Warwickshire

1 mile NW of Warwick

No haunted house in the kingdom rivals Guy's Cliffe for a romantic, gloom-laden atmosphere – yet the place does not have a documented ghost story. However, many people who visit the abandoned house are overcome with a feeling of unnatural fear and hurry away without investigating further. The Palladian mansion was abandoned after the Second World War, but the adjacent chapel (which has a deep dungeon beneath its crypt) is used as a Masonic lodge. Piers Gaveston, favourite of Edward II, was beheaded on nearby Blacklow Hill in 1312. A horse decorated with ribbons and bells (to mock his apparently effeminate taste) carried him to his death, and the ghostly tinkling of these bells is sometimes heard near the monument on the summit of the hill.

Hampton Bishop Hereford and Worcester

3 miles SE of Hereford

In past centuries the stretch of the River Wye that runs through this parish was dreaded by those travelling on it. Most boatman avoided sailing here at eight in the evening for fear of seeing the Spectre's Voyage. The Spectre was the figure of a young woman, travelling in a small boat which glided rapidly, often against wind and current, to take its passenger to the east bank of the river near

Hampton Bishop. Once she disembarked the ghostly lady made 'the most fearful lamentations' on the riverbank before re-boarding the vessel and heading upstream to Hereford. Both the Spectre and her vessel disappeared abruptly about half a mile from the city at a point where the current flows particularly strongly. Anyone unlucky enough to catch sight of the Spectre's Voyage usually dies soon afterwards. The ghost may be that of Isobel Chandos, the daughter of the governor of Hereford Castle in the reign of Edward II. Her lover betrayed the King and was hanged for his treachery, and Isobel, deranged by grief, drowned while rowing on the river.

Harborne West Midlands 🍺

4 miles SW of Birmingham

The ghost of John Wentworth (Jack Harborne in some accounts) haunts the White Swan. Wentworth was a well-to-do local businessman who, in the nineteenth century, used the inn for clandestine meetings with a local beauty. The woman was fatally injured on her way to the rendezvous one day and died in the arms of her lover. Soon afterwards the broken-hearted Wentworth shot first his dog and then himself.

Harbury Warwickshire

5 miles SE of Leamington Spa

The village has the ghosts of a woman and her child who were thrown into a pond by her husband, who watched them both drown. The spectres appear when there is a harvest moon.

Harrington Northamptonshire 💀

6 miles W of Kettering

There is a field known as the Falls behind the Tollemache Arms, which was once the site of Harrington Manor – the Falls being its terraced gardens. A White Lady appears here at twilight, wringing her hands and weeping. She is supposed to be the ghost of Lady Jane Stanhope, who had a violent temper and was feared and hated by all except an ancient gardener – the only person who dared to stand up to her. However, one day she found him standing on her favourite plants and in a fit of rage seized a spade and struck his head, killing him instantly. Anyone who catches sight of the remorseful Lady Jane will die within the next few months.

Harvington Hall Hereford and Worcester

3 miles E of Kidderminster

The medieval hall – the present building dates from Elizabethan times (and is open to the public) – was the home of Sir Peter Corbett who caught his daughter *in flagrante delicto* with her lover. Sir Peter set his deerhounds on the young man with the result that only the man's hands and feet remained (apparently dogs never devour human hands and his feet were in his boots). On hearing of this Sir Peter's daughter threw herself into the moat and was drowned. Sir Peter died of grief and remorse soon afterwards. His restless spirit may still be heard on wild nights in remote parts of Wyre Forest, urging on a spectral pack of deerhounds.

Henley-on-Thames Oxfordshire

In 1752 Mary Blandy was hanged for poisoning her father, a Henley lawyer, who had discovered the body of her lover, Captain Cranstoun. Mary wrongly suspected that her father, who had disapproved of the alliance, had killed him. 'Seeing Mary Blandy' was the local saying for seeing a ghost. Subsequently there were two dramatic productions of the story – on both occasions people reported seeing a strange figure watching rehearsals from the back of the stalls of the theatre at Henley. Mary Blandy is also said to appear at Kingston House at Kingston Bagpuize, Wiltshire (where, presumably, the murder took place); on the execution mound behind Westgate shopping centre in Oxford (where she was executed); and on a lane at Hambleden (where she rides a white horse and appears for no particular reason).

Hereford Hereford and Worcester ✥

From 1926 until 1932 both St Peter's church and the environs of the cathedral were the haunt of a phantom monk. The ghost became so celebrated that crowds turned out hoping to see it in the cathedral close, disturbing the residents and eventually the ghost itself, which ceased to appear.

The city centre also has the ghost of Old Taylor. He may have been an apothecary who accidentally poisoned his apprentice and then killed himself.

Hergest Court Hereford and Worcester 🐇

3 miles SW of Kington

 Black Vaughan is probably the most famous ghost of old Herefordshire. It is connected with the fifteenth-century manor house of the Vaughans near Kington. Black Vaughan is supposed to be the nickname of Thomas Vaughan, who was beheaded after the Battle of Banbury in

Hergest Court

1469 and lies in the Vaughan chapel of Kington church. He began his ghostly career with trifling matters such as appearing to farmers' wives as they rode to market, but soon his behaviour became so outrageous that it affected the trade of the town. Thus it was resolved that his ghost should be laid and twelve clergymen were assembled to perform the rite, which entailed persuading the spirit to confine itself in a silver snuffbox (unusually, a new-born baby also attended the service – perhaps as a symbol of innocence). Each priest held a lighted candle and Black Vaughan succeeded in extinguishing every light except one, this held by a particularly brave and virtuous parson who continued reading the exorcism while his candle flickered. After a long struggle Vaughan's spirit was conquered, imprisoned and committed to the bottom of Hergest Pool for a thousand years, which should give local residents another four centuries of peace. Black Vaughan's dog, a black bloodhound, is still supposed to haunt the house and its surrounds, where its appearance foretells a family death (Conan Doyle often visited Hergest Court and borrowed part of the story for *The Hound of the Baskervilles*). Legend has it that at his master's execution the faithful hound made off with the head. The dog's ghost has often been heard in a room at the top of the house, clanking its chains, and was also seen by a pond on the way from Kington, a gloomy spot once greatly feared by local people.

High Wycombe Buckinghamshire

Hughenden Manor (open to the public) was the home of Benjamin Disraeli who, even though he died in London (in 1881), haunts the home that he cherished, appearing clutching a sheaf of papers by his portrait on the staircase.

Hoarwithy Hereford and Worcester

4 miles NW of Ross-on-Wye

This very haunted village has a White Lady, a Grey Lady, the cowled figure of a nun, and a lady who sails down the Wye in a boat at uncanny speed. (See also Hampton Bishop, above.)

Huddington Hereford and Worcester ●

6 miles NE of Worcester

The headless shade of a woman walks round the moat and up the avenue of oaks each year on 31 January, the anniversary of her husband's execution. Thomas Winter of Huddington lost his head in 1606 for his part in the Gunpowder Plot of the previous year.

Ilmington Warwickshire ● ☻

7 miles S of Stratford-upon-Avon

The 'night coach' of this neighbourhood passes noiselessly over fields and hedges. The ghostly horseman is the spirit of a huntsman named Simon who, disturbed by his hounds, went out to quieten them in his nightshirt. They failed to recognise him and tore him to pieces. (See also Broadway, above.) This is a malignant ghost which appears on Christmas Eve and New Year's Day. The rider may command anyone he meets to open a gate, but if you do so your soul will be lost to him.

Kenchester Hereford and Worcester

5 miles W of Hereford

Roman soldiers march through the village on nights when there is a full moon.

Leigh Hereford and Worcester

4 miles W of Worcester

Old Colles' Shade is the ghost of Edmund Colles who owned Leigh Court in the early seventeenth century but was forced to sell the mansion to settle his debts. When even this failed to meet his obligations he took to highway robbery. Disguised, he waylaid a friend who was returning home from Worcester carrying a sum of money. As Colles grabbed at the reins of the horse the friend struck out with his sword and urged his steed on. When the friend dismounted at home he found a bloody hand still grasping the reins. The signet ring on one of the fingers identified the hand as that of Colles. After Colles's death his ghost disturbed the neighbourhood each St Catherine's Eve (29 April) by driving a coach thirteen times around the Court before reaching the River Teme, passing over the great tithe barn thirteen times en route. His spirit was eventually committed to a pond by twelve parsons. The pond was then filled in and the ghost was laid. The servants of the household used to tell of a giant raven which haunted the cellar. This, like a similar story told at nearby Holt Castle, was an invention designed to safeguard the stocks of cider.

Lenchwick Hereford and Worcester

2 miles N of Evesham

A spectral coach runs between the village and Evesham. The horses snort fire, and flames flash from their eyes and from the whip of the coachman. The man inside the carriage has a vivid weal on the side of his neck, probably the mark of a noose, for this is said to be the ghost of John Wybon, executed in 1615 for murdering Gabriel Bigge.

Little Compton Warwickshire ✠

6 miles S of Shipston-on-Stour

In the 1870s Mr Drane, the curate at St Denis's church, became enamoured of a woman who sang in the choir. However, the woman – Miss Fielding – favoured Captain Brandon, who lived in the Grange. When they became engaged, Miss Fielding cruelly asked Drane to perform the marriage ceremony. He did so, but then, having kissed the bride, he hanged himself in the belfry. Drane's ghost walks in the church.

Little Lawford
Warwickshire

3 miles NW of Rugby

The hall, apart from the stables, was pulled down in 1784 after being seriously disturbed by the ghost of One-Handed Boughton. Lord Boughton lived here in Elizabethan times and lost his hand when he was struck by lightning in the park. This event utterly changed his personality, and from being mild and inoffensive he went to being intolerant and violent. Many people put down his survival to the intervention of the Devil, a view confirmed after Lord Boughton's death when the room in which he died became haunted by all manner of spirits, and the estate was terrorised by a spectral coach-and-six bearing a one-handed passenger. A

Little Lawford

service of exorcism was held in 1752 which, after a protracted fight, managed to confine the evil spirit to a small glass bottle which was thrown into a marl pit. The bottle remained there for twenty years until it was dredged up, causing the haunting to resume. The bottle was then kept by the Boughton family at Brownsover Hall (2 miles east), which seems to have been a very disturbed house until the family left and the hall became a hotel. At the family's departure the infamous bottle was finally laid to rest in a block of concrete at a secret location, and this has put an end to One-Handed Boughton's restlessness.

Loughton Buckinghamshire

1 mile W of Milton Keynes

Three times each year the ghost of Dick Turpin gallops up Trap's Hill, where he once ambushed coaches on Watling Street.

Mapledurham Oxfordshire

3 miles NW of Reading

The mansion (open to the public) is haunted by the ghost of a servant who was killed by his master in a fit of temper. The murderer is also seen, dragging the corpse across the floor.

Mickleton Warwickshire 🦎

8 miles S of Stratford-on-Avon

The Mickleton Hooter was the name given to a beast which produced spine-chilling cries on still nights, and was said to be a huge ghostly cow similar to the Dun Cow of Dunsmore Heath (see above). Another theory is that the noise and accompanying legend of an evil goblin were invented by a landowner to deter poachers.

Nearby Meon Hill has strong connections with witchcraft, and is haunted by a pack of ghostly hell-hounds led by a damned huntsman who dared to hunt on a Sunday.

Minster Lovell Oxfordshire

4 miles E of Burford

The ruined hall (open to the public) is haunted by the spirit of Lord Lovell who unwisely chose to support the cause of the pretender, Lambert Simnel, in 1487. After the rebellion was quashed Lord Lovell hid in a secret room, looked after by one servant – the only person to know his whereabouts. However, the servant died suddenly, and Lord Lovell's body was only discovered in 1718 when structural alterations revealed his skeleton seated at a table, the bones of his dog at his feet.

Napton-on-the-Hill Warwickshire ✟

2 miles E of Southam

St Lawrence's Church is haunted by two unknown Elizabethan women who are sometimes seen kneeling in a front pew.

Naseby Northamptonshire ✕

6 miles SW of Market Harborough

Although for a time there were reports of the Battle of Naseby being subsequently re-enacted in the sky above the battlefield (see also Culloden, Scotland), the phenomenon gradually grew faint and after a hundred years ceased altogether. However, apparitions have since been seen on an old drovers' way near by, which suddenly becomes filled with dusty, grim-faced figures pushing low wooden carts. They wearily plod past without a sound, even though chains hang down from the carts. This evocative commemoration of 1645 is most likely to happen on a hot and humid summer's day, though the part they played in the conflict is unclear.

Netherton West Midlands

1 mile S of Dudley

The ghost of the Dudley Devil, Theophillus (sic) Dunn, haunts Bumble Hole which he frequented. It is said to be 'a most mysterious and strange place'. Dunn, who died in 1851, specialised in finding lost or stolen articles.

Oundle Northamptonshire 🍺 👑

The Talbot Hotel is haunted by the sound of a woman crying at night. The ghost also appears in a long white dress (although some say it is black) and stands at the top of the stairs or by the windows of the conference rooms opposite. Expect to see her between February and April, especially if building work is taking place. The staircase and windows where the ghost appears were brought here from Fotheringhay (see above) when the castle was demolished. It is usually assumed that the ghost is that of Mary, Queen of Scots who, while standing at the top of these stairs, received the news that she would be executed on the following day.

Drumming Well Yard is the passageway that leads from the main street to the rear of the hotel. It takes its name from the well that was once located here, which warned of impending national disasters by emitting loud drumming noises for days on end. Thus it predicted the Fire of London and the deaths of King Charles II and Oliver Cromwell, as well as other events before it drummed its last in the late eighteenth century.

Owlpen Gloucestershire ♛
5 miles SW of Stroud

Margaret of Anjou, Queen Consort of Henry VI stayed here before the Battle of Tewkesbury in 1471, after which she was imprisoned and her son, Prince Edward, was killed. Owlpen Manor (open to the public) is haunted by her ghost, seen during the Second World War by evacuee children who asked about the lady in the beautiful clothes.

Oxford Oxfordshire ✛

Exeter College
The college is haunted by the headless spectre of John Crocker, whose tomb may be seen in the chapel. The Elizabethan scholar appears dressed in a yellow jacket, gown and brown breeches.

Magpie Lane
The half-timbered building on the corner belongs to Barclays Bank and is haunted by a gentle, grieving Brown Lady who is generally believed to be the shade of Prudence Burcote. The Burcotes supported Cromwell and Prudence imprudently fell in love with a dashing Cavalier. When her lover deserted her (or was killed), Prudence died of a broken heart, disowned by her family.

Merton College
The Fellows' Garden is haunted by the ghost of Colonel Francis Windebank, who was shot here by Cromwell after surrendering to him in 1645.

St Giles's churchyard
The Grey Lady seen here is the restless spirit of a lady who left a legacy to the parish charities that was never paid, possibly because her relatives found the money before her executors.

St John's College
In 1645 Archbishop Laud suffered under the axe for his belief in the Church against Parliament and was buried beneath the altar in the chapel of his college. His ghost is unconventional. In its most spectacular form it bowls its head towards the feet of anyone unlucky enough to meet it, often causing them to faint. In quieter mode he walks in the normal way but a few inches above the ground, probably reflecting the way the earth has settled over the centuries.

University College

Obadiah Walker, master of the college during the reign of James II, haunts the room he occupied three centuries ago – room 1 on staircase 8 in the front quad.

Westgate

Mary Blandy was executed at the castle in 1752 for the murder of her father (see Henley-on-Thames, above) and her ghost walks in the vicinity. It is said that a blackbird perched on the scaffold during the execution and that no blackbird has sung here since.

Prestbury Gloucestershire ✛ 🕐 🐗 🗡 💀

2 miles NE of Cheltenham

This is the Cotswolds' most haunted village. It has a Black Abbot that walks from the church at Easter, Christmas and on All Saints' Day; a cavalier on horseback (the ghost of a messenger who was unseated by a rope across the road), and a knight in armour on horseback, both of which haunt the Burgage; an elderly lady in old-fashioned clothes who peers through the windows in the main street; a phantom shepherd with a ghostly herd in Swindon Lane; Mrs Preece's ghost in Mill Lane; a supernatural being that plays the spinet in Sundial Cottage; Old Moses, the ghost of Walnut Cottage near the racecourse, and the malevolent ghost which haunts Cleeve Corner, the rambling old house by the church. A young bride was strangled in her bed here and those who sleep in the room run the danger of feeling themselves being throttled, a danger which passes only if they can gasp out a prayer.

Preston-on-Stour Warwickshire 🕐

3 miles S of Stratford-upon-Avon

An unusual ghost haunts the countryside around this village. It is described as half man, half calf, and in bygone days so frightened the inhabitants that they remained indoors after dark.

The main road from Stratford to Shipston is haunted by the figure of a man that appears, always at midnight, where the road passes the drive to Alscot Park. The ghost is a farmer who, in 1882, wagered that he could ride from Atherstone to Alderminster in record-breaking time. Rashly, he attempted the ride at night and failed to see a low bough which struck him fatally from his horse.

Princethorpe Warwickshire

6 miles SE of Coventry

A ghostly nun and priest haunt Princethorpe Wood, famous for its bluebells.

Ragley Hall Warwickshire

2 miles S of Alcester

The Palladian house (open to the public) is the home of the Marquess of Hertford. Its park is haunted by three White Ladies, though there is a possibility that they may be one and the same ghost. A woman's skeleton was found in the park in the nineteenth century wearing rich jewellery and with an iron dagger close by. The brooches and rings were of Anglo-Saxon date and it is presumed that one of the ghosts may be the shade of this lady.

Ringstead Northamptonshire ✠

8 miles SE of Kettering

A young woman named Lydia Atley was seduced by a local farmer. When she announced that she was pregnant, he murdered her and hid the corpse. Her sad spirit lingers by the church gate, and seems to want to lead people eastwards, perhaps to where her body was hidden so that she may be properly buried.

Rycote Chapel Oxfordshire ✠

3 miles W of Thame

A Grey Lady walks here, usually outside the lovely building. She is called Arabella, and is said to be one of the county's most active ghosts. There are also ghosts of a brown-robed monk; the Earl of Leicester who supposedly murdered his wife, Amy Robsart, at nearby Cumnor Place (see above); and Sir Thomas More, whose daughter Cicely married Giles Heron of Rycote. Giles Heron and Thomas More were executed together.

St Leonards Buckinghamshire ◔

3 miles E of Wendover

Margaret Pole, Countess of Salisbury, is supposed to be the ghost at Dundridge Manor. She was executed for treason at the Tower of London (see Greater London) in 1541. Her ghost, affectionately known as Silkie from the noise her skirts make as she walks, favours late afternoons from August to October. (See also Warblington, Southern England.) The different, scuffling noises heard on the stairs are psychic echoes of a fight between two young boys, when one killed the other with a ploughshare.

Shelsley Walsh Hereford and Worcester

11 miles NW of Worcester

The Court House has the ghost of Lady Lightfoot who was imprisoned and murdered here. She returns in a phantom coach which circles it, then drives straight through it, accompanied by dreadful screaming.

Snodhill Hereford and Worcester

12 miles W of Hereford

The old manor house was built by the Prosser family in about 1660. A ghostly funeral procession, bearing fiery torches, foretells of a death in the family, and the rustling of silks and tapping footsteps are another manifestation here.

Spetchley Hereford and Worcester

3 miles E of Worcester

The Red House has a woman on the stairs who was seen by many people including the son of the author Joseph Conrad. It is a helpful ghost which holds steps and generally assists people.

Stanton Harcourt Manor Oxfordshire

6 miles W of Oxford

Two ghosts were laid in the pond here, but one, the spirit of a woman who drowned herself, escapes to haunt the ruins if the pond dries out – sometimes in a coach-and-four. The spirit of Lady Alice Harcourt was successfully exorcised, however. She was murdered in Pope's Tower while the family were at mass.

Stoneleigh Warwickshire

3 miles S of Coventry

The ghost of a Victorian cyclist, killed while descending the steep hill down to the River Sowe, haunts the scene of his death.

Stratford-upon-Avon Warwickshire

Shakespeare's Birthplace (open to the public) was haunted in the 1940s by an old lady with white hair and rosy cheeks. She was occupied at a spinning wheel but when she found herself being watched murmured, 'Good day, my dears,' and disappeared.

Clopton House, on the northern edge of the town, has been converted into luxury apartments but part of the house is medieval, and it was greatly enlarged in the sixteenth and seventeenth centuries. It was the home of Charlotte Clopton in 1564 when an outbreak of plague came to Stratford. Charlotte was infected, and was quickly buried in the Clopton vault at Holy Trinity church when it was thought she had died of the pestilence. When, after two weeks, the vault was unlocked to bury another victim, Charlotte's coffin was found open. Her corpse was by the door, which was marked by her efforts to escape. Charlotte's ghost, and that of a priest killed in his hiding place, haunted Clopton House before its conversion.

Sudeley Castle Gloucestershire

1 mile SE of Winchcombe

The restive spirit of Janet, once housekeeper at the castle (now open to the public), appears dressed in a long pink-and-white skirt, white blouse and mobcap.

Thame Oxfordshire 🍺

A bedroom at the Birdcage Inn suffered from the sound of persistent knocking and an accompanying feeling of intense cold. A seance was held, which revealed that the disturbance came from the spirit of a leper who was locked up here before being stoned to death by townsfolk.

Walmley West Midlands

2 miles S of Sutton Coldfield

In 1745 a patrol of the Duke of Cumberland's army pursuing the forces of Bonnie Prince Charlie encountered the idiot of Erdington, a neighbouring village. When this poor soul proved incoherent, the soldiers shot him and then cut off his head, which was thrown into an oak tree at New Shipston Farm, Walmley. There it remained until 1827, when the tree was felled. The skull is the macabre ghost that haunts the district, looking for its body.

Warwick Warwickshire

The castle (open to the public) has a 'Bogey Room' haunted by the ghost of Sir Fulke Greville, the Elizabethan chancellor who was murdered in London by his valet. I once experienced the unnatural chill of a haunting here. I was taking photographs in the castle when a powercut forced me to walk through the room in semi-darkness. The chill seemed unwholesome, a head-high floating mist like odourless cigarette smoke. I was aware of the room's reputation at the time.

Weobley Hereford and Worcester

10 miles NW of Hereford

Dunwood Farm is haunted by 'Old Gregg', poisoned by a member of his own family who served him stewed toad for his supper.

West Bromwich West Midlands 🍺

4 miles NW of Birmingham

The ghost of the White Horse Inn, responsible for an assortment of rather tame phenomena such as pacing footsteps and ghostly shoulder tapping, seems linked to the macabre discovery of a mummified human arm in an attic here in 1890. The gruesome object was the severed hand of an executed man, known as a Hand of Glory and carried as a talisman by thieves. The hand was usually obtained from a gibbet and thieves would bend the fingers to hold a candle. They believed the candle had magical power, as long as it burned, to keep a household asleep while they ransacked it.

West Wycombe Buckinghamshire 🍺

West Wycombe Park (open to the public) is a magnificent Palladian mansion built by the notorious Sir Francis Dashwood, rake and Devil worshipper. Thus it is not surprising that it is haunted, one of its ghosts having been seen by Noël Coward in the Music Room. The ghost leaned elegantly against his piano as he played, 'an amiable smiling monk' which disappeared as suddenly as it had materialised. The Music Room also has a female ghost 'of the utmost charm and respectability'.

The George and Dragon is haunted by the ghost of Sukie, a serving girl who threw over three local suitors for a visiting gentleman. She was duped by the local lads into thinking that her noble lover wished to rendezvous with her in the caves. She was to dress herself in a bridal gown so that the couple might speed off to a clandestine wedding. When she was met by the jeering lads instead of her gentleman, she threw herself at them in rage, lost her footing on the slippery floor and shattered her skull as she fell. Her ghost returns to haunt the hotel where she died soon after the incident, and although she is seldom seen these days, the tenants speak of a mischievous presence which delights in playing pranks. Most recently she has enjoyed hiding the VAT accounts.

Weston-on-the-Green Oxfordshire 🍺

7 miles N of Oxford

Weston Manor Hotel was once a monastery and Maude was a nun who made indiscreet visits to a monk here from her convent nearby. One night she was caught in the monk's cell and burnt at the stake in front of the monastery. The hotel is quite pleased about her haunting the place. She favours the best bedroom with its magnificent four-poster bed, but no one knows the reason for her nickname, 'Mad Maude'.

Wichenford Hereford and Worcester

5 miles NW of Worcester

The ghost of Lady Washbourne walks at Wichenford Court, with a bloody dagger in one hand and a goblet in the other. She is supposed to have killed a French prisoner here in 1405 who rejected her advances. She gave him a sleeping draught and then stabbed him in the back. This left a bloodstain on the floor that endured for five centuries. When the stream is in flood the ghosts of French and Welsh soldiers also appear. They died at Wichenford in 1405, at the time of Glendower's uprising.

Winchcombe Gloucestershire ✠ 🗡

The abbey church sometimes has echoes of ghostly music and there is a monk, known as the Winchcombe Ghost, that haunts the Cheltenham road near Postlip.

Wolvercote Oxfordshire ◐ 🗡

3 miles NW of Oxford

Henry II's mistress, Rosamund Clifford – the Fair Rosamund – haunts the derelict Godstow Nunnery where she died in 1177. Rosamund bore Henry two sons before being poisoned by his queen, Eleanor. When the monasteries were dissolved in the sixteenth century, grave-robbers desecrated Rosamund's tomb, allowing her ghost to escape and haunt the ruins to this day, in the form of a Grey Lady. You will also hear ghostly voices chanting medieval psalms if you are at the nunnery at dawn on 1 May, and happen to see the first rays of the sun shine through the broken lancets of the nunnery chapel.

Woodchester Park Gloucestershire

3 miles SW of Stroud

The Victorian mansion was abandoned after the Second World War and now lies derelict. It is haunted by a Roman centurion, a dwarf wearing rags, a gamekeeper torn to death by guard dogs, and a headless horseman. However, its unique spectres are a pair of American soldiers – Woodchester Park housed a secret laboratory staffed by Americans during the Second World War.

Woodstock Oxfordshire 🍺

The ghost of Blenheim Palace (open to the public) is to be found in one of the innumerable bedrooms, a figure that sits huddled over an empty grate. He is usually supposed to be a Roundhead soldier.

The medieval Woodstock Palace which stood by the lake was a garrison during the Civil War, and was haunted by a malicious poltergeist called the Devil of Woodstock, which once forced the Royal Commissioners to leave the palace.

Room 12 of the Bear Hotel in Woodstock is haunted by a workman who fell from the roof about three hundred years ago – some say he was pushed.

Wootton Wawen Warwickshire

5 miles NE of Alcester

Wootton Hall is haunted by a Grey Lady, said to be the spirit of Mrs Fitzherbert, mistress and then wife of the Prince Regent, who made it her home. These days her apparition is seldom seen, but the haunting continues with a sudden smell of unusual perfume which wafts into rooms for no obvious reason.

Wales

Conwy Castle

To the English, the Welsh words for ghosts and other supernatural beings seem to offer an extra dimension of menace and fear. Gwrach-y-rhibyn is the Welsh banshee, while the Cwn Annwn are the black hell hounds that hunt for the souls of those who have led an evil life. Their prey are already doomed, but should you, an innocent bystander, be unfortunate enough to catch sight of them, you may die before the end of the year. The Canwyll Corph (corpse candle) at Plynlimon struck down a man as dead as a horse, but sounds deceptively gentle under its English name, Will o' the Wisp.

In the mountains beware of Bwbach Llwyd (Brown Hobgoblin) and the fearsome Brenin Llywd (Monarch of the Mist), both of whom attempt to lead travellers and climbers into perilous situations.

UFOs are frequently reported from North Wales and it is interesting to speculate whether the sailing ship in the sky described by an Anglesey farmer in 1743 (see Holyhead) would be identified as an alien space craft if seen today.

WALES

Aberbeeg Gwent

1 mile S of Abertillery

The ghostly figure in a tall hat seen on the Cwm road (A4046 to
Ebbw Vale) may be the shade of Hosea Pope, a policeman who was
killed in 1911 while trying to handcuff James Wise, a local vagrant.

Abergele Clwyd ⚓

Prince Madoc sailed from Abergele in the twelfth century and is
supposed to have reached America. His magic vessel, the *Gwennan
Gorn*, is seen off the resort. The vessel used staghorn instead of
iron for nails so that Madoc could use a lodestone for navigation. In
the late eighteenth century the Mandan tribe of Indians were
encountered in America – they could understand Welsh and had
legends and habits that seemed to belong to Wales. To many this
confirms that Madoc's fleet actually arrived in America and that
his settlers thrived there.

Aberglaslyn Pass Gwynedd 🐾 💀

4 miles N of Portmadoc

The pass is haunted by the ghost of a huge mastiff, an unnerving
spectre to meet on a dark night, but harmless. By contrast,
encountering the apparition of the White Lady invariably means
that an accident, and often sudden death, will befall the onlooker.

Aberystwyth Dyfed 🐾

Pen Parcau on the southern road from the town is the haunt of a
headless dog. He is supposed to be the ghostly reminder of a dog
kept by a young giant of the district who saw his father in distress
and rode off at such speed to rescue him that the dog's head came
off in the leash.

Beddgelert Gwynedd 🍺

6 miles N of Portmadoc

The Goat Hotel is haunted by the ghost of an early proprietor,
David Pritchard, who was landlord in the latter years of the
eighteenth century. His spirit returned a hundred years after his
death to tell staff the whereabouts of his savings, hidden beneath a
hearthstone. Room 29 is particularly auspicious for this ghost.

Borth Dyfed

7 miles N of Aberystwyth

The Cors Fochno, the marshland at the mouth of the River Dovey, is
the haunt of Yr Hen Wrach (the Old Hag). She is seven feet tall and
has black teeth and a yellow skin. She brings illness to people by
breathing into their faces on misty nights (the deadly power of her
breath may have something to do with her diet which reportedly
consists of bog beans and toadstools).

Boverton Castle South Glamorgan ♛

1 mile E of Llantwit Major

The Black Lady of Boverton who haunts the site of the castle is the ghost of Wissie, the divorced wife of wicked King John. She loved him in spite of being cast off to spend years of exile here, and wore mourning clothes as a symbol for the love that died in her husband.

Brecon Powys

The Welsh Bookshop in The Struet is haunted by a woman in eighteenth-century clothes who glides through the wall into the house next door. The only explanation for this haunting is that the property had once been the Surgeon's House and thus the scene of many gruesome events in the past.

Brecon Beacons Powys

The legend of the Old Woman of the Mountains is a recurring one in Wales and it is uncertain whether these creatures are witches or ghosts. On these mountains the woman is supposed to be a descendant of the Druids and probably a witch. She ceaselessly roams the ridges looking for those she can beguile with bewitching music. Thus entranced, the unfortunate person is lured to the lonely Llyn Cwm Llwch – the Devil's Pool – on Carn Du and thrown into its waters to drown. Her task is to cast nine hundred victims into the pool and if she accomplishes this she will lose her repugnant appearance of 'unutterable age' and become beautiful again and able to make a human fall in love with her. This will break the ancient spell and allow her to lead a mortal life.

Broad Haven Dyfed

6 miles W of Haverfordwest

This seaside village caught the headlines in 1977 when children claimed that a spacecraft had landed next to their school in the lunch hour. The report would have been ridiculed had it not been one of a series of sightings of UFOs in the district. Others witnessed a spacecraft driving up to Stack Rocks in St Bride's Bay and saw small figures scrambling over the rocks. This part of western Wales is famous for its stories of fairies and this makes it difficult to distinguish between figures from the realms of magic, the supernatural, or space.

Caerphilly Castle Mid Glamorgan

7 miles N of Cardiff

The Green Lady with large head and bulging eyes which haunts the castle (open to the public) is more correctly a Gwrach-y-rhibyn, a Welsh hag resembling the banshee of Ireland. She flits from turret to turret above the ghostly soldiers sometimes seen on the battlements. Staff at the castle feel that the Flag Tower is an especially evil place.

WALES

Cardiff South Glamorgan
Castle
The ancient stronghold was made into a flamboyant palace (now open to the public) by the second Marquess of Bute who engaged William Burges for the work. The marquess died in the castle in 1848 and his ghost appears by walking through the fireplace of the library and progressing through various thick walls to reach the dressing room in which he died. Another ghost inside the castle is that of Sarah – a faceless apparition in flowing off-white skirts. At times she is a troublesome spirit but she calms down if addressed as Sarah. A phantom coach drives up to the castle when a member of the Bute family is about to die (as it does at their Scottish home, Mount Stuart), and an eleven-foot giant wearing a helmet of dullish metal is a ghost seen in the park surrounding the castle. A Grey Lady waves towards the castle from the bridge over the River Taff. Some believe that she waves to attract the attention of Duke Robert of Normandy, eldest son of William I, who was held prisoner here for twenty-eight years. This would have been in vain, however, since he had already been blinded by his captors.

National Museum of Wales
The architect of the building, Dunbar Smith, is said to haunt the building and make work difficult for attendants patrolling at night by moving chairs into their way. He was annoyed that his ashes were moved when new gents toilets were added.

Carew Castle Dyfed
4 miles NE of Pembroke

The White Lady is generally supposed to be the ghost of Nest, daughter of the last king of the district, who was taken from the castle (now open to the public) in the eleventh century.

Carreg Cennen Castle Dyfed
4 miles SE of Llandeilo

This romantic castle (open to the public) has a wonderful passageway descending deep into the crag on which it is built, lit at first by loopholes cut from the side of a cliff. Later the darkness is Stygian and one may well believe, scrambling over the slippery slates, that Owen of the Red Hand and his fifty-one warriors are asleep here. They will wake after a thousand years of slumber and purge Wales of its enemies and bring peace to all the world.

Castell Coch South Glamorgan
5 miles NW of Cardiff

EDITOR'S CHOICE This building (open to the public) must be one of the loveliest castles in Britain, with its turrets and magnificent situation giving it fairytale character. Castell Coch was a crumbling ruin for two centuries before its extravagant restoration in 1865–85 by the Marquess of Bute. The ghost of Dame Griffiths dates from this time. Her young son fell into a

136

bottomless pit in the precincts and was drowned, and she died of grief. The phantom Cavalier haunts the castle because he concealed a treasure in a secret room beneath it and was then killed when a cannon exploded. Others believe that the treasure belonged to Ivor Bach, a fierce Welsh soldier, who bewitched two of his men into eagles and left them to guard his wealth. Over the ages there have been countless attempts to overcome the enchanted eagles (some involving exorcism and silver bullets) but all have proved unsuccessful and the eagles still keep watch in the underground chamber.

Conwy Gwynedd 🍺

The haphazard array of buildings from all periods within the town walls gives Conwy a magical charm and an environment suitable for supernatural activity. Thus there is a cloaked figure haunting the ramparts of the castle (open to the public), a hooded monk walking the churchyard and waterfront, and the bewhiskered ghost of a sailor named Albert who appears in a house in Berry Street. The Castle Hotel has the wraith of a housemaid as well as an entity that thumps down on the beds of guests making them reach out, expecting to find a cat. Of course, they touch nothing.

However, the great Tudor mansion of Plas Mawr, hidden away off the High Street, is most treasured by ghosthunters. The story of Doctor Dic dates from the early years of the house, built by the adventurer Robert Wynne between 1576 and 1595 ('adventurer' was a contemporary euphemism for pirate). The story begins with one of Wynne's descendants leaving Plas Mawr to fight abroad, leaving his wife pregnant and with a three-year-old child. One gloomy November afternoon she climbed to the tower of the house with the child to look out over the estuary for any sign of her husband's return. The way back down the twisting stairs was difficult and, while attempting to help the child, she slipped, and they both fell, suffering terrible injuries. The housekeeper called the town doctor. Unfortunately he was away and his young deputy, Doctor Dic, came instead. He saw the patients in the Lantern Room where they had been taken and realised that he could do little for either of them. Gravely he explained this to the housekeeper who, fearing the wrath of her master, panicked and fled from the house, but first locked Doctor Dic in with the dying mother and her child. Only hours later the master of the house arrived back at Conwy and received news of the accident. When the door of the Lantern Room was unlocked a dreadful sight met his eyes – both the mother and her child were dead and the pitiful corpse of a premature baby was laid out on a window ledge. There was no sign of Doctor Dic. It was believed that he had attempted to climb the wide chimney to escape and became stuck there, as he was never seen in Wales again. It is the ghost of the poor woman's husband, however, who haunts the Lantern Room, looking for Doctor Dic whom he blamed for the tragedy. This spectre has not been seen recently but instead there is a charming little girl in blue Victorian dress whose ghost has been seen many times, and an ancient goose-roasting spit, worked by clockwork, which would suddenly and inexplicably burst into action. Unfortunately when this occurred (and it has done so on two occasions within the last decade) unexpected death came to people close to those who lived or worked in the house. Thus the curator (Plas Mawr is open to the public) thought it advisable to jam the mechanism of the spit.

Cwm Clwyd 🍺

4 miles SE of Rhyl

The Blue Lion is a well-haunted pub suffering from poltergeist activity and from the harmless appearance of the ghost of John Henry, a farm labourer who was murdered here in 1646 when the building was a farmhouse.

Denbigh Castle Clwyd

The castle itself (open to the public) has a White Lady but the more interesting ghost is the one haunting the Goblin Tower, situated a short way below the castle. The tower was built by Henry de Lacy, Earl of Lincoln, to protect the castle's water supply. His fifteen-year-old son was killed when he fell from the wooden scaffolding during the building of the tower, and his unhappy face may be seen peering from its dark, narrow windows.

Dixton Gwent 🐾

1 mile NE of Monmouth

A tramp was once drowned in the river and his spirit, clutching a parcel, haunts the lanes and fields between the rectory and river. A white dog with its owner is another apparition to be encountered in these waterside meadows.

Egryn Gwynedd

9 miles S of Harlech

In 1905 this hamlet was the scene of a series of strange phenomena which seemed to have mystical origins. Mary Jones was an evangelist who claimed to receive messages from Christ and her presence is said to have generated spectacular displays of light when she preached.

Glyder Gwynedd 🐾

5 miles SE of Llanberis

A strange phenomenon has been seen on this mountain, which lies just to the east of Snowdon. Showell Styles wrote of seeing his only mountain ghost on the saddle between the two peaks of the Glyders. He described it as a transparent bear that made a rushing sound like a strong gust of wind though it was a perfectly still day.

Gwrych Castle Clwyd

2 miles W of Abergele

The drama of its position overlooking the A55 makes this one of the most memorable of Welsh castles even though it dates from only 1820. It has both a White and a Red Lady, the latter being the most famous as she was seen in 1950 by the British heavyweight boxer, Bruce Woodcock, when he was preparing for a title fight at the castle. One theory is that the lady was killed in a hunting accident, which is why she wears red.

Hay-on-Wye Powys

17 miles W of Hereford

Mol Walbee, who also haunts Corfe Castle (see South West England), was supposed to have had magical powers and to have used them to build the castle here in a single night. She and her family died horrible deaths at Corfe for their opposition to the tyranny of King John.

Henllan Clwyd 🍺

2 miles NW of Denbigh

For many years the Llindir Inn was thought to be haunted by Sylvia, murdered at the pub by a jealous husband. Recent investigation, however, suggests that the ghost is male and thus likely to be that of the murderer rather than his victim.

Holyhead Gwynedd

In 1743 a farmer was ploughing a field near the town with his ploughboy when they were amazed to see a ketch (a sailing boat) approaching them – from the sky. It was bearing down on them from the east, about half a mile above the ground, with its sails well filled with the wind. They saw a flock of birds mob it and then hastened to the farmhouse to fetch more witnesses to the sight. When they returned they found the ship had turned and was drifting back the way it had come, but with its sails now neatly furled. This haunting could well be the visit of a UFO since the farmer later admitted that he had seen a similar vision about ten years previously. UFOs usually appear in ten-year cycles.

Hyssington Powys ✠

6 miles E of Montgomery

The ghost of a wicked squire was exorcised and now lies in an old boot beneath a flagstone at the entrance to St Etheldreda's church. If the stone is ever moved the evil spirit will resume haunting the village in the shape of a massive and malevolent bull.

Kidwelly Dyfed

7 miles NW of Llanelli

A headless Grey Lady may be encountered on Mynydd-y-Garreg, which overlooks the town from the north-east. She is Gwenllian, the beautiful wife of a twelfth-century Welsh prince, who with her children was executed by the Normans. She searches for her missing head.

Laugharne Dyfed 🐾

9 miles SW of Carmarthen

Dylan Thomas lived here and some claim to have met his ghost at the Boat House that was his home (see also Shepherd's Bush, Greater London). Laugharne also has a phantom Black Dog which is seen near a wayside pit at Pant-y-Madog. This beast seems to be a harmless spirit.

Little Haven Dyfed 🍺

6 miles SW of Haverfordwest

The Castle Hotel has many manifestations: a White Lady whose corpse was found on the beach opposite the pub; the ghost of a hunchback; two apparitions of men in modern clothes (one of them appears gradually, from the feet upwards); and a 'bedroom-invader' (Guy Lyon Playfair's categorisation, see his *Haunted Pub Guide*). This feels like a cat landing on the foot of the bed but is an invisible, supernatural force.

Llanafan Dyfed

8 miles SE of Aberystwyth

Surprisingly for a semi-highland location, it is pirates that are the ghosts here. They are supposed to have hidden treasure in the cave of Craig-y-Rogof.

Llanbadrig Gwynedd

11 miles NE of Holyhead

The New Zealand operatic star Rosina Buckman lived at Galan Ddu and her ashes were buried in the grounds of the house. When Wylfa Nuclear Power Station was built in 1964 her ashes were moved and this caused her ghost to walk as a White Lady, who hums melodically.

Llandysul Dyfed 🍺

15 miles E of Cardigan

The Pool of the Harper on the River Teifi has the ghost of a harpist who drowned here. Listen carefully; you may still hear his music.

Llanfaglan Gwynedd ✠

2 miles SW of Caernarvon

A strange procession of people in eighteenth- and nineteenth-century costumes is sometimes seen in June approaching the churchyard. Once inside the gates they move in an orderly way to the graves where they raise their arms and jump, disappearing into them. They are the ghosts of people drowned at sea and cast up on the shore below the church. The tombstones decorated with skull and crossbones are popularly taken to mark the graves of pirates but in fact the symbol has long been an emblem of man's mortality.

Llangefni Gwynedd

8 miles W of Bangor

The phantom coach that trundles along the Penmynydd road is a psychic reminder of an incident in which a highwayman held up a mail coach and killed its passengers.

Llangollen Clwyd

Plas Newydd (now open to the public) was the home of Lady Eleanor Butler and the Hon. Sarah Ponsonby two hundred years ago. They were famous eccentrics and became known as the Ladies of Llangollen, entertaining Wordsworth, Byron and Shelley at their home where they wore the distinctive traditional dress of Wales. The ghosts seen here are taken to be theirs, though it is not known whether the ghost of their maid, Mary Carryll, also appears. She had the intriguing nickname of Molly the Basher.

Llanhilleth Gwent

2 miles S of Abertillery

Llanhilleth Mountain, to the east of the village, is the haunt of an old woman who may be a ghost or a witch. She is a distinctive figure in a four-cornered hat carrying some sort of pot and delights in leading travellers astray. She greets walkers with the cry, 'Wow up!' and then an unknown influence forces the walkers to follow the woman away from their path into remote areas of the hill.

Llanrhidian West Glamorgan 🍺

10 miles W of Swansea

A phantom coachman named Henry by the locals sits quietly in the parlour of the Welcome to Town Inn. He is dressed in Regency style but there is no story to account for his spirit lingering here except the notion that he might like the pub. To the east of Llanrhidian is the lost village of Llanellan, deserted after shipwreck victims brought plague to the village. It is haunted by a White Lady.

Llanvihangel Court Gwent 🕐

4 miles N of Abergavenny

The White Lady always walks at midnight from the hall of the Court to nearby Lady Wood, where she vanishes. There is also the spirit of a little green man.

Llanvihangel Crucorney Gwent 🍺

4 miles NE of Abergavenny

The Skirrid Inn claims to be the oldest pub in Wales and has good cause to be haunted since at least 182 people were executed on the premises on the orders of Judge Jeffreys after the Monmouth rebellion. The stairwell served as a gallows and mysterious helmeted figures are seen flitting past the Skirrid's windows. Once a woman was taken ill at the inn and when her clothing was loosened she was found to have the mark of a rope imprinted on her neck.

Llyn Cwm Bychan Gwynedd

4 miles E of Harlech

The Roman steps at the upper end of the lake were used by miners in Roman times. Their ghosts have been seen, accompanied by legionaries.

Llyn Cynwch Gwynedd 💀

2 miles N of Dolgellau

The remote lake holds a man-shaped monster which drags itself from the water crying, 'The hour is come but not the man.' If a man happens to be near he will be dragged below the surface of the lake and never seen again.

Maes y Neuadd Gwynedd 🍴 🛏

3 miles NE of Harlech

Described as one of Wales's most treasured hotels, the Maes y Neuadd occupies a building that dates back to the fourteenth century. Robert Graves said that it was the most haunted house he had ever known, and some of its ghosts are extraordinary in that they are seen in mirrors. A little yellow phantom dog also walks on the lawn early in the morning, and the ghost of a nanny visits and soothes children when they are sick.

Mallwyd Gwynedd

11 miles NE of Machynlleth

In the sixteenth century the district was infamous for its brigands, big men with coppery hair whose lawlessness lead to an expedition being mounted against them in 1554. Eighty of them were executed, but the remainder swore vengeance. The judge who had passed sentence and his party were ambushed and savagely murdered at Mallwyd on the following Christmas Day, as they returned from an assize at Montgomery. There were thirty arrows in the judge's body and the screams of his death agony are heard in the ravine where the attack took place (on the A458 near the Brigands' Inn, 1 mile north of the village).

Marford Clwyd

4 miles NE of Wrexham

The village is famous for its picturesque 'gingerbread' cottages, many of them adorned with strange windows made in the form of crosses, which contrast strangely with the Strawberry Hill gothick windows also used in the same buildings. In 1713 Margaret Blackbourne of Rofft Hall (later replaced by Rofft Castle) was murdered by her unfaithful husband. He escaped punishment and married again, continuing to live at the hall with his young bride. Margaret's ghost, known locally as Lady Blackbird, began to haunt the village, looking in at the windows of the cottages (but avoiding the ones with crosses) on her way to the hall where she confronted her wicked husband. She became such a nuisance that he was forced to leave his home and take up residence elsewhere, but this was in vain, since Lady Blackbird followed him and continued to haunt him relentlessly.

Margam Castle West Glamorgan

4 miles SE of Port Talbot

The ruined castle (a mansion dating from 1840) has a White Lady, while the neighbouring Cistercian abbey (also in ruins) is the haunt of a ghostly monk. Both are open to the public.

Monmouth Gwent 🐾

Monmouth could justifiably claim to be the best-haunted town in Wales – it has no fewer than four phantom stagecoaches haunting its approaches and there are also a host of spectral animals as well as ghostly soldiers and babies and a strange leaping figure. There are no explanations for most of these hauntings.

Nannau

Montgomery Powys ✠

In the churchyard is the grave of John Newton Davies, executed for robbery in 1821, who protested his innocence on the scaffold and said that grass would never grow where he was buried as a mark of the injustice he was suffering. His grave has remained remarkably grassless ever since, the bare earth showing the pattern of a cross, and misfortune comes to anyone who attempts to cultivate the plot.

Nannau Gwynedd

2 miles N of Dolgellau

The mansion of Nannau was once the home of the Vaughan family. In 1402 Owain Glyndwr (Owen Glendower) visited his cousin, Hywel Sele, at Nannau in an attempt to

143

persuade him to join in the rising against Henry VI. Together they walked in the Deer Park but Glyndwr returned alone. Forty years later a skeleton was discovered in a hollow oak tree. Nannau was haunted by Hywel Sele's ghost until on a hot sultry night in 1813 the oak toppled to the ground and put an end to the ghost's walking. However, Nannau is still haunted by the ghost of a mistress of one of the Lords of Nannau, who killed the lady and her pet dog when she became too demanding. Her spirit haunts the crossroads where the drive from the house crosses the Dolgellau to Llanfachreth road to reach the Deer Park. Another Nannau haunting takes place at Ffynnon-y-mulod, the Mules Well, where a groom once took a stallion to water. The horse shied suddenly when a gust of wind shook the daffodils surrounding the well, and it trampled the groom to death. This tragic scene is re-enacted in spring and the shouts of the groom and snorting of the horse are heard again.

Nannerch Clwyd

7 miles NW of Mold

The lane which goes to Afonwen is the haunt of a Black Lady – a woman in Victorian clothes who was killed in an accident on her way to chapel. Many motorists have left the road attempting to avoid the figure, which flits across the road in front of the car and then vanishes into the opposite hedge.

Nanteos Dyfed

3 miles SE of Aberystwyth

The Georgian house is famous for being the home of the Holy Grail used at the Last Supper. Nanteos has three ghosts. A Grey Lady, a member of the Powell family who built the house in 1739, is one of the ghosts. She appears bearing a candelabra to warn of the death of the head of the household. The ghost of a lady who left her deathbed to hide jewellery which was never found, and a phantom horseman who rides up the drive late at night, are the other two.

Nantgarw South Glamorgan 🐾

7 miles NW of Cardiff

The district is famous for its spectral black dog, an omen of death called the Cwn (Ci) Annwn. Its deadly effect can be overcome by showing it a crucifix, or you may say in Welsh, 'The blood, the blood which flowed from Jesus's side one afternoon,' in which case the dog will never trouble you again.

Newport Gwent

The castle has the ghost of a giant said to represent its Norman founder, Robert FitzHamon. The apparition fades as quickly as you focus on it.

Ogmore Castle Mid Glamorgan 💀

2 miles SW of Bridgend

The White Lady that guards treasure here can be a malevolent spirit if upset. She once allowed a man to see the hoard and gave him half of it. When he returned for the rest she drove him away and scratched him with her long fingernails – he eventually died from the wound. (The castle ruins are open to the public.)

Oxwich West Glamorgan ✛ 🐇

10 miles W of Swansea

A phantom white horse, walking on its hind legs, has been seen in the churchyard. There is also a vague apparition that floats among the tombstones.

Oxwich

Oystermouth Castle West Glamorgan

4 miles SW of Swansea

A White Lady walks in the ruins of the eleventh-century stronghold (open to the public). For some reason she has a deep, bleeding wound in her back and seems to be weeping.

Pembroke Dyfed 🍺

The Port Hotel was once a residence for officers seconded to the dockyard but became a hotel after 1947 when the dockyard closed.

It is haunted by the ghost of a serving girl who leaves a strong scent of lavender.

Penally Dyfed

2 miles S of Tenby

In the nineteenth century a phantom funeral here preceded a real one, and all the details of the earlier funeral tallied with the later, real one. Even the unusual path taken by the ghostly cortège – it passed over hedges – was also taken by the real funeral, when it was necessitated by a heavy fall of snow.

Penhow Castle Gwent

7 miles E of Newport

The ghost of a serving girl in a blue-grey apron hurries about the castle (open to the public) on an urgent duty.

Pentre Meyrick South Glamorgan

3 miles W of Cowbridge

A curious phenomenon has often been seen on the stretch of the A48 known as Crack Hill. What resembles a short fat man rolls down the hill into an old quarry where it disappears in a shower of sparks. This is usually attributed to the Devil's work.

Plas Pren (Gwylfa Hiraethog) Clwyd 💀

8 miles SW of Denbigh

Few people can fail to notice the romantic ruins on the northern side of the A543 near the Sportsman's Arms. If you chat to locals in this pub they will tell you that the ruined hunting lodge is haunted by a terrible luminous skeleton, but the more authentic ghost haunts a stone bridge nearby. A Roman soldier stands guard on the bridge but it is not a ghost to seek out because if you see him you will shortly suffer a violent death.

Plas Teg Clwyd

7 miles NW of Wrexham

The beautiful Jacobean house is said to be the most haunted house in Clwyd. Two spectres linger as reminders of a sixteenth-century tragedy when the daughter of the house fell into the well and drowned. Her overwrought sweetheart killed himself soon after and both return to the scene, the girl as a White Lady. The main road close to the house, a fast section of dual carriageway, is haunted by the figures of three horsemen who have been known to chase walkers and harass poachers nearby.

Plynlimon Dyfed

9 miles W of Llanidloes

George Borrow, author of *Wild Wales*, was told a story of a man being struck down ('dead as a horse') on this mountain by a corpse candle or Will o' the Wisp. This natural explanation seems unlikely since the incident happened on a wet and windy night when any accumulations of methane would have been quickly dispersed.

Pontypool Gwent 🍺

7 miles N of Newport

Twm Barlwm on Mynydd Maen overlooking the town from the south-west is a prehistoric fort which emits ghostly organ music so sweet that it attracts children within the hill itself. Another legend tells of a great house that stood here until it was buried by a landslide after its lady owner refused to feed a starving relative.

Pwyllywrach Manor South Glamorgan ●

5 miles SE of Bridgend

The huntsman here went on a three-day drinking spree, completely neglecting his hounds. When he returned to the kennels he heard the sound of hounds, but the baying came from the sky and not from the ground, and was followed by the 'Tally Ho!' of a huntsman, also from above. The drunkard impetuously answered this call with his own and at that moment his hounds broke out of the kennels and tore him to pieces. It was said that he had called the Cwn Annwn (the hell hounds of Wales) and locals swear that on the night of the first Monday in August a ghostly huntsman's cry is heard from the sky.

Raglan Castle Gwent

7 miles SW of Monmouth

A ghostly bard has been reported from the remains of the fifteenth-century castle (open to the public), a famous bardic centre when it was first built.

Rhossili West Glamorgan

16 miles W of Swansea

The Old Rectory, the lonely building standing between the downs and the sea, is haunted by a nameless horror that comes out of the sea and enters the house. A phantom coach also races across the sands on stormy nights, driven by a man named Mansel. He was the first to reach the wreck of a Spanish treasure ship and made off with a fortune that rightfully belonged to the lord of the manor.

Roch Castle Dyfed

6 miles NW of Haverfordwest

Lucy Walters, the first mistress of Charles II, was born here in 1630 and it is her ghost which, dressed in white, floats through locked doors. The sound of running footsteps are another cause of sleepless nights.

Rossett Clwyd 🍺

5 miles NE of Wrexham

The Golden Lion is haunted by a morose ghost known as Old Jeffrey. He was a seventeenth-century murderer who was hanged at Ruthin and his body sent to Rossett Green (the scene of the crime) to be gibbeted. The local blacksmith was unable to provide the usual iron cage for this purpose so Jeffrey's corpse was simply

fixed with iron staples to a wooden backboard. Once his remains
had disintegrated, the timber was used in the construction of
outbuildings at the Golden Lion, which is why Old Jeffrey haunts
here, dressed in a ploughman's smock. Room 2 and the upstairs
landing are his favourite venues.

Ruthin Castle Clwyd 🍺

The castle, garrisoned by the English under Reginald de Grey, was
besieged by Owain Glyndwr in 1400. De Grey was a repressive
governor of North Wales and it was his cruelty that incensed the
Welsh and caused them to rally around Glyndwr. The drowning pit
used by de Grey at the castle may still be seen: it was a small
dungeon which could be gradually flooded with water from the
moat. The remains of this Plantagenet stronghold stand in the
grounds of a hotel where, appropriately, a Grey Lady is the most
active ghost. She is the shade of a woman who lived in the castle in
the time of Edward I and was married to the deputy commandant.
When she found that her husband was being unfaithful she killed
her rival with an axe and was executed for the murder. There is
also an apparition of a man in armour who has only one gauntlet,
and a strange, glowing ball of light is sometimes seen. The castle is
now a hotel.

St Athan South Glamorgan 🕐

6 miles W of Barry

A White Lady, Lady de Clare, haunts the site of West Norchète
(West Orchard) Castle. Her husband, Sir Jasper, went to the
Crusades and when he returned accused Lady de Clare of being
unfaithful. Borrowing a form of punishment from the infidels, he
had her buried up to the neck in sand and forbade anyone to tend
her. She survived for ten days. Her ghost (or that of her sister who
used to visit her) is seen early in the mornings where she died.

St David's Dyfed 🕐 ☕ ✚

St David, patron saint of Wales, is supposed to have been born near
to the ruined chapel that was dedicated to his mother, St Non,
which overlooks a bay just to the south of the city. If you are here on
the nights before and after St David's Day (1 March), you may hear
other-worldly hymn singing that seems to come from the tumbled
walls of the chapel.

St Donat's Castle South Glamorgan 🐎 ☕

1 mile W of Llantwit Major

The castle featured in *Lord Halifax's Ghost Book* and he listed four
separate manifestations: a ghostly panther that roamed its
corridors, a bright, glaring eye that could be seen in one of the
bedrooms, a hideous old woman in the armoury, and a piano that
played by itself, even with the lid closed. He might also have
mentioned the ghost of Lady Stradling, which walks in the Long
Gallery and is seen before disaster or death, and another portent

of doom, the Gwrach-y-rhibyn or Welsh banshee, which flies around the castle at night emitting fearsome shrieks when a member of the Stradling family is about to die. Finally, there is Mallt-y-nos, poor Matilda of the night, who appears once each year seeking the soul of Colyn Dolphyn, a Breton pirate who once terrorised the coast of Glamorgan and whose effigy used to be burnt by the people of Llantwit.

St Donat's Castle

Sker House
Mid Glamorgan ⚓

3 miles NW of Porthcawl

The chilling sound of chains being dragged across a floor is the psychical phenomenon in this lonely place. It echoes the miserable existence of a girl who was kept fettered by her father who had a pathological mistrust of her. A supernatural light is seen over Sker Rocks before storms, and a phantom shipwreck takes place to herald a real event that follows soon after.

Snowdon Gwynedd 💀

5 miles SE of Llanberis

The mountain ghosts to be wary of are the Bwbach Llwyd (Brown Hobgoblin) and the awesome Brenin Llywd (the Grey King or Monarch of the Mist). The former is adept at leading travellers astray. His figure is seen ahead and can be mistaken for that of a shepherd. At first he follows the path but then, almost imperceptibly, diverges from it, leading anyone following him towards dangerous ground. Brenin Llywd's throne is among the clouds that clothe the summits and he eats anyone who becomes lost in his domain. When climbing mountains first became popular, the guides who were paid to accompany climbers were genuinely terrified of Brenin Llywd and would never venture away from the recognised paths, much to the frustration of their customers.

The Brocken Spectre phenomenon (see Glossary) has been witnessed from ridges near the summit of Snowdon.

Southerndown Mid Glamorgan

3 miles S of Bridgend

The ghost of a mad Earl of Dunraven haunts the beach here. He caused many ships to be wrecked on the shore by showing false lights. One of them, however, carried his son, whose body was washed up on the beach and discovered by the earl. Dunraven Castle, just to the east, was demolished after the Second World War and was haunted by an old lady in a blue dress who left a scent of mimosa behind her.

Stradey Dyfed 🐚

2 miles NW of Llanelli

The ghost of Lady Mansel haunts Old Stradey House where mysterious organ music also emanates from the thick walls.

Strata Florida Abbey Dyfed

14 miles SE of Aberystwyth

The remote Cistercian abbey (it's ruins open to the public) has a ghostly monk who is seen on Christmas Eve attempting to rebuild the ruined altar. Flickering candles are also seen.

Swansea West Glamorgan

The Grand Theatre has a White Lady who leaves behind the aroma of violets. She is believed by some to be the ghost of Dame Adelina Patti who opened the theatre in 1897, though others say she may be the spirit of a young actress named Jenny who performed at the Grand shortly before embarking on the *Titanic*.

Talley Dyfed

6 miles N of Llandeilo

The ghost of a cloaked man has been seen at Talley House but his connection is probably with the ruined abbey (open to the public) to which the old manor house is linked, it is said, by a secret passage.

Tintern Abbey Gwent

4 miles N of Chepstow

One of Tintern's ghostly monks was happily put to rest about a hundred years ago after he had appeared to tourists and indicated (by automatic writing) that he wished two masses to be said for his soul. The other occasionally makes an appearance kneeling by an archway at the western end of the ruin (open to the public).

Trelawnyd Clwyd

5 miles SE of Rhyl

Gop Hill (or Gop-y-Goleuni) is a forty-foot-high cairn which is popularly believed to be the burial place of a Roman centurion. His ghost has been seen, mounted on a white horse, at the head of a squadron of foot-soldiers.

Usk Gwent 🍺

9 miles NE of Newport

Room 3 of the Cross Keys Hotel has the ghost of either a serving girl who committed suicide or, according to another theory, a monk who was killed in Elizabethan times.

Valley Gwynedd

4 miles SE of Holyhead

Roman soldiers have been seen marching round the perimeter of the airfield. Their appearance commemorates a battle fought here in 60 AD when the Welsh tribespeople (or Druids) were defeated by the Romans. It may be that the curses shouted at the legionaries by the Druids before the battle commenced have proved effective in preventing the Romans' spirits from ever obtaining peace.

North
Midlands

The Tudor House, Chester

Shropshire, Staffordshire, Cheshire, Derbyshire, Nottinghamshire and Leicestershire

This region, the midriff of England, provides an excellent selection of hauntings from its diverse districts of countryside and industry. The Wild Hunt roaming the Shropshire hills is led by Wild Edric attended by his wife Lady Godda. They appear whenever danger threatens the nation, riding towards its source. Beware of catching sight of them – they can send you mad or blind.

Much more friendly is the Boy in Pink at Renishaw in Derbyshire, famous for the passion of the kisses it bestows on women guests. Hauntings involving people still living (doppelgängers) have been reported from this region, and the North Midlands also has unique ghosts such as those of the Irish mercenaries brought in to support the doomed cause of Lambert Simnel. They are seen naked, the condition in which they fought against the royal army, at East Stoke near Nottingham. The village of Wanlip in Leicestershire has the ghost of a black man, a freed slave named Rassalas Morjan who died in 1839 and was buried in the churchyard.

A ghostly barge sailing down the River Severn at Ironbridge bears a macabre cargo, a pile of corpses, victims of an outbreak of plague in medieval times. A sinister hooded figure steers the craft – Death the Helmsman rather than Death the Reaper.

Albrighton Shropshire

8 miles NW of Wolverhampton

The Aerospace Museum here was formerly RAF Cosford and is haunted by a ghost called Fred by the staff. He seems to be attached to the Lincoln bomber in the collection and wears a white polo-necked sweater and blue battledress jacket.

Alderley Edge Cheshire

5 miles NW of Macclesfield

A ghost that behaves like a peeping-tom appears here. He is naked, with long hair, but disappears into thin air if approached.

Annesley Hall Nottinghamshire

10 miles N of Nottingham

The grounds are haunted by several ghosts – the White Lady is said to be the wraith of a servant who died in childbirth after she was made pregnant by the squire; her relatives stole the money she had put by for the upkeep of the child. Another female ghost rises from a well and sits on a tree trunk combing her hair, and a black-robed monk has been seen near the ruined church.

Annesley Hall

Ashford in the Water Derbyshire 💀

2 miles W of Bakewell

Shady Lane, which goes to Longstone, sees a spectral procession of twelve headless men carrying a coffin that is said to be empty – but how is this known? This is a portent of death.

Astley Abbots Shropshire 🐸

2 miles N of Bridgnorth

The shade of Hannah Phillips haunts the riverside road between Severn Hall and The Boldings. Hannah was drowned in the river on the day before her marriage and her wedding gloves and basket still hang in the church. The district also has the ghost of a lion, and a vision of a farmhouse which vanishes.

Atcham Shropshire 🍺

3 miles SE of Shrewsbury

The Mytton and Mermaid Hotel is haunted by the eccentric squire from whom it takes part of its name. 'Mad Jack' Mytton lived at Halston and died penniless in London, having squandered his fortune on drink, hunting and endless daring escapades. His body was brought back for burial at Halston, the cortège stopping at Atcham overnight, and such was his popularity that three thousand people came to the funeral.

Attenborough Nottinghamshire

5 miles SW of Nottingham

Fishermen on the banks of the River Trent at Barton Ferry are used to the sight of a bedraggled platoon of mounted Roundheads, who wade across the river towards St Mary's Church.

Barrow Shropshire

5 miles NW of Bridgnorth

Tom Moody, the famous horseman and 'whipper-in' of foxhounds, died in 1796 and rests in Barrow churchyard. He was terrified of being buried alive and his elaborate funeral ended with three halloos from the huntsman's trumpet. Tom believed that this call had the effect of waking anyone not properly dead. However, the halloos failed to revive him, and Tom's ghost roams the district accompanied by that of his favourite foxhound.

Beckbury Shropshire

6 miles NE of Bridgnorth

Lower Hall was the birthplace of Squire Stubbs in 1671. He was famous for his love of hunting, following the hounds six days a week. It is usually supposed to be his ghost riding up the long drive to the hall, a presence that is heard but never seen.

Bleaklow Hill Derbyshire

5 miles NE of Glossop

The spectres of Roman soldiers have frequently been reported from this locality by walkers on the Pennine Way. They are particularly likely to appear at the time of the first full moon in spring, sometimes in small groups and sometimes as marching legions. The lonely western side of the hill is the scene of the Longendale Lights, on some occasions pinpricks of light as though a group of walkers are carrying torches, at other times a searchlight-type beam of blue light that seems to emanate from the far side of Torside Reservoir and lights up the landscape for three or four minutes. Rescue teams are often called out because of the lights and have frequently reported seeing them themselves.

Blithfield Hall Staffordshire

4 miles N of Rugeley

The mansion, the family home of the Staffordshire branch of the Bagot family from 1086 until 1979, has now been converted into flats. Before this the house was haunted by ghosts: a priest heard walking in the lower gallery, usually at 11.20 p.m.; a man wearing dark clothing and a large and unusual ring on his left hand; a lady wearing a long dress covered by a mackintosh; and a Grey Lady wearing a lace collar and cap, and shoes with brilliant silver buckles. There is also the wraith of an elderly gardener. He attempted to rescue a child who had fallen into a well, but he himself fell and was killed, along with the child.

Bosley Cheshire

4 miles S of Macclesfield

John Naden died on the gallows at Gun Hill in 1731 for the murder of his employer. He haunted the site of his execution until the gibbet which displayed his bones was dismantled. Its timber was used to build a stile and he haunted this instead. Gun Hill still retains its sinister atmosphere.

Bottesford Leicestershire 🏏

7 miles W of Grantham

A ghost bomber is heard over the abandoned airfield at dusk and mysterious lights have been reported in the control tower. The bomber may have been one of the two-engined Manchester aircraft stationed here when the airfield opened in 1941. These proved to be very unreliable and many lives were lost before the squadron was re-equipped with Lancasters.

Bradgate Park Leicestershire 👑

6 miles NW of Leicester

The mansion, now in ruins, was the early home of Lady Jane Grey, the sixteen-year-old queen who reigned for only nine days before being beheaded in 1554. On Christmas Eve a spectral coach drawn by four headless black horses drives up to the ruins and Lady Jane alights, carefully carrying her head in her hands.

Bradwell Derbyshire

6 miles E of Chapel-en-le-Frith

Hazelbadge Hall was a home of the Vernon family. Margaret Vernon was a lady disappointed in love in Tudor times and her ghost makes a headlong ride up Bradwell Dale on nights when the weather is particularly wild.

Braunstone Leicestershire

2 miles SW of Leicester

Braunstone Hall, built in 1776 for the Winstanley family, has served as a school for the city council since 1933. It has a White Lady, said to be the ghost of May Winstanley who joined a convent when she was seventeen but died of tuberculosis within a year (novices wear white robes).

Bridgnorth Shropshire 🍺

The Magpie House Restaurant at the bottom of Cartway has the apparition of a Black Lady, the mother of two children who were accidentally locked in a cellar during a game of hide-and-seek. Unhappily, the river was in flood and rose quickly to fill the cellar and drown the children, whose ghostly voices are also heard on stormy nights, crying for help. A Black Lady is also seen in the High Street. This may be the same spectre as that haunting Cartway, though one account maintains that the apparition is that of a living person, which would make it a 'doppelgänger' form of haunting.

Broughton Astley Leicestershire

8 miles SW of Leicester

The Grey Lady is the spirit of a young woman who lost her sweetheart in the Civil War and spent the rest of her life grieving for him. She walks by the stream and is usually seen at dawn.

Broughton Hall Staffordshire

5 miles E of Market Drayton

One of the oldest manors in the county, Broughton supported the King during the Civil War. When the young heir to the estate saw a party of Cromwell's soldiers approaching the house he unwisely opened a casement and shouted, 'I am for the King,' whereupon they shot him, and he crawled to die in the adjoining room (where his bloodstains remained until the floor was replaced in the 1920s). The boy's ghost walks the Long Gallery, a distinctive wraith wearing red stockings.

Burtonwood Cheshire 🔨

4 miles NW of Warrington

The old airfield was the receiving depot for new bombers flown from America during the Second World War. It is haunted by the macabre figure of a headless airman, a pilot who attempted to quit his aircraft just before it crashed and was decapitated by the canopy. The museum that occupies one of the hangars has an old bus on display where the ghost of the old gamekeeper, who lived in it after its withdrawal from service, has been seen.

Buxton Derbyshire

In 1973–4 there were reports of a phantom helicopter flying over the moors around Harpur Hill to the south-east of the town. Its night-time flights were a mystery to the police and an intriguing story for the press.

Capesthorne Hall Cheshire

6 miles N of Congleton

The mansion, home of the Bromley Davenport family (and open to the public), was built in 1722 and is the home of a Grey Lady as well as a group of ghostly figures who glide down to a vault beneath the chapel. Even more disturbing is the severed arm which has been seen attempting to open a bedroom window.

Capesthorne Hall

Castleton
Derbyshire 🍺

The Castle Hotel is well endowed with ghosts, but not with explanations for them being here. The veiled White Lady is a jilted bride; there is also an elderly Grey Lady, a gentleman in a pinstripe suit, and the ghost of a woman who walks below the level of the present floor, reflecting the changes to the building over the years.

Checkley Staffordshire 🐾

5 miles NW of Uttoxeter

Mrs Hutchinson, a vicar's wife who died in 1895, haunts the rectory and the memorial school which she endowed. She was a formidable lady, greatly feared by those who had been absent from church without a reasonable excuse. Sometimes accompanied by a small white dog, Mrs Hutchinson's ghost wears a mobcap, grey dress, waistcoat and frilly blouse.

Chester Cheshire 🍺 ✠

Bridge Street
The Tudor House (number 29) has the immaculate wraith of a Royalist gentleman killed by a Roundhead cannonball. It took off his head and this may impair his elegance a little. The Falcon Inn is haunted by a maidservant harshly treated by a former landlord. It suffers from frequent poltergeist disturbance.

City Walls
A Roman centurion and a Cavalier haunt the Roman walls that encircle the city. Near Morgan's Tower a blast of intensely cold air precedes the sight of a ghostly cavalcade of Royalist gentry.

Eastgate Street
The premises of Thornton's Chocolates have the presence of Sarah, a girl who was jilted on her wedding day and hanged herself. She particularly resents Valentine's Day displays, which she likes upsetting, and has been known to push downstairs a person who expressed scepticism about her.

George and Dragon Hotel

Although the hotel in Liverpool Road is a twentieth-century building it is troubled by ancient ghosts, being built on the site of a Roman cemetery. Residents hear heavy footsteps marching through the upstairs corridor – ignoring all the fire doors that would interrupt normal progress.

Roman Amphitheatre

The ghost of the Roman soldier seen here appears so vividly that he has been identified as an officer (decurion) of the Eleventh Legion Adiutrix. He was lured from the garrison by a local girl and killed by her confederates.

The Rows

A sailor who, dressed in old-fashioned sailing gear, looks as though he might have appeared in HMS Pinafore, haunts The Rows. He seems to be searching for someone or something and has been mistaken for a pantomime actor.

St John's Church

The ghost of a monk in a grey habit has been seen here and, remarkably, spoke to witnesses in Anglo-Saxon (perhaps it is even more remarkable that they recognised the tongue). The collapse of the church tower in 1881 seems to have triggered the haunting. This may be the same ghostly monk that appears at the Anchorite Cell and walks through a tunnel to the church.

Stanley Palace, Watergate Street

This lovely house was the home of James Stanley, Earl of Derby, who was held prisoner here in 1651 before being executed at Bolton. He haunts the downstairs part of the house in unusual form, appearing like a photographic negative so that his flesh is black, his clothes white. A Grey Lady haunts the rooms upstairs.

Chesterfield Derbyshire

The Pomegranate Theatre was built in 1898 as an extension to the civic hall, which was erected as a memorial to Chesterfield's most famous son, the great engineer George Stephenson. The theatre is haunted by a man in grey and some say this is Stephenson's ghost, which is also supposed to haunt his nearby home, Tapton House.

Christleton Cheshire

2 miles SE of Chester

Plough Lane has the ghosts of two Irishmen hanged on the gibbet that once stood at the end of the lane.

Combermere Abbey Cheshire

4 miles NE of Whitchurch

The appearance of the ghost of a little girl, agonised with grief or worry, used to presage a death in the Cotton family, who owned the abbey after the monks left. Spectres of monks have also been seen.

Crewe Cheshire

The Lyceum, a splendid Victorian theatre, is haunted by the wraith of a young ballerina who hanged herself in a dressing room, while the shade of a bygone actor lingers by the stage door (though once he was seen at the back of the theatre standing with the ghost of the ballerina).

Croft Leicestershire

7 miles SW of Leicester

Croft Hill was the scene of terrible brutality in December 1124, when Ralph Basset put to death forty-four local men for tax evasion – six of them had their eyes and testicles removed before execution. Their cries of agony are heard on wild nights in December. There are also reports of ghostly white figures on the hill; they may be the spirits of Druids, who considered the hill a sacred place.

Darley Derbyshire

3 miles NW of Matlock

Ghost Lane, skirting the churchyard, gets its name from the other-worldly form of a pedlar murdered here about 350 years ago.

Easthope Shropshire ⊕

9 miles W of Bridgnorth

The church and village enjoy the friendly presence of William Garmston, murdered here in 1333 by the squire, John de Easthope, who subsequently killed himself. William is seen as a short figure in grey, usually at dusk in the churchyard. He also visits people who have newly moved to the village and gazes benevolently at them from the foot of their beds.

East Stoke Nottinghamshire ✕ ⊕

12 miles NE of Nottingham

In June 1487 the village was the scene of a massacre when the raggle-taggle army gathered by the Earl of Lincoln to support the pretender, Lambert Simnel, was decisively defeated by the forces of King Henry VII. Seven thousand died, many of them naked Irishmen armed only with pikes and knives. This probably accounts for the ghosts of naked men that haunt the district, particularly in the vicinity of the road to Fiskerton Ferry, still known as Red Gutter because it saw the worst of the slaughter. The churchyard has a stone angel supposed to weep real tears.

Eyam Derbyshire 🦌 🍺

5 miles N of Bakewell

The rectory is haunted by the presence of Catherine Mompesson – the wife of the rector, who bravely isolated the village when the Plague struck in 1665–6. Catherine was one of the first of the three hundred people who died of the outbreak here. Eyam Hall (open to the public) has the ghosts of a white horse and an old man, while at the Miner's Arms pub there is the spectre of an old lady dressed in cape, bonnet and boots. She may be the murdered wife of a seventeenth-century landlord. Hanging Flatt Mine is haunted by the ghost of an old miner with a spade on his shoulders, who wanders about the deserted workings muttering, while Eyam Dale has a phantom cyclist.

Farndon Cheshire
6 miles NE of Wrexham

If you stand on the bridge across the River Dee on a stormy night you may hear the sad cries of two children, the sons of Prince Madoc, who were pushed into the river and drowned on the orders of Roger Mortimer. This took place in the fourteenth century, before the building of the bridge.

Fradley Staffordshire 🛶
4 miles NE of Lichfield

RAF Lichfield is now an industrial estate, but it was a training depot for bomber crews at the end of the Second World War. The headless ghost here is that of a tail gunner who killed himself by walking into the spinning propellers of a Lancaster.

Gawsworth Cheshire ✛
3 miles SW of Macclesfield

The shade of Mary Fitton, Queen Elizabeth I's lady-in-waiting, walks in the church. She emerges from behind the altar to visit the Fitton memorials in the chancel and is also seen to walk to the church from the Old Rectory where she once lived. The capering ghost of 'Maggoty' Johnson, England's last jester and a celebrated eighteenth-century dramatist, has been seen near his grave in Maggoty Wood.

Glossop Derbyshire ✛
The churchyard is said to be haunted by a Grey Lady – contrarily described as being dressed in brown – the ghost of a vicar's wife reputed to have killed her husband. The vicarage is also haunted, possibly by a different ghost.

Gonalston Nottinghamshire
8 miles NE of Nottingham

Waifs and strays from workhouses throughout England were sent to Gonalston to work in the mill. Used as slave labour, they were clad in rags and often cruelly treated. The many who died were buried without formality in makeshift graves in the surrounding woods and fields, and their spirits remain restless. Their sobs and cries are often heard in the vicinity of the old mill.

Grace Dieu Priory Leicestershire

3 miles N of Coalville

A White Lady roams the ruins and has been seen on the main
Ashby to Loughborough road which passes close by. Buses and
motorists have stopped for her but she immediately vanishes.

Grindleford Derbyshire 🍺

5 miles NE of Bakewell

Stoke Hall was built in 1755 and was once a residence of the earls
of Bradford. It is now a country-house hotel which has inherited the
headless ghost of Fair Flora, a girl murdered in or near the hall so
long ago that the circumstances of the crime have been forgotten.

Handforth Cheshire

2 miles N of Wilmslow

The Old Parsonage has the restless spirit of a woman said to have
died of fright when Bonnie Prince Charlie visited in 1745.

Harlow Wood Nottinghamshire

3 miles S of Mansfield

A memorial stone lies hidden in the undergrowth by the main road
near the hospital, which is soon to close, and marks the spot where
Bessie Sheppard was murdered on 7 July 1817. Her ghost is seen
here whenever the stone is moved – usually after roadworks or, on
one occasion, after it had been hit by a car.

Hassop Derbyshire

2 miles N of Bakewell

A ghostly Cavalier is a traffic hazard on the road here, as is a
phantom stagecoach. In September 1501 Prince Arthur, son and
heir of Henry VII, rested by the Great Cross at Hassop and had a
vision of a sinister White Lady, who told him that he would shortly
be married but that this would be his final 'earthly pageant'.
The prophecy came true – within weeks he married his Spanish
bride but soon afterwards he died. Hassop Cross is now in
Bakewell churchyard.

Hathersage Derbyshire

9 miles SW of Sheffield

Highlow Hall, on the south-west outskirts of the village, was the
seat of the Eyre family and has a White Lady as well as a
complementary White Man on a white horse, though the man has
not been seen for some years. The White Lady is supposed to be the
ghost of a girl rejected by Nicholas Eyre, the founder of the dynasty,
who, in about 1340, preferred to marry her younger sister. The
elder girl killed herself, but her ghost appeared to Nicholas some
years later prophesying that the Eyres would prosper, but only for
fourteen generations. This is exactly what happened – the Eyres
were forced to leave Highlow in 1842.

Moorseats Hall is the 'Moor House' where Jane Eyre sheltered from the blizzard in Charlotte Brontë's novel. It has a White Lady ghost which walks in the orchard, and another 'doppelgänger' ghost (see Bridgnorth, above) which appears as a likeness of someone alive and living at the hall.

Hockenhul Hall Cheshire

5 miles E of Chester

The elderly housekeeper was tortured by Roundhead troops after she had refused to reveal the hiding place of the valuables. The Royalist owners had stashed the valuables away and fled after Charles I's defeat at Rowton Moor. The Roundheads cut off the housekeeper's head and it is her ghost that walks from the hall to the pub, dressed in white and carrying her head beneath her arm in traditional style.

Holwell Leicestershire 🐕 💀

3 miles N of Melton Mowbray

The black dog that roams Holwell Mouth, a famous bluebell wood, is known locally as Black Shug. It is seen either at dusk or dawn and its appearance heralds the death of someone close to the person who sees it.

Hope Derbyshire 🍺

7 miles E of Chapel-en-le-Frith

On Christmas Eve a Lady in Black glides along the upstairs corridor of the Travellers' Rest inn. She is the ghost of a young woman who fell to her death down a staircase while avoiding the attentions of a drunken customer.

Hopton Castle Shropshire

10 miles W of Ludlow

The idyllic setting of the ruins makes it hard to believe that this was the scene of one of the bloodiest incidents of the Civil War. Colonel Samuel More had held Hopton for three weeks against the Royalists with thirty-one defenders against a siege-force of five hundred. When he at last surrendered, the Royalists made the Colonel watch as they shot all of his men, disposing of their bodies in the pond. Colonel More was spared and held prisoner at Ludlow. Many visitors to Hopton have watched the last walk of the Roundhead soldiers as they leave the castle, their ghostly bodies slowly disappearing from the neck downwards, leaving their heads floating in the air as they move from the castle to the place of execution.

Husbands Bosworth Leicestershire

6 miles E of Lutterworth

The Bow Room of Bosworth Hall is haunted by a Victorian maidservant. In 1881 the house belonged to Sir Francis Fortescue-Turville, a Catholic, who married a Protestant widow, Lady Lisgar. She refused to call a priest to administer the last rites at the deathbed of the Catholic maidservant, and so the maid's spirit remains earthbound here. (An alternative version says that the ghost is the remorseful Lady Lisgar.) There is also a bloodstain said to be the relic of an incident in Cromwellian times when a Jesuit priest was celebrating mass and Roundhead troops came to the house. The priest made for a secret hiding place, but in his haste spilt the consecrated wine and cut his hand on the chalice – blood and wine mingled to make a stain that never dries.

Ipstones Staffordshire 🐾

5 miles SE of Leek

Two Black Dogs haunt this village – one is seen in the lane to Hermitage Farm, the other at Indefont Well.

Ironbridge Shropshire 🍺

5 miles S of Telford

Room 5 at the Tontine Hotel is haunted by the ghost of a man who was arrested here and later hanged for the murder of a woman at Ketley. On the river a phantom trow drifts slowly with the current, a hooded figure at its tiller. As the boat comes closer, corpses can be seen, piled on deck. At times of plague, bodies were moved from villages to remote plague pits by means of such craft.

Kidsgrove Staffordshire

6 miles N of Stoke-on-Trent

Kit Crewbucket is the lady boggart of the canal tunnels. She has often been seen in the Harcastle tunnel.

Kinver Staffordshire

4 miles N of Kidderminster

The benign ghosts of George Grey, 7th Earl of Stanford, and his beautiful second wife, an orphaned gypsy girl he found working in a stable in 1850, walk hand-in-hand on Kinver Edge on balmy summer nights.

Knutsford Cheshire 🍺

The Royal George Hotel is a coaching inn haunted by a former habitué who lived a double life. Edward Higgins followed the hunt as a country gentleman by day but at night would muffle the hooves of his horse and indulge in burglary and highway robbery. He was caught and executed in 1767 and his ghost seems particularly attracted to the Round Room.

Leicester Leicestershire ✣

Blackfriars' Hall

The hall in New Walk was once Holy Cross Church, and before that a Dominican monastery. It has two ghosts – one is a former prior, the other is Father Norbert, a priest at the church in 1918, who seen approaching the altar.

Castle

The transparent top-hatted figure which haunts the courtyard of the castle is the ghost of William Napier Reeve, a Victorian historian who particularly liked this spot. The shade of John of Gaunt is also supposed to haunt the castle.

Cathedral

A hooded ghost in the churchyard is to be seen, kneeling with its ear to the ground. Should one of its lengthy arms reach out and succeed in touching the beholder, that person will be dead within the year.

Police Station, Asfordby Street

The building used by the police in the city centre was once a fire station and is haunted by the ghost of a chief fire officer from the Victorian era.

Lilleshall Abbey Shropshire

4 miles NE of Telford

The black-robed figure of an elderly Augustinian monk has been seen, and is unusual in being a ghost that speaks, inquiring of the beholder whether that person has discovered the hidden treasure of Lilleshall Abbey.

Linley Shropshire

4 miles NW of Bridgnorth

Mysterious balls of light have frequently been seen in the district, attributed to energy produced by the geological faultlines underlying the village. Although sightings of these ethereal shapes may have resulted in the reports of a White Lady here, they do little to explain the poltergeist activity, or the Black Monk that also haunts Linley.

Lubenham Leicestershire

2 miles W of Market Harborough

Papillon Hall stood one mile to the west of the village until its demolition in 1950. However, Old Pamp, its sinister ghost, survived this trauma and still haunts the stables of the house which remain. A portrait of Old Pamp that was kept in the house was also reputed to be haunted, the likeness leaving the frame to haunt the neighbourhood. Certainly his hypnotic stare is well caught by the artist (it gives credibility to the local belief that he had the Evil Eye). Papillon Hall was built by David Papillon who lived between 1691 and 1762. As a young man he acquired a Spanish mistress who was kept locked in the house and only allowed to exercise on the roof. She died in mysterious circumstances in 1715 and Papillon was married shortly afterwards. A pair of shoes, supposed to have belonged to the Spanish lady, carried a curse that brought disaster if they were ever taken away from the house. The curse was fulfilled on the several occasions when the shoes left Papillon, most notably when the hall was bought by Lord Hopetoun in 1866, and when they were sent to the Paris Exhibition in 1889.

In 1903 the hall was rebuilt by Lutyens and a woman's skeleton, taken to be that of the Spanish lady, was found concealed in a wall. During the Second World War the house was occupied by the USAF, and on the two occasions when the shoes were absent, pilots who took off on bombing raids were killed. Both Pamp's portrait and the shoes remain with the family.

Ludlow Castle Shropshire

The Hanging Tower of the castle (open to the public) is so called because it was once used for executions. This may explain the haunting here – a gasping sound like snoring. A more romantic version of events concerns a lady named Marion de la Bruyère who lived during the reign of Henry II. She had a lover who courted her by climbing up to her window on a rope. One day, however, he proved himself false by leaving the rope for soldiers attacking the castle. She killed her lover with his own sword and then threw herself from the top of the tower. Presumably in this case the gasps would be those of the young man as he climbed the rope.

Lyme Hall Cheshire ♕

7 miles SE of Stockport

 The classical façade of the mansion is misleading – it dates from 1570 and was the home of the Legh family until 1946 when it was given to the National Trust and Stockport Corporation were persuaded to maintain and administer the house and parkland (it is open to the public). It has several ghosts, though that of Martha Benet is unlikely to appear since her shade haunted only when an heir to the property paid his first visit. She married Piers Legh in 1737 and had five children, none of

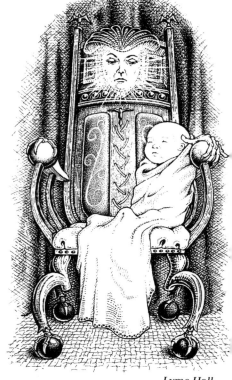

Lyme Hall

whom survived infancy, and so disliked the nephew who inherited the property from her husband that she used to return to make sure that his successors were better prospects.

Lady Blanche was the daughter (some say mistress) of an earlier Piers Legh, who died in battle in 1421, and who occupied the medieval house in the park which preceded the Tudor one. When she heard of his death she threw herself into the stream by the park entrance and drowned. She is frequently seen at the head of a ghostly cortège making its sombre way to the house, and she may also be the White Lady seen inside the house. There is a phantom priest, too, whose presence may be explained by the skeleton found in a hiding place under the floor of a room off the Long Gallery.

The most illustrious ghost is saved for last – this is the lingering presence of Mary, Queen of Scots who was imprisoned here. Her bedroom is often redolent of freshly peeled oranges. It was Mary who introduced the recipe for marmalade to England.

Market Bosworth Leicestershire

11 miles W of Leicester

Bosworth Hall (open to the public) dates from 1680 and in modern times has served as a hospital, nursing school and conference centre. In 1758 it was the home of Sir Wolstan Dixie, an arrogant and ill-tempered man feared by his neighbours. When he found that his daughter, Anne, was having secret meetings with the gardener's son, he set mantraps in the grounds to catch him. However, one of these snared his daughter instead. She suffered terrible injuries and was taken to her room where she eventually died from loss of blood – an indelible stain in the shape of a woman's hand may be seen on one of the ceilings, blood having dripped through from the floor of her room above. The ghost of Anne Dixie walks as a Grey Lady.

Milford Staffordshire

3 miles E of Stafford

A phantom cyclist haunts Weetman's Bridge on the Rugeley road – presumably he was killed in an accident here.

Minsterley Shropshire 💀

9 miles SW of Shrewsbury

Wild Edric (see also Ratlinghope, below) and his band of ghostly warriors haunt the old lead mines here and they emerge when Britain is threatened by war. They tear across the skies, blowing horns and waving great swords on their mission of waking the dead to defend the nation. It is as well to shield your eyes if you suspect they might be leaving the old workings, for if you catch sight of them you will either go mad or become blind.

Morville Shropshire 🍺

3 miles W of Bridgnorth

In 1973 Marc Alexander described the Acton Arms as 'England's most frequently haunted inn'. It is haunted by an apparition said to be the shade of Richard Manners, the Prior of Morville when the monastery was dissolved in the sixteenth century. The ghost sometimes appears more than once during the day, like a sheet flicking from one door to another. Motorists passing through the village may see a large house on the hill with many people outside in Victorian costume. This is a scene from the past, just before the house burned down and its occupants died.

Newstead Abbey Nottinghamshire 🐇

8 miles N of Nottingham

The Byron family bought the Newstead estate when the abbey was dissolved in 1540 and, as was usual, the departing abbot cursed the property and all who lived there subsequently. In the case of Newstead this curse seems to have been effective and by the time of Lord Byron, the famous poet, the family was impoverished and the mansion derelict. Byron himself saw the Newstead ghost – the Goblin Friar – on the eve of his marriage to Anne Millbanke, and knew then that it would be a disastrous match. Byron sold the property in 1818 but the curse remained to bring early death and misfortune to later owners. It now belongs to the City of Nottingham and is open to the public. The famous monument to Lord Byron's dog, Boatswain, is sited on the high altar of the abbey, and perhaps this is the reason for Boatswain's reincarnation as a phantom black hound. However, it may be because Byron's request to be buried next to his faithful dog was not fulfilled.

Nottingham Nottinghamshire 💀 🍺

Castle

Queen Isabella haunts the subterranean passageways of this castle (which is open to the public) where in 1330 she was captured with her paramour, Roger Mortimer, after she and Mortimer had killed her husband, Edward II, at Berkeley Castle. Mortimer was killed immediately but Isabella was kept prisoner at various places for thirty years, notably Castle Rising in Norfolk (see Eastern England), where she also haunts. The Countess of Nottingham walks the Long Gallery of the castle, and seeing this ghost means death before the year is out. The Bonnington Room is also haunted, the ghost often setting off burglar alarms. However, reports that a black alsatian, brought in by the police in response to one such alarm, turned white overnight are apocryphal.

Colwick Hall

The hall, on the south side of the city by the river, dates from 1776 and is now a hotel. Its White Lady may be the ghost of Mary Ann Chaworth-Musters (who, in girlhood, was called 'the Morning Star of Annesley' by Byron). She was forced from her home when Reform Bill rioters marched on Colwick Hall in 1831, and, hiding in the shrubbery, caught a chill from which she died (though at Wiverton Hall, not Colwick). The White Lady haunts the grounds and east wing of the hall.

Wollaton Hall

The great mansion built by Sir Francis Willoughby between 1580 and 1588 was bought by the City of Nottingham in 1925 for £200,000 on the deaths of Lord and Lady Middleton. It is now a museum with a notable natural history collection. Enough supernatural activity takes place in the hall and its grounds for a small book to have been written on the subject (*Ghosts of Wollaton Hall* by Keith Taylor, 1990). The most enduring haunting seems to take place in Room 19, which houses a fossil collection. In the past this was occupied by a Lady Middleton who suffered spinal injuries when she fell down the stairs. She spent the rest of her life confined to the room and is said to haunt it. Often, when the house is viewed from outside in the evening, the soft glow of candlelight comes from its windows even though all the lights are switched off.

Ye Olde Salutation Inn

The fifteenth-century pub is frequented by the ghost of a highwayman who wields a pair of flintlocks (guns), and that of a landlord who unintentionally poisoned himself, perhaps by drinking his own ale.

Ratlinghope Shropshire

11 miles S of Shrewsbury

The Church Stretton road over the Long Mynd is haunted by a spectral funeral, while the other (western) side of the village is visited by Wild Edric (see also Minsterley, above), a ghostly rider who appears with his wife, Lady Godda, whenever the safety of the nation is threatened or our soldiers are to die on distant shores. The pair always ride towards the source of the danger, thus they were seen heading eastwards before the start of the Crimean War and to the south three days before the start of the Falklands conflict. Edric was a Saxon landowner who stoutly opposed the Norman invasion.

Renishaw Derbyshire

8 miles SE of Sheffield

The home of the Sitwell family has several ghosts, all suitably eccentric. The Boy in Pink is also known as the Kissing Ghost and visits one particular bedroom (marked on the bell board as the 'Ghost Room'). He enjoys kissing female occupants, not timidly on the cheek but passionately on their lips, three times, though his own lips are cold. He is the spirit of Henry Sacheverell who died in 1716. A dark-haired young lady in crinolines is a daytime apparition and casts no shadow, gliding rather than walking. Sir Reresby Sitwell lists eleven more hauntings and said that ghosts 'are about the whole blooming place, generally'.

Rothley Leicestershire 🚂 🐕

5 miles N of Leicester

The splendid Great Central Station is haunted by a phantom stationmaster, as well as by a farmer and his dog who were killed on the line during the Second World War.

Rowarth Derbyshire

3 miles SW of Glossop

Long Lee Farm is haunted by a White Lady, the ghost of a miserly old woman, and has a Boggart Room which used to contain the coffin of an infant, kept here to avoid paying the Shroud Tax levied in the seventeenth century.

Rufford Abbey Nottinghamshire

2 miles S of Ollerton

The ruins of the Cistercian monastery are situated in one of the great parks of the Dukeries. A phantom monk, his black cowl pulled over a grinning skull, walks here. Apparently, an entry in the Edwinstowe church register tells of a man dying of fright after encountering this ghost early in the twentieth century.

Sankey Cheshire

2 miles W of Warrington

Buttermilk Bridge takes its name from the buttermilk sold by a lady to the navvies constructing the canal. Hers is a formidable ghost and one that is often seen, a figure wearing a black shawl with ghastly face and terrible, cackling laugh.

Scrooby Nottinghamshire

2 miles S of Bawtry

The village is on the original course of the Great North Road and was the scene of a brutal murder in 1779 when the toll keeper and his wife were killed. John Spencer, the murderer, was quickly caught and his body was hanged in chains at the scene of the crime at the northern end of the village. A ghostly re-enactment of the murder sometimes takes place here.

Sheldon Derbyshire

2 miles W of Bakewell

The abandoned Magpie Mine is both cursed and haunted. Its ghost is an old miner apparently able to stand on water.

Shocklach Cheshire ✠

7 miles E of Wrexham

The isolated church is to the north of the village by the River Dee. Many of the Brereton family are buried here, and their ghosts are said to drive up to the church each year for a family gathering.

Shrewsbury Shropshire 🍺

Castle

One of the most terrible of ghosts haunts the fourteenth-century stronghold – perhaps it is fortunate that public access is currently restricted. An enormous figure is seen dragging a screaming woman by the hair. The psychopathic phantom is that of an ogre who once menaced the town, and the woman is his ninth and final victim. After her terrible death the townspeople were rallied by her sister, and the ogre, who kept the fingertips and toes of his victims as keepsakes, was tracked down and brought to justice, being hanged, drawn and quartered.

Dun Cow

Some of Prince Rupert's Dutch military staff stayed at the Dun Cow during the Civil War. One of them killed a servant at the pub and was sentenced to death. On the scaffold he complained it was unfair that he, a Dutchman, should be executed for the killing of only one Englishman. It may be his ghost that is sometimes seen in the pub, dressed in the uniform of a cavalry officer of the period. Certainly this ghost cannot be confused with the one that haunts the rooms above the bar. This is a monk in a glittering brown robe, seemingly bespangled with fairy lights. It is a bad-tempered presence and sometimes throws things at people.

Nag's Head

The Nag's Head on Wyle Cop was troubled by haunting which broke out when the pub was being altered in the 1980s. A sealed-up room was discovered and thought to be the cause of the trouble, so it was hastily bricked up again. Heavy breathing and the appearance of an apparition in a long coat and tall hat were the manifestations, but they have not recurred recently.

Prince Rupert Hotel

The name of the hotel commemorates the visit of Prince Rupert to the town during the Civil War, when he lodged here. However, it is not a royal ghost that haunts the hotel but that of an unfortunate man who lost his prospective bride to his best man on the eve of the wedding. The groom-to-be hanged himself and his ghost is seen in Room 7 and the passage leading to it.

Spondon Derbyshire ✛

3 miles E of Derby

St Werburgh's church has a Blue Lady who was photographed in the 1970s. She leaves the church by the vestry door and also haunts the former vicarage, which has several other ghosts.

Spurstow Cheshire

6 miles NW of Nantwich

Dead Man's Lane takes its name from an incident concerning the wicked squire of the village. He was overheard plotting the murder of one of his tenants – he planned to carry off his daughter – but the tenant was forewarned and thwarted the ambush, striking off the squire's head in the process. The headless ghost of the squire haunts the lane, following the route taken by corpse going to the church for burial.

Stiperstones Shropshire 🌑 💀

11 miles SW of Shrewsbury

On 22 December all the ghosts of Shropshire gather at the Stiperstones and are seen in debate (but anyone witnessing the sight is sure to die).

Stoke Dry Leicestershire ✠

2 miles SW of Uppingham

The church is haunted by the ghost of a woman who was imprisoned by a rector in the small room above the porch. He believed her to be a witch and left her there to starve to death.

Sutton Cheney Leicestershire ⚔

4 miles N of Hinckley

The Battle of Bosworth Field took place in this parish in 1485 and brought about the defeat of Richard III. The battlefield is haunted by a phantom horseman and a headless foot-soldier.

Swinscoe Staffordshire 🐕

3 miles NW of Ashbourne

The 'Padfoot' (black dog) which haunts the village is supposed to guard the graves of three Jacobites ambushed here when Bonnie Prince Charlie's army was in retreat from Derby in 1745.

Tamworth Castle Staffordshire

The castle (open to the public) has a terrace haunted by a White Lady, supposed to be the mistress of Sir Tarquin, who was killed in the jousting grounds here by the noble Sir Lancelot. The castle's other ghost, the Black Lady of Tamworth, is connected with another famous figure, the evil Baron Marmion immortalised by Sir Walter Scott. She is the spirit of a medieval prioress who caused Marmion to restore her monastery's property by making him dream of horrible consequences that would ensue if he ignored her petition. The Black Lady appears in the Ghost Room. Visitors to the castle are also shown a 'Murder Room', also supposed to be haunted.

Tideswell Derbyshire 🍺

6 miles NW of Bakewell

The George Hotel has the ghost of Old Sarah, a Victorian barmaid who is eternally looking for her husband. Tideswell also has the spectre of a fair-haired lady in a nightgown who leaves her grave in the churchyard to visit Wheston Hall, about a mile to the west of the village. She murdered her husband at Wheston and buried his body in the orchard there.

Tunstead Farm Derbyshire

2 miles W of Chapel-en-le-Frith

The skull of Dickey o' Tunstead which made this location famous for at least two centuries has now been taken from the farmhouse and buried in the garden, the owners of the property tiring of the publicity that Dickey attracted. The legend dates from the reign of Henry IV, when the yeoman farmer of Tunstead, Ned Dickson, joined the King's army to fight in France, leaving his farm in the care of his cousin. Dickson was gravely wounded at Navarre, but eventually managed to return to Tunstead, where his appearance caused consternation to his cousin, who had assumed him dead. The cousin, with his wife, ensured his inheritance by murdering the invalid as he slept, hiding the body in the garden. Subsequently, everything went wrong for the murderers and they were seriously troubled by the ghost of the murdered man, until a witch advised them to bring Dickey's skull indoors. She warned that should it ever leave the farm, disaster would ensue. Certainly on the several occasions when tenants or owners disregarded the warning, the farm became violently disturbed, while if treated with respect Dickey proved to be a benign talisman to the property. As with most legends, experts have found flaws in the story, the major one being that the skull is of a young woman (certainly the ghost most often seen at Tunstead has been female). It will be interesting to hear whether Dickey's recent removal from the house generates further psychic activity.

Twycross Leicestershire

7 miles S of Ashby

A gibbet post stands close to the A444, on the side of the road to Bilstone. It was erected in 1800 to display the body of John Massey who killed his wife by throwing her into the millrace at Bilstone. Massey was famous as a wrestler and was nicknamed Topsy-Turvy because of the ease with which he upended opponents. He had thrown his young daughter into the water at the same time as his wife, but she survived. Her ghost may be seen gazing at the gibbet where her father's body hung for twenty years, with the dripping ghost of her mother.

Utkinton Hall Cheshire

9 miles E of Chester

In Tudor times the house was troubled by a very disagreeable ghost, which a priest managed to 'consign' into the body of a blackbird in the walled garden. The blackbirds that sing around the rambling old farmhouse are descendants of the one holding the spirit of the ghost.

Wanlip Leicestershire

4 miles N of Leicester

The ghost of a black boy has been seen here and is supposed to be that of Rassalas Morjan, a rescued slave who died in 1839 and is buried in the churchyard.

Warslow Staffordshire

6 miles NE of Leek

The lonely moorland between Onecote and Warslow is roamed by a headless rider mounted on a white horse. This gruesome apparition follows the road over Butterton Moor to Onecote, and is said to be the ghost of a knight whose horse brought his headless body home after a skirmish with the Scots.

Weston Rhyn Shropshire 🏞

3 miles N of Oswestry

Parts of Tyn-y-Rhos Hall go back to medieval times, but its White Lady is the ghost of a Miss Phillips whose family occupied the hall during the rule of Cromwell. She was tortured by Roundhead troops after they found a priest concealed at Tyn-y-Rhos, and then taken away for execution at Chirk.

   Another ghost is seen lying on a day-bed in the drawing room. He was the young son of the house, gassed in the First World War, who was brought back to England to die at home.

Whitchurch Shropshire

After the Battle of Evesham in 1264, a straggling remnant of Prince Edward's defeated army was cornered and butchered at Whitchurch. Blaney's Lane is haunted by the ghosts of these poor souls, whose bodies were thrown into the river at Dead Man's Ayot.

Whittington Staffordshire 🍺

4 miles N of Kidderminster

Dick Whittington, the celebrated Lord Mayor of London, owned land here, and not surprisingly his ghost haunts the place. The ghost is claimed by the Whittington Inn, but there is a more lavish spectacle on the main road outside, where the ghostly Lord Mayor rides by in his coach-and-six. Lady Jane Grey also lived at the inn for a time and her spirit has been seen, but the most unsettling presence is that of a 'bedroom intruder', an unseen ghost which keeps people pinned down in their beds. One bedroom in particular is notorious for this phenomenon.

   On Whittington Common in 1812, William Howe murdered a local farmer. Local opinion dictated that after execution his body should be gibbeted at the scene of the crime. His ghost haunts Gibbet Lane, as does that of a girl whose skeleton was found at the site of the old gibbet in 1906, a rusty dagger protruding from her ribs.

Wilderhope Shropshire

7 miles SW of Much Wenlock

The manor house here is now a youth hostel, but at the time of the Civil War was the home of Major Smallman, a Royalist supporter. He was imprisoned at the house but managed to escape and was riding along the crest of Wenlock Edge when he came face to face with a Roundhead patrol. The only way to escape was to ride over the 100-foot-high precipice to the left, which he did, breaking his fall at the bottom by clinging to the branches of a crab-apple tree. His horse was killed and haunts the scene of the incident close to the Plough Inn. The road past the pub on the top of the Edge has a bad reputation – drivers complain of an unnatural mist which causes electrical circuits to fail, and of steering which suddenly gains a mind of its own and leads to collisions.

Winnats Pass Derbyshire

1 mile W of Castleton

A young couple called Henry and Clara were on their way to a clandestine marriage when they were waylaid by three ruffianly lead-miners and cruelly murdered here in 1758. When the rain beats down and the wind howls through the pass, their ghosts are seen here, although more often it is only their voices that linger, begging for mercy. The three miners were never caught but natural (or supernatural) justice prevailed, one being crushed to death in a rockfall, another going mad, and the third hanging himself.

Wombourne Staffordshire

4 miles SW of Wolverhampton

The bloody finale of the Gunpowder Plot took place in November 1605 here at Holbeche House, where the remaining conspirators were either killed or captured. Phantom riders are the last memorial to the conspirators – hooves are often heard, and gates and hedges are damaged by their passing, usually on the Bridgnorth road.

Youlgreave Derbyshire 🐾

3 miles S of Bakewell

The supernatural re-enactment of a duel between a Cavalier and a Roundhead takes place at Youlgreave Hall each year on a night in November. The road to Middleton is haunted by a phantom coach-and-four which sometimes has dogs running alongside.

North West England

Cumbria, Lancashire, Greater Manchester and Merseyside

Boggart, skriker and cappel are three of the names carried by ghosts in this region, which includes the Lake District and the Pennine fells of Cumbria and Lancashire as well as the industrial hinterlands of Liverpool and Manchester. The industrial revolution generated surprisingly few ghosts – remarkable in view of the suffering inflicted on the young and the poor which led to so many premature and painful deaths – and in this region, as in many others, a great number of the hauntings derive from the religious persecutions of the sixteenth and seventeenth centuries.

Britain's most interesting vampire story also comes from this region, from Croglin, a village in the remote hills of eastern Cumbria. No one who visits the place can fail to be impressed by the windswept isolation of the old house where the incident occurred three hundred years ago.

A typical Cumbrian ghost is that of a good-natured farmer who, many centuries ago, was wont to spend much of his time in the taverns of Egremont, relying on his faithful pony to find the way back to his fellside farm. One Christmas Eve he set off for home in his usual intoxicated state and was never seen in earthly form again, though his merry ghost is occasionally encountered riding a plodding pony up a lonely lane.

Appleby Cumbria

Hanging Shaw, the moorland to the north of the town, was where felons were executed and gibbeted – hence the name. The place is notoriously well-haunted by the ghosts of those who suffered there and a proposal to move the famous horse fair to Hanging Shaw from its traditional site was opposed by the gypsies who knew of Hanging Shaw's reputation.

Ashton-under-Lyne Greater Manchester ☕

7 miles E of Manchester

The Tameside Theatre is haunted by Ernie, a ghostly violinist, as well as by other entities, some of them malevolent.

Askerton Castle Cumbria

6 miles N of Brampton

A White Lady haunts the parkland surrounding the castle and is noteworthy in having the ability to speak. She once appeared in front of a horseman and grabbed his bridle, telling him that she would let go only if he gave a promise that he would undertake a task for her which he would never divulge, on pain of death. The White Lady disappeared once the promise was given and the horseman, not unnaturally, kept her secret.

Astley Greater Manchester

8 miles W of Manchester

A Grey Lady may be seen searching for something near the canal. She may be the ghost of eighteen-year-old Anne Mort who died of a broken heart after her parents banished her suitor because he was a Catholic.

Barrock Fell Cumbria

7 miles SE of Carlisle

A highwayman named John Whitfield suffered a particularly nasty death here in 1768: he was strung up alive in a gibbet by the roadside. He swung in his metal cage for some days before a coach driver shot him. His cries of agony have been heard on the A6 at the spot where the gibbet once stood.

Bebington Merseyside ⊕

3 miles S of Birkenhead

The church and churchyard are haunted by grey-robed monks whose apparitions glide about eighteen inches above the ground (this is supposed to reflect the changes in level since Norman times). There have also been reports of a ghostly nun and a phantom hitch-hiker in Poulton Road.

Beetham Cumbria 🐾

8 miles SW of Kendal

The Cappel is the ghostly black dog of Cumbria – a fearsome creature with its blazing eyes and terrible ferocity. One of these phantoms once dwelt in a barn at Cappleside Hall near Beetham where it helped the farmer both with his stock and as a guard dog that terrorised locals and strangers. It was even heard to talk to its master, and this probably lead to the vicar exorcising it to spend eternity in the waters of the Bela River. Only one wall of Cappleside Hall survives today and there have been no recent sightings of the Cappleside Lady that formerly haunted here.

Blackpool Lancashire

A ghost tram is sometimes heard rumbling along by the promenade in the early hours of stormy nights and at Bispham a long-dead pointsman is seen with his lantern walking the tracks.

Blease Hall Cumbria
3 miles SE of Kendal

A dobbie stone protects the house from evil. These are common in Cumbria; they are three-faced prehistoric hammerheads which, like certain skulls, have the power of returning to their homes if ever taken away. In spite of this the old house has a haunted bedroom, and the ghostly funeral procession seen outside is the re-enactment of the burial of a girl who died of a broken heart when her lover was killed fighting in a Crusade.

Bramhall Hall Greater Manchester
4 miles S of Stockport

The Red Rider is the spectre that haunts the hall each New Year's Eve, galloping into the courtyard. The haunting commemorates the occasion in 1630 when a traveller dressed entirely in red came to the house. As was the custom at Bramhall, he was received hospitably and, after dining, shown a room in which to sleep. On New Year's Day William Davenport, owner of Bramhall, was found murdered in his bed, and the guest had disappeared.

Brampton Cumbria

Just to the south of the town is a monument marking the site of the Capon Tree where judges, on their way from Newcastle to Carlisle, would pause to feast on plump capons. Many Jacobite rebels were put to death at this place and their ghosts are to be seen flitting about 'with airy ropes about their necks'.

Brindle Lancashire
5 miles SE of Preston

The district is favoured by a malevolent boggart named Old Scrat. In bygone times he delighted in slyly climbing on to a cart, his unnatural weight making it impossible for the horses to move it. He once climbed on to a hearse approaching Brindle churchyard but the accompanying clergyman was on to his tricks and saw him off with an appropriate prayer.

Burnley Lancashire ✠ 🐎

Manchester Road

Terence Whitaker wrote in *North Country Ghosts & Legends* that Manchester Road, the main southwards route out of town, is haunted by at least six ghosts and there may well be a dozen haunting its large Victorian houses once occupied by prosperous mill-owners. The ghostly lady in a spectral pony and trap is the shade of Lady O'Hagan, the last private owner of Towneley Hall, who often used to 'visit' in Manchester Road.

St Peter's Church

The district around the parish church is haunted by a phantom hound known in these parts as Skriker or Trash. The second of these names is supposed to derive from the noise his great paws made as he loped along.

Caldbeck Cumbria 🐎

11 miles SW of Carlisle

John Peel's village (that of the huntsman not the disc jockey) has a phantom Black Dog that haunts the lane to Branthwaite, a ghost that rattles chains in a room in the rectory overlooking the churchyard, and a mysterious light that floats about the garden of Bushay House.

Carlisle Cumbria

The female ghost haunting the castle (open to the public) may be that of the woman whose body was found immured in the wall of an upper part of the keep. She was dressed in a robe of silk tartan and wore valuable rings on her fingers. In 1842 a sentry saw the ghost and struck at it with his bayonet before fainting (leaving the bayonet embedded in the wall). He died of shock the next day. The west walls of the city are haunted by a Cavalier dressed in white who smiles warmly at anyone who sees him.

Cartmel Cumbria

12 miles SW of Kendal

The fells above the town are haunted by a sad wraith who is heard (but seldom seen) calling her lover's name. Her lover was a charcoal burner who was struck by lightning. She refused to leave the hut where he died and eventually died of exposure.

Chingle Hall Lancashire

3 miles N of Preston

The house dates from the thirteenth century, is the earliest brick-built house in the country, and is often promoted as 'the most haunted house in England'. Its manifestations range from apparitions of monks to inexplicable loud noises that shake the house, though it is the various malaises affecting cameras and tape recorders here that are the most common and interesting phenomena. The haunting may arise from the suffering endured by John Wall, one of the last Catholic martyrs, who was executed at

Worcester in 1679. He was born here and his head, exhibited all over Europe after it was struck from his body, is said to have finally found its resting place at Chingle, in a secret location.

Claife Cumbria

6 miles S of Ambleside

 In the summer season a car ferry operates across Windermere but formerly humble rowboats served. One winter night an eerie voice was heard calling for a ferry from the Nab on the western side of the lake. A ferryman left the comfort of the pub to row across to fetch the passenger. Some long time later he returned, his face ashen. He had been struck dumb with fear and died the next day without being able to describe the terrible vision he had seen. Similar calls were heard on other wild nights by the ferrymen who ignored them at first but then called on a priest to exorcise the spirit, now known as the Caller of Claife. Even after the exorcism the Nab remained a fearful place. It was said that hounds in full cry would suddenly stop here and let their quarry go, becoming fretful and whimpering. It may be that the haunting derived from a tragedy in 1635 when forty-seven wedding guests drowned on the sinking of their overladen boat (there is also a ghostly boat sailing the lake with fiendish crew and passengers). Another theory is that the Caller is the spirit of Thomas Lancaster who, in 1671, poisoned his wife, six of her family and a young servant at Threlkeld, near Keswick. As was the custom then, he was brought back to be hanged at his birthplace, High Wray, just to the north of Claife, and afterwards his body swung from a gibbet on the road to the ferry.

Clayton-le-Moors Lancashire 🍺

4 miles E of Blackburn

The Dunkenhalgh is a luxury hotel on the outskirts of Accrington that was the home of the Petre family until 1940. The ballroom and the grounds are visited on Christmas Eve by the shroud-draped wraith of Lucette, a French governess who was seduced and abandoned by one of the Petres and threw herself to her death from the aptly named Boggart's Bridge.

Coniston Cumbria

7 miles SW of Ambleside

The area around Coniston was intensively mined for lead and copper and, as is the way in many mining districts, tales abound of 'bogies, kobolds, gnomes and all manner of evil influences'. Rock climbers know of Simon's Nick as a spectacular slice taken from a rock face encountered on the ascent of Swirl How from the Coniston direction. It got its name from a miner named Simon who was guided by the 'little people' to a rich lode of copper. However, bad luck followed his discovery and he failed to prosper, suffering a series of accidents culminating in his death when a charge of powder exploded prematurely. The old miner's ghost is seen hanging precariously on the rockface to which he gave his name. Climbers also hear disembodied voices when climbing the Nick.

Corby Castle Cumbria 💀

5 miles E of Carlisle

No one knows the identity of the Radiant Boy, the figure of a beautiful child dressed in dazzling white surrounded by an aura of unnatural light. Those who see him enjoy wealth and power for a time before meeting violent ends. Lord Castlereagh saw the apparition before he became Foreign Minister – later he became insane and took his own life in 1822.

Crackenthorpe Cumbria

2 miles NW of Appleby

'Peg Sneddle' is the affectionate name given by locals to the ghost of Elizabeth Sleddall, who lived at the hall in Cromwellian times. She was married to Lancelot Machell but reverted to her maiden name after his death when she found herself disinherited. After her own death her ghost made banshee-like appearances to Machells on their deathbeds until her body was re-buried beneath a huge boulder in the riverbed. However, her ghost was allowed to walk once a year, in September, from the river to the hall. Another ghostly lady (or perhaps the same one) dashes around the locality in a phantom coach drawn by four black horses and attended by coachman and outriders.

Croglin Cumbria

9 miles S of Brampton

This remote village was troubled by a vampire in the late seventeenth century. Its activity chiefly centred on Croglin Low Hall where the victim was a young woman, but the beast also attacked a three-year-old girl at Croglin High Hall before it was shot and driven into a vault in the churchyard which at that time stood close to Low Hall. The vault was opened the next day and its occupant found to have a recent gunshot wound, whereupon the body was burned and the vampire ceased to roam Croglin. (There is no mention of an oak stake being driven through its heart.)

Dent Cumbria ✕

5 miles SE of Sedbergh

A spectral army haunts the fells to the south of the village and is seen descending into Dentdale from Whernside. It is conjectured that the ragged soldiers may be Scots mosstroopers who made forays into the district in the fourteenth century (though another account says firmly that this is a Danish army). As many as a hundred ghostly figures have been counted.

Dunham Massey Hall Greater Manchester

2 miles W of Altrincham

The eighteenth-century hall (open to the public) replaced an Elizabethan manor house. When the manor house was being built its architect mysteriously fell to his death. Many suspected that he was pushed from the roof after a dispute with the builders. His ghost is still seen wandering in the grounds of the newer building.

Egremont Cumbria 🐾 🕐

5 miles S of Whitehaven

The story of the pony and rider who haunt the village goes back to the Middle Ages when a fell farmer spent too much time in the taverns of Egremont one Christmas Eve. He set off for home but neither he nor his beast were seen again – except as ghosts, on the night before Christmas.

Elterwater Cumbria

3 miles W of Ambleside

There have been many reports since 1979 of a ghost at the Langdale Outdoor Education Centre. It is believed to be the spirit of John Foxcroft, one of four men killed in 1916 in an explosion at the gunpowder factory that occupied the site at the time.

Formby Merseyside 🐾

6 miles SW of Southport

An enormous Black Dog is frequently seen on the beach but never leaves tracks in the sand. Nearby Tower Grange is a medieval house that once belonged to Whalley Abbey and its ghost is that of a small monk who may have preferred to starve to death in his hiding place than to betray the household that sheltered him. As in so many houses of this date, a skeleton is said to have been discovered in the priest's hole. The ghost is sometimes sensed by the family dog before it becomes visible to humans.

Godley Greater Manchester 🐾

1 mile W of Hyde

The district is haunted by a spectral hound which is unusual in being a yellowish-brown rather than black. It is still a terrifying ghost to meet, however, being as big as a bull and just as fierce, but with the ability to appear and vanish instantaneously. At one time people believed it to be a lion escaped from Bellevue zoo.

Formby

Greystoke Castle Cumbria

5 miles W of Penrith

There is a disused room here haunted by a monk who was bricked up in a secret passageway that went to the church. He is usually seen in February. Another ghost haunting the same room is that of a man, a guest of the Duke of Norfolk at the castle, who joined his host in hunting on a Sunday. When servants went to his chamber the following morning they found it empty and the man was never seen in earthly form again.

Hall i th' Wood Greater Manchester

3 miles N of Bolton

The beautiful timber-framed manor house now serves as a folk museum. It has at least three ghosts: an old lady in the kitchen, a man in black upstairs, and – also upstairs – another man dressed in green silk and fine lace who seems to be carrying a sack.

Hawkesdale Hall Cumbria

5 miles SW of Carlisle

The ghost of a young boy with a lantern walks here at Hallowe'en, coming out of the front door and walking to the river where he disappears. He is supposed to be the shade of a young lad who hanged himself at the hall long ago .

Heskin Hall Lancashire

3 miles SW of Chorley

A modern conference centre masks the ancient hall, haunted by a White Lady. She is the ghost of a Catholic lady who, during the Civil War, was betrayed by a priest. He was caught at the house and offered to hang her himself to gain his freedom. The Roundhead commander kept him to his promise and the woman was hanged from a beam still to be seen at Heskin. The ghost seems to be particularly attached to the Scarlet Room.

Hob Stones Lancashire

1 mile NW of Colne

The name of Hobstones Farm betrays the ghost it houses. A hobgoblin is an evil dwarf and at Hobstones in the 1950s just such an entity appeared to the tenant farmer as he was sitting in the outside lavatory. The door burst open and he was confronted with a scowling dwarf bearing a mangled arm, almost severed at the elbow. This occurred several more times and in the end the couple left the farm. Later occupants were forced to have the place exorcised and Terence Whitaker (in *North Country Ghosts & Legends*) reports that all is peaceful there now.

Hoghton Tower Lancashire

4 miles W of Blackburn

A lady in green velvet haunts this ancient house. She may be the ghost of Ann, a Protestant who saw her Catholic lover shot at her feet by her father as they prepared to elope. The young man is supposed to have come from nearby Samlesbury, and this story has a parallel with the ghost story there (see below).

Hollinwood Greater Manchester

5 miles NE of Manchester

The ghost of Birchen Bower is a celebrated British haunting, the shade of Miss Beswick being active for more than a hundred and fifty years. She used to live in Birchen Bower, the ancient manor house in the village. When her brother was laid out in his coffin she visited him to pay her last respects but saw signs of life. He recovered and lived on for some years but this experience so affected Miss Beswick that she stipulated in her will that her body should always be kept above ground and for a week in every twenty-one years it should rest at Birchen Bower. This wish was obeyed when she died in 1768, the body being embalmed in tar and bandaged leaving only the face exposed. It was a famous exhibit at the Manchester Museum for a century and was taken to Birchen Bower every twenty-first year as the will dictated (after the house was demolished it was kept in the granary). Even at this time, with the conditions of the will being obeyed, Miss Beswick's ghost appeared in the village, the figure of an old lady wearing black silk with a white bonnet. The ghost remained active after 1868 when her body was buried in Harpurhey cemetery. A related phenomenon was the strange light seen in the granary – as though it was on fire – and this was supposed to be the hiding place of the old lady's fortune. The last report of the ghost came in the 1920s.

Hyde Greater Manchester

8 miles NE of Stockport

The A57 between Hyde and Mottram-in-Langendale, the village to the east, is haunted by a phantom lorry that was blamed for several fatal accidents in 1929 and 1930.

Kirkby Stephen Cumbria

The ghost of the sadistic Lord Wharton haunts the road between the town and Ravenstonedale. He was struck blind one day as he rode home to Ravenstonedale and his ghost still gropes and fumbles his way along the main road.

Lancaster Lancashire

The ghost of tragedienne Sarah Siddons is claimed by the Grand Theatre where her brother was once manager (see also Baker Street, Greater London). There is also a Grey Lady, who is seen in the auditorium.

Leasowe Castle Merseyside 🍺

2 miles W of Wallasey

The castle dates from 1593 when it was built for the Earl of Derby. Later, delapidated, it became known as Mockbeggar Hall, whose name survives as that of the shoreline here. The castle is now a hotel and has a bedroom haunted by the ghosts of a man and his young son. The father killed the boy and then committed suicide.

Leigh Greater Manchester

10 miles W of Manchester

Hooten Lane (near Warrington Road) has a ghostly nineteenth-century bombardier who runs up behind people. He is the shade of a soldier who drowned in one of the ponds that were once a feature of the district. Whether his death was suicidal or an accident is unknown.

Levens Hall Cumbria 🐘

5 miles S of Kendal

The Grey Lady of Levens is the ghost of a gypsy who, dying of exposure, staggered up to the front door of the house (now open to the public) about three centuries ago. Uncharitably the owners of the hall (the Bagot family, as nowadays) told her to walk to the kitchen at the back of the house. The gypsy died before reaching the warmth of the kitchen but as she did so she cursed the Bagots, saying that there would be no male heir to the property until the year came when the River Kent ceased to flow and a white fawn was born in the park (white offspring are extremely rare to the herd of Norwegian black fallow deer that graze there). The curse was effective until 1896 when both provisos were met and a male Bagot was born who survived to become head of the family. The gypsy's ghost, however, still walks at Levens and on the busy road outside its gates. Levens also has a Pink Lady (probably a housemaid as she wears a mobcap) and the appealing ghost of a small dog, black and woolly, which welcomes visitors to the house.

Liverpool Merseyside 🍺

Adelphi Hotel

'George' is the name given by staff to the ghost at the famous city-centre hotel. He is an innocuous presence and comes within the 'bedroom invader' section as categorised by Guy Lyon Playfair in *The Haunted Pub Guide*.

Prison

If you are unfortunate enough to occupy cell G2 in Liverpool Prison you may encounter the ghost of William Kennedy who went from the cell to his execution for the murder of a policeman in 1927.

Longridge Lancashire 💀

8 miles NW of Blackburn

A particularly unnerving boggart is native to this village. It appears as the figure of an old lady always walking in the same direction as yourself. She carries a basket and wears a long skirt and a bonnet that conceals her face. The old dear seems delighted to have the company of anyone walking alongside. But suddenly she turns her 'face' and her victim finds that she is faceless beneath the bonnet. Then she lifts the cloth from her basket and lets out her head, which pursues the victim over hill and dale, snapping at their heels and uttering shrieks of manic laughter.

Lowther Castle Cumbria

4 miles S of Penrith

It is unfortunate that the ruined castle, one of Britain's most romantic buildings, is no longer accessible because of its dangerous condition. The estate used to be haunted by the ghost of 'Jimmy' Lowther, first Earl of Lonsdale. He was a flagrantly wicked landowner who was hated throughout the county and his ghost proved hardly less troublesome than he had been until it was laid beneath Wallow Crag, overlooking Haweswater. However, some local people say that Jimmy was never properly exorcised and his boggart still tears about the district on occasion, causing havoc wherever it goes.

Lowton Common Greater Manchester

6 miles NE of Warrington

Joshua Rigby was murdered at Cheetham Fold Farm in 1883 and the man arrested for the crime was acquitted. The ghost of Josh was particularly active in the locality in the two years after the murder, but there have been reports of a haunting here right up to the present time. It usually takes the form of a misty figure, which seems to be less distinct these days.

Maghull Merseyside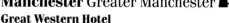

7 miles N of Liverpool

The ghostly sounds of battle are occasionally heard at dusk just to the south of Maghull, probably the psychic echoes of a skirmish after the siege of Preston in 1715.

Manchester Greater Manchester 🍺

Great Western Hotel

This Moss-side hotel has the ghost of a former employee, a young man wearing a grey sweater, most frequently seen in the cellar.

Shakespeare Hotel

The hotel is haunted by the presence of a maid who died there nearly fifty years ago when she accidentally set her clothes ablaze.

Marple Greater Manchester 👑

4 miles W of Stockport

The riverside is haunted by the ghost of a daughter of Henry Bradshaw, an ardent supporter of Cromwell. She fell in love with a young Royalist who was murdered by her father when the affair was discovered. The daughter died of a broken heart. The headless spectre of Henry's brother, John Bradshaw, haunts Marple Hall at the stroke of midnight (a busy ghost, this, who appears at several other locations, such as Red Lion Square, Greater London). He was one of the Cromwellian leaders who signed the King's death warrant, and when the Royalists returned to power they exhumed his body from Westminster Abbey, hanged it at Tyburn, and then removed the head for exhibition around the kingdom. The hall also has the nebulous shade of Lady Brabyn, a troublesome lady thrown out by her brother, and, unreasonably, the ghost of Charles II.

Melling

Melling Merseyside
🍺 🐇

6 miles N of Liverpool

Melling Hall is now a hotel but its ghosts are still active. The spectral lady wearing a purple dress is Lady Darlington who occupied the house during the First World War. There is also an excitable dwarf-like figure with bird-like legs, and a ghostly dog that pads about the place, name tag clinking against collar.

Mersey Tunnel Merseyside

A girl riding pillion on a motorcycle is the phantom hitch-hiker-in-residence of the tunnel. She died in an accident in the 1960s.

Middleton Greater Manchester 🍺 ⊕

5 miles NE of Manchester

Ring o'Bells Pub
The pub stands close to the church at the centre of the village. At the time of the Civil War, Royalist supporters met here and used the escape route to the churchyard from the pub's cellar. However, the son of Lord Stannycliffe was betrayed and found a party of Roundheads waiting for him at the exit of the tunnel. They left him for dead, but he managed to crawl back to the Ring o'Bells where he died (perhaps in the Cavalier's Seat in the Snug). His ghost haunts the pub and so, too, does the shade of a man in a grey suit. However, the present landlady says that neither ghost has been seen recently.

St Leonard's Church
The parish church is haunted by the figure of a thin clergyman who moves behind a pillar and vanishes, and the ghost of a lady here has appeared in a photograph.

Miterdale Cumbria

9 miles NW of Broughton-in-Furness

Bakerstead is the topmost farm of this remote valley between Eskdale and Wastwater. Its ghost story is one that recurs throughout the northern counties. A traveller arrives at a lonely farm or inn and is given refreshment. In some way, as he dozes in front of the kitchen fire, he betrays that he is in fact a robber (in some tales the traveller is dressed as a woman and inadvertently reveals that he is wearing trousers as he stirs in his sleep). The maidservant or farmer's wife, realising his real nature, pours hot tallow down his throat as he snores. At Bakerstead this proved fatal to the robber who haunts the location as a particularly revolting ghost – his face a shapeless white blob (the lady of the house overdid the boiling wax) which nevertheless issues terrible choking noises. Similar legends belong to Bewley Castle in Cumbria and the old Spital Inn on Bowes Moor in Durham.

A Corpse Road descends from Burnmoor and passes Bakerstead. This is haunted by a spectral packhorse carrying a coffin. Both went missing one day when a funeral party got caught in a snowstorm on the tops.

Moresby Hall Cumbria

3 miles NE of Whitehaven

A tale told of many houses belongs to the time of the first Jacobite uprising here. The Fletcher family supported the Stuart cause and the head of the family was taken to London for interrogation. Unfortunately he neglected, or was unable, to tell anyone that another Jacobite supporter was hidden in the house in a secret room. The man died of thirst and starvation before Fletcher's return, and his ghost haunts the hall.

Muncaster Castle Cumbria

16 miles SE of Whitehaven

Thomas Skelton, who died in 1600, was the fool or jester to the household of Sir Ferdinand Pennington but also seems to have been a thoroughly unpleasant character. He undertook all manner of tasks for his master who on one occasion asked him to get rid of another servant whom he suspected of being on over-friendly terms with his daughter. Skelton killed the young man and then presented Sir Ferdinand with his head. Both the jester and the headless young man haunt the castle (open to the public), the young man mainly frequenting the Tapestry Room.

Newton-le-Willows Merseyside ✗

5 miles N of Warrington

Cromwell rounded up a party of Royalists here in August 1648 and hanged them on the spot. The sounds of marching heard on nights in August are the ghostly memorial to this 'chok'd Battalion'. A white figure, sometimes described as a White Lady, sometimes as a tall white monk, haunts Castle Hill on the way to Golborne.

Oldham Greater Manchester ◔

The Colosseum Theatre is haunted by an actor, Harold Norman, killed during a stage fight in a production of the Scottish play (*Macbeth*) in 1947. Look out for him on Thursdays, the day on which the accident occurred.

Pendragon Castle Cumbria 🐎

4 miles S of Kirkby Stephen

The castle takes its name from Uther Pendragon, a man of enormous stature and considerable evil who used sorcery to seduce Igraine, Duchess of Cornwall. The offspring of this union was King Arthur, the founder of the rule of chivalry. Uther Pendragon died when his enemies, besieging the castle, poisoned the water supply. However, his is not the only ghost haunting the scant ruins – there is also that of Sir Hugh de Morville, a later occupant and one of the knights who murdered St Thomas at Canterbury, and a ghostly black hen that frustrates those who attempt to find treasure concealed in the castle by scrapping back all the soil they have laboriously excavated.

Penrith Cumbria

A spectral skeleton haunts Beacon Hill – the ghost of Thomas Nicholson executed and then gibbeted for murder in 1767.

Rainford Merseyside 🍺🖾

9 miles NE of Liverpool

The Golden Lion was built as a farmhouse and later became a girls' boarding school before finally becoming an inn. It has two ghosts, one being that of a schoolgirl raped and killed in the nineteenth century, the other that of a soldier, the son of the landlady at the time, who was killed in the Second World War.

Renwick Cumbria

9 miles NE of Penrith

A cockatrice flew out of the old church when it was being demolished in the eighteenth century. This was a dragon-like creature which, like a basilisk, could kill with its glance. Local people say that some such entity still haunts the lonely village and fear that it may be a vampire (but see Croglin, above).

Reston Hall Cumbria

3 miles E of Windermere

The ghost that lingers by the gates of the hall is probably that of Robert Bateman who built the house in 1743 and died (and was buried) abroad. His spirit managed the long journey home, however, and Bateman's dislike of women is supposed to be the reason that no woman has been able to live at Reston for long either as owner or tenant.

Rochdale Greater Manchester

Rochdale Market is built on the site of a graveyard that was disturbed when the new St Mary's church was built in 1909. This seems to have triggered ghostly activity in the form of a male spectre whose misty shape may still be seen drifting across the market from the direction of the Baum (originally a field where medicinal balm was grown).

Rufford Old Hall Lancashire ♛

7 miles E of Southport

One would expect a ghost wearing a bridal gown to be a White Lady but here she is Grey. Perhaps it is because she had to wear the gown for so long, since she swore, when her husband went off to fight in Scotland immediately after their marriage, that she would remove it only when he returned. She waited in vain, as does her ghost, here at the hall (open to the public). A motionless vision of Elizabeth I also appears here.

Rydal Mount Cumbria

1 mile NW of Ambleside

William Wordsworth died at Rydal Mount (open to the public) in 1850 and his ghost has been seen in the corner room on the first floor once occupied by his sister, Dorothy.

Saddleworth Moor Greater Manchester

6 miles E of Oldham

The victims of the Moors murderers were concealed in this boggy wasteland, infamous for its boggarts (troublesome ghosts) and mysterious lights. In 1975 a motorist encountered a glowing egg-shaped vision as big as a double-decker bus on the crest of the A635 at Wassenden Head and there have been innumerable other reports of UFOs from this locality.

Samlesbury Old Hall Lancashire

4 miles E of Preston

Sickly Dorothy is the ghost here, so called because of her greenish complexion, though she falls within the White Lady category. Dorothy was the daughter of Sir John Southworth, an ardent Catholic who suffered much for his faith during the reign of Elizabeth I. She fell in love with a Protestant but a tryst was discovered by her brother, and in the ensuing mêlée both her brother and her sweetheart were slain. Dorothy's ghost appears in the house and grounds and has been known to haunt the road outside (note the close similarity of this story to that of Ann at neighbouring Hoghton Tower).

Selside Hall Cumbria

4 miles N of Kendal

Electricity came late to this isolated house but its advent brought an end to the haunting here. Previously a troublesome (but unseen) ghost would rush through the house extinguishing every lamp and candle. Sheep stealers used to be hanged from the ancient yew tree in the grounds and it has been suggested that their unquiet spirits caused the haunting.

Shap Cumbria ✿

10 miles SE of Penrith

The A6 over Shap Fell was one of the busiest roads in the country before the advent of the motorway. It was haunted by a phantom Black Dog whose appearance invariably presaged a bad accident. It was always seen at the same spot, running for a few moments in front of traffic before leaping over a stone parapet that guarded a sheer drop of three hundred feet.

Sizergh Castle Cumbria ♛

4 miles S of Kendal

The castle has belonged to the National Trust since 1950 (and is open to the public), after having been the home of the Strickland family for more than seven hundred years. It is haunted by a lady who was locked in the main tower of the house when her husband went off to fight the Scots. He terrified the servants with threats of death should they ever release her, so that when he failed to return she eventually went mad and died. Catherine Parr, sixth and last wife of Henry VIII, often stayed at Sizergh and her ghost haunts the Queen's Room.

Skinburness Cumbria

17 miles W of Carlisle

A ferry here used to provide a quick way across the Solway Firth for runaway lovers eager to reach Gretna Green. One night the ferry was lost in the tide-tumbled waters – the screams of the drowning lovers may still be heard on stormy nights from the shore at Skinburness (see also Solway Firth, Scotland).

Smithills Hall Greater Manchester

2 miles NW of Bolton

The wonderful black and white house (open to the public) is haunted by the ghost of George Marsh, the Protestant martyr, who was brought here in 1555 for examination by the Catholic owner of Smithills, Sir Roger Barton. Marsh is said to have been so exasperated by the questioning that he stamped his foot as he left and prayed that this might leave a constant reminder of the injustice of his tormentors. Where this occurred, on the flagged floor of the passageway leading to the chapel, there is the impression of a foot that is supposed to show traces of blood at times. The Coach House adjacent to the hall has a Grey Lady.

Souther Fell Cumbria ✗

5 miles NE of Keswick

A farmhand first saw the remarkable phantom army marching along the outlying ridge to Blencathra in 1735. The vision occurred between eight and nine in the evening and the procession continued until fading light made it invisible. The farmhand told his master, who disbelieved him until on the same date (Midsummer Eve) two years later he witnessed the spectacle himself and called up his family to see it too. For some reason it was not until 1745 (shortly before Bonnie Prince Charlie's rebellion) that the army marched again. This time its march was witnessed by twenty-six people who had gathered on the fellside in case it appeared. They all agreed on the details, and in the morning climbed the fell to look for hoof prints or the tracks of the carts but found nothing. It was as though the mountain had swallowed the thousands of marching men, and they were never seen again.

Speke Hall Merseyside

7 miles SE of Liverpool

A female wraith, a White Lady, appears in the Tapestry Room of the famous half-timbered mansion (open to the public). She vanishes through a wall which was once the entrance to a secret passage. In its early years the house was notorious for sheltering priests and was riddled with concealed passageways and hiding places. Ghosts were frequently invented to explain away the glimpses that visitors may have caught of the fugitive priests.

Stainton Cumbria

2 miles SW of Penrith

A monastery here was dissolved by Henry VIII. The local baron, a violent and profane despot, acquired the property and soon had it demolished so that he might build himself a fine new house. In doing this he disturbed the monks' cemetery and failed to have the bones of the monks re-buried in sacred ground. With the site cleared he rode off but as he looked back his horse shied and the baron was thrown and had his neck broken. Baron's Hill overlooks Stainton and is where the accident happened. The ghost of a man on horseback has been seen here.

Stockport Greater Manchester 🎺

One of the earliest records of poltergeist activity comes from Dukinfield chapel which now stands in ruins at the heart of an industrial estate. In 1646 a service at the chapel had to be abandoned because of the unbearable noise of a phantom drummer who moved about the congregation incessantly beating his drum.

Stockport

Talkin Cumbria 🍺

3 miles SE of Brampton

The spirit of a former landlady lingers at the Blacksmith's Arms. This is the ghost of old Maggie Stobbart who kept the pub about ninety years ago.

Tallentire Hall Cumbria

3 miles N of Cockermouth

The headless spectre of a young woman walks at the hall and a red fungus grows below the window of the room where she was savagely murdered.

Thirlmere Cumbria 💀

6 miles SE of Keswick

When the valley was flooded in 1894 the waters rose over Armboth House which Harriet Martineau, nineteenth-century author and philanthropist, described as a remarkably haunted house where all the phantoms of the Lake District met at Hallowe'en. Perhaps its ghosts have migrated to the northern end of the reservoir where climbers on the demanding north face of Castle Rock often complain of an evil presence imperilling them.

Thurnham Hall Lancashire

5 miles S of Lancaster

The Green Lady haunting this ancient house is the wraith of Elizabeth Dalton who lived here in the mid-nineteenth century. There is also a mischievous boggart and a ghostly Cavalier.

Thurstaston Merseyside

5 miles SW of Birkenhead

The hall is haunted by an old lady who once murdered a child left in her care here, while Thurstaston Common is haunted by smugglers killed by Revenue men. Their groans and screams are heard on stormy nights.

Turton Tower Lancashire

4 miles N of Bolton

A Lady in Black is the ghost at Turton Tower (open to the public), most often seen on the spiral staircase leading to the top of the tower. The infamous Timberbottom Skulls are kept at the tower and are usually blamed for the various poltergeist activities. The skulls used to belong to Timberbottom Farm and created violent disturbance when moved from there. However, the farm was demolished many years ago, and their malign influence seems now to have waned.

Wharton Hall Cumbria

2 miles S of Kirkby Stephen

The Wicked Lord Wharton who lived here in Tudor times was the archetypal evil squire who terrorised his tenants and neighbours.

His downfall came when he had a stroke while riding alone on Ash Fell and was left blind. His ghost haunts the nightmare path he took home, outstretched hands groping for the long wall surrounding the estate.

Whiston Merseyside

9 miles E of Liverpool

A seaman's ghost haunts Delph Lane. He took a shortcut home after saying goodnight to his sweetheart and fell to his death in a quarry.

Wigton Cumbria

An energetic ghosthunter named Tom Jackson catalogued innumerable ghosts in the Wigton area, making it the most haunted, or at least the most documented, place in Cumbria. He listed more than a dozen ghosts, including the Church Street Phantom, the Clinic Ghost, the Burnfoot Spirit and the New Street Headless Horror. Unfortunately most of the stories behind the hauntings have been lost to living memory.

Wycoller Hall Lancashire 🐾

3 miles E of Colne

Charlotte Brontë described the fearsome Black Dog that roams the district in *Jane Eyre*. He is Guytrash Lightfoot, a portent of death or disaster, who may be met on the moorland paths that lead down to the ruined Wycoller Hall. The Cunliffe family occupied the hall until its last member died in 1819, propped up on his deathbed so that he might watch a cockfight. Many of the family led blighted lives, and one was a wife-killer who is fated to re-enact the murder on one night each year. Invariably the weather is vile when the Spectral Horseman gallops through the village to the hall. He climbs up stairs which crumbled and fell long ago and then dreadful screams are heard before the reappearance of the fiendish Cunliffe, who charges off on a horse that breathes flames from its flaring nostrils. Another Cunliffe also killed his wife: he married a black West Indian lady but rid himself of her during the voyage home by arranging to have her thrown overboard. Her wraith followed him home to Wycoller Hall where she predictably appears as a Black Lady.

North East England

Tom Crudd of Ripon

Northumberland, Durham, Tyne & Wear, Cleveland, Yorkshire and Humberside

Even hard-headed Yorkshirefolk are susceptible to ghost stories, but at least in York these have been put to good use, where the ghosts of the ancient city earn its citizens a bit of brass from the innumerable ghost tours that throng its lanes and alleys in the evenings. The wild coast of North Yorkshire was adopted by Bram Stoker for Count Dracula's landfall in England and thus it comes as no surprise to find that Whitby too has its ghost tours, often led by a guide dressed as the vampire.

Many of this region's best stories come from its least accessible places – the gloomy border strongholds, for example, few of which are without a good haunting. Chillingham Castle is the epitome of these, with a ghostly atmosphere in keeping with its sinister appearance. It has a fine selection of psychic activities, and the advantage of being open to the public.

The Simonside Hills are not far from Chillingham and they are roamed by a deugar, a hideous dwarf with cannibalistic tendencies, while even further to the north many people have witnessed re-enactments of the battle of Flodden Field. The battle originally took place in 1513 and resulted in the death of James IV of Scotland and a devastating defeat for his army.

Alnwick Castle Northumberland

William de Newburgh, a monk writing in Yorkshire in the latter part of the twelfth century, told the story of a wicked lord of the castle (now open to the public) who was supposed to be a vampire. After his death he flew about the town, seeking to feed off the blood of the living, and leaving such a stench that it caused an outbreak of plague. His corpse was disinterred and found to be grossly swollen, but when a spade cut into it fresh blood flowed out. The body was then burned and this put an end to the trouble. The neighbouring town of Berwick-on-Tweed also has a vampire story.

Alwinton Northumberland

9 miles W of Rothbury

A cowled figure without hands, feet or face haunts the moorland near this remote village and was investigated in the 1960s.

Appletreewick North Yorkshire 🐗

6 miles NE of Skipton

Norse influence hereabouts led to boggarts being called trolls and the phantom hound a barguest (it has a yellow coat, the usual saucer-like eyes, and is as big as a 'smallish' bear). The latter may well be encountered on dark nights in Trollers Ghyll, a very haunted place.

Askrigg North Yorkshire 👑

10 miles W of Leyburn

Mary, Queen of Scots is supposed to haunt Nappa Hall, the fifteenth-century fortified manor house. She stayed there in 1568 possibly as a break during her period of captivity at Bolton Castle. A vivid account of the apparition was written by a visitor in 1878.

Aston South Yorkshire

7 miles E of Sheffield

The former rectory (now known as High Trees) is haunted by the ghost of a rector who caught his wife in the arms of the butler and murdered her. There is an indelible bloodstain on the bedroom floor where the deed was done.

Attercliffe South Yorkshire ✗

2 miles NE of Sheffield

A silent phantom army was seen by the river here in 1661 dressed all in white, the cavalry riding white horses. The troops took more than an hour to pass William Bloom, the vicar of Attercliffe, who recorded the phenomenon in his diary.

Bamburgh Castle Northumberland

12 miles N of Alnwick

Green Jane is the wraith clad in a green cloak that is seen to fall from a crag on the landward side of the castle (open to the public), near the Clock Tower. A path used to ascend from the crag to a postern gate and it is believed that she falls from this, clutching a bundle (a baby?) and with the sound of mocking laughter accompanying her appearance, or rather, her disappearance.

Barnard Castle Durham ✛ ☠

The tomb of George Hopper in St Mary's churchyard is particularly gruesome with its emblem of Death the Reaper. It may be best to avoid examining this closely, however, because if you see the scythe move it means that you or a loved one will soon be part of the Reaper's harvest.

Barnard Castle

Barrasford Northumberland

6 miles N of Hexham

The original Barrasford Arms Hotel, a famous coaching inn, was burned down about a hundred years ago. The ghost of an unfortunate man who perished in the flames is occasionally seen dashing across the road, his clothes ablaze.

Batley West Yorkshire

8 miles SW of Leeds

It was a Yorkshire highwayman named William Nevison who achieved the remarkable feat of riding from London to York in fifteen and a half hours on Black Bess in 1678, a journey often mistakenly credited to Dick Turpin. Nevison undertook the ride to establish an alibi, but in spite of this he was eventually arrested and executed at Tyburn. His reason for haunting at Batley is nebulous but is probably because he killed a man named Fletcher there in 1681, shortly before his capture.

Beauchief Abbey South Yorkshire

5 miles SW of Sheffield

This is a well-haunted location, being visited by a White Lady, a monk and other less identifiable phantoms.

Belsay Northumberland

10 miles NW of Newcastle

The Silkie here (a northern White Lady) was a malevolent ghost that haunted a wide area and delighted in dropping from a tree to ride behind unsuspecting horsemen, terrifying the mounts and causing them to bolt. She was also blamed for causing ploughing teams to misbehave. The demise of the working horse seems to have brought Silkie's influence to an end.

Berwick-on-Tweed Northumberland

The town suffered serious disturbance from a vampire in the Middle Ages. After the death from pestilence of one of the town's merchants (who had acquired his wealth by dubious means), Berwick became seriously troubled by his ghost. The citizens demanded that his body be dug up and destroyed by burning and when, in the course of this, a spade struck through the corpse and fresh blood spouted, this was taken to prove that he was a vampire. The haunting ended with the destruction of the body.

Beverley Humberside

It is surprising that so few old workhouses, scenes of so much unhappiness, have worthwhile stories of ghosts. Thus the old workhouse here, in the grounds of Westwood Hospital, is exceptional. It has a Grey Lady who wears a nurse's (or matron's) cap. She lost her lover in the First World War and committed suicide. There is also the shade of a man with a small dog, and residents are sometimes disturbed by the sounds of horses being fed, accompanied by human voices in conversation. However hard you try, it is impossible to make out what is being said.

Sir Jocelyn Percy, who died in 1670, drives a spectral coach from Percy Castle at Leconfield to Beverley Bar and then through the town to the minster. Sir Jocelyn, the son of the fourth Earl of Northumberland, rides as a headless, skeletal passenger in the coach which is drawn by four black horses, also without heads.

Birstall West Yorkshire

2 miles N of Dewsbury

On 30 December 1684 William Batt rode up to his home, Oakwell Hall (now open to the public), where he was son and heir, passed his family without speaking and climbed the stairs to the main bedroom where he disappeared. A bloody footprint there was the only sign of his presence and this may still be seen. A few days later his family learned that he had been murdered in Barnet at the exact time his apparition had appeared. His distracted ghost is still seen at the house from time to time.

Blanchland Northumberland 🍺

9 miles S of Hexham

The Lord Crewe Arms is famous for the ghost of Dorothy Forster who helped her brother Tom escape to France after the 1715 Jacobite rebellion. Her presence makes itself felt by a strange weight that bears down on the feet of guests as they lie in bed. The hotel was originally the guest house of Blanchland Abbey, which accounts for its other spectral visitor, a red-haired monk.

Blenkinsopp Castle Northumberland

2 miles W of Haltwhistle

The White Lady here usually appears only to children and is said to be the wraith of a lady whose husband suddenly went missing, after saying that he would always prefer wealth to women. One theory is that she attempts to lead children to treasure she had hidden from her spouse.

Bolton Abbey North Yorkshire ✠

5 miles NW of Ilkley

King George V was one of the witnesses to the Marquis of Hartington's account of seeing the ghost (a monk) in the rectory in 1912, but the black-robed spectre that haunts the church accompanied by a strong smell of incense is probably a different entity, possibly the spirit of the last prior. Daytime sightings are particularly likely in July.

Boroughbridge North Yorkshire

6 miles SE of Ripon

The old course of the Great North Road to Scotch Corner is haunted by the shade of Tom Hoggett, a notorious highwayman, who drowned in the River Swale while escaping from troops who had captured him. His apparition wears a long, strangely glowing coat and travels along the road at considerable speed.

Bradford West Yorkshire

Bolling Hall (open to the public) has the ghost of the nineteenth-century freethinker Richard Oastler who vowed that he would return here if there was a hereafter. On the day of his death in 1861 he appeared to the son of the owner of the hall and there have been reports of his ghost being seen ever since. In 1643 Bolling was the scene of a famous supernatural intervention when the Earl of Newcastle, the Royalist commander who had made the hall his headquarters and vowed to wipe out the citizens of Bradford because of their support for Cromwell, was visited by a female ghost who persistently beseeched him to 'pity poor Bradford'. He was so troubled by this that he obeyed the ghost's request and spared the town.

Burton Agnes Humberside

6 miles SW of Bridlington

'Awd Nance' is a famous talisman, one of those skulls which create havoc if they are ever taken from the house where they belong. Anne Griffith was the youngest of three sisters who grew up in Elizabethan times as Burton Agnes Hall (open to the public) was being built. One day she went to visit neighbours and on her way was mugged and left for dead by two ruffians. She was taken back to Burton Agnes where she made her family promise that if she died her head would be kept in the house. Shortly afterwards she died and was buried intact, whereupon the place became violently disturbed. When things became so bad that the servants left en masse, the sisters went to the vicar, who reminded them of the deathbed promise. Thus the coffin was opened and the skull discovered already detached from the body. Once it was installed at the hall the supernatural activity ceased, and only resumed on the few occasions when the skull was taken from its resting-place. Awd Nance's ghost still occasionally walks at Burton Agnes – it seems an unfortunate nickname for the ghost of a young girl.

Burton Constable Humberside ✖

7 miles NE of Hull

The principal ghost at Burton Constable Hall (open to the public) is that of Nurse Dowdall, the family's greatly loved nanny, who died in the nineteenth century. She is a frequent visitation, wearing a shawl over her long dress and a lace bonnet. There is also a nun that floats down the Long Gallery and a spectral black Labrador that passes people on the tower stairs. A modern ghost is of a woman in brown check skirt and brown shoes – the shoes appear clearly but the upper part of her body has so far been indistinct. A phantom Roman legion has been seen marching along the road at the top of the drive.

Byland Abbey North Yorkshire

8 miles E of Thirsk

The district is interesting for being the location of some of the earliest recorded ghost stories in Britain. Around the year 1400 a monk of Byland Abbey wrote down twelve tales in Latin on blank pages in a volume of Cicero and these were translated by M. R. James. The locations include Kilburn, Rievaulx and Newburgh and the stories concern ghosts restless because of remorse or unjust excommunication. One tells of how the ghost of Robert de Boltby of Kilburn was captured and questioned in a churchyard. He answered with a voice 'from the inside of his bowels, and not with his tongue, but as it were in an empty cask and he confessed his different offences'. After absolution he rested in peace.

Calverley West Yorkshire

6 miles NW of Leeds

In 1604 the local squire, Walter Calverley, beset by financial difficulties caused by his heavy drinking, went mad and killed two of his children and grievously wounded his wife. His horse fell when he was on his way to kill his remaining child and he was captured and brought to trial. Because he refused to plead he was executed by being pressed to death at York and buried there. Later, however, the family dug up the body and took it for burial at the churchyard at Calverley. Walter still haunts the village, riding a headless horse.

Capheaton Northumberland ☕

12 miles SW of Morpeth

In this village a phantom piper gives warning of danger. The sound of his pibroch was heard before fires in 1783 and 1821 and served as an air-raid warning in 1940 when German bombers passed over.

Carter Bar Northumberland ✗

11 miles SE of Jedbergh

In 1575 the last Border battle, the Redeswire Raid, took place on Leap Hill just to the east of Carter Bar. In the course of this an Englishman, Thomas Ellesden, was beheaded by a blow from a Scottish claymore and his headless ghost haunts the boggy moorland here, the first and last of English ghosts.

Catcleugh Reservoir Northumberland

12 miles SE of Jedbergh

The ghost of an ancient Keeper of Redesdale named Percy Reed haunts the remote moorland around the reservoir. He is a helpful spirit, leading lost travellers away from danger and on to their correct routes. Percy was murdered by members of the Hall family who invited him to join them hunting and then killed him, though the reason for this has been forgotten.

Chillingham Castle Northumberland

12 miles NW of Alnwick

A twelfth-century tower house is at the heart of the castle (open to the public) which was extensively enlarged and fortified in Elizabethan times. Chillingham is an awesomely haunted house, as befits its appearance. It has a Radiant Boy (see also Corby Castle, North West England) who appears in the Pink Room at midnight, crying and moaning. These sounds cease as the apparition is seen in more detail, wearing a blue suit and surrounded by a remarkable, figure-hugging halo. The bones of a child were found in one of the walls of the room about a hundred years ago and after they were buried in consecrated ground the Radiant Boy was quiet, though recently he has been seen again walking through a wall in the north-west tower. Several other skeletons have been discovered in different parts of the castle. Workmen altering the building in the eighteenth century found the perfectly preserved body of a man sitting in a chair in a sealed room. The body crumbled before their eyes as the air reached it. Chillingham's Grey Lady, Lady Mary, is appropriately a member of the Grey family, who were earls

Chillingham Castle

of Tankerville and owned the castle from Norman until modern times. Abandoned by her husband for her sister, Lady Mary's spirit walks leaving a sound of rustling skirts and an icy chill in its wake. (The family connection continues as the wife of Sir Humphry Wakefield – they are the present owners – is a descendant of the Greys.) A phantom funeral has been seen walking through the Topiary Garden – it may have been this that Lady Tankerville witnessed shortly before the outbreak of war in 1914. The famous herd of white cattle that have grazed the parkland for seven hundred years are the surviving wild cattle of Britain and are supposed to possess magical powers.

Coverham North Yorkshire

3 miles S of Leyburn

A Black Lady walks from the church over the moor towards Middleham. The ghost is said to be that of a woman whose body was discovered by peat diggers about fifty years ago.

Cresswell Northumberland

7 miles NE of Morpeth

A White Lady haunts the shore near the tower from which she watched her Viking lover being killed. He unwisely landed from his galley at Cresswell and was killed by the local fishermen who

204

believed him to be a pirate. The phantom dogs on the shore here seem to resemble sporting dogs rather than the fiendish hell hounds of other parts.

Darlington Durham

Civic Theatre
This was originally the Darlington Hippodrome, opened in 1907 by Rino Pepi whose benevolent ghost still walks its aisles. The less friendly ghost of this theatre may be that of the stagehand who hanged himself with the fly-ropes.

Town Hall
This occupies the site of a twelfth-century manor house, which had the one-armed spectre of murdered Lady Jarrett. The robber who killed her cut off the arm to take her bracelet and rings. It is disappointing that her ghost seems not to like the civic building.

Dilston Castle Northumberland

2 miles E of Hexham

The last occupant of the now-ruined castle was James Radcliffe, Earl of Derwentwater, who was executed on Tower Hill in 1716 for his part in the Jacobite uprising. He had been forced to join the cause by his wife who mocked his lack of courage. The spirits of both haunt Dilston, the ghost of the young earl galloping over the countryside with his men while his remorseful wife haunts the castle itself, wringing her hands. There were remarkable events at the castle at the time of Derwentwater's execution: blood issued from the gutters while corn ground in the mill was tinged with red.

Drighlington West Yorkshire

6 miles SW of Leeds

Lumb Hall is haunted by a ghost which the owners have named Charlie. He has appeared as a cloaked figure said to be like a Civil War fugitive but is more frequently heard making a shuffling noise at the front door.

Dunstanburgh Castle Northumberland ♛

6 miles NE of Alnwick

The wonderful clifftop fortress (open to the public) has the ghost of the wandering knight Sir Guy, disappointed in his love for the White Lady of Dunstanburgh whom he failed to release from magical imprisonment here. The wife of Henry VI, Margaret of Anjou, also appears in spectral form here and might be confused with the White Lady. The castle was built in 1316 by Thomas, Earl of Lancaster, who fell foul of Edward II and was executed at Pontefract Castle, the executioner bungling his work and taking eleven strokes to separate head from body. Thus this is a very unpleasant ghost to meet, the mangled head carried with its face uppermost, the features contorted in agony. It is surprising it appears here rather than at Pontefract.

Durham Durham

At Neville's Cross on the western side of the city, the path to Cradlewell is haunted by a woman dangling a child. She was the victim of a murderer and her wraith appears on St Thomas' Eve (20 December).

East Riddlesden West Yorkshire 🐾 💀

1 mile NE of Keighley

East Riddlesden Hall is a National Trust property (open to the public) and has four ghosts: a Grey Lady who was starved to death by her husband (she is a kindly spirit who leaves an ancient cradle rocking gently as she passes and appears on New Year's Eve); the ghost of a Scottish merchant murdered by a treacherous steward for his money; a White Lady who died near the duck ponds when she was knocked from her horse by a low bough, and a Blue Lady whose reasons for lingering 'betwixt and between' are unknown.

This district is notorious for its unfriendly spirits – beware of a giant scrawny black cat and a black dog the size of a donkey which bring death to those they meet, while a black bear serves as a banshee, howling at the windows of someone soon to die.

East Scrafton North Yorkshire

4 miles SE of Leyburn

A flickering light that defies explanation and disconcerts motorists haunts the minor road through the hamlet. Known as the Pennine Light, it could be connected with the ruined St Simon's Chapel by the riverside.

Ellingham Northumberland

6 miles N of Alnwick

The village had a strange and recurring haunting in the early years of this century. It was the spectral re-enactment of a man pursuing a horse down the street and was last seen in 1921.

Elsdon Northumberland

9 miles SW of Rothbury

Steng Cross, or Winter's Gibbet, is to the east of the village on the Morpeth road. William Winter was a petty thief who, after his return from transportation, was egged on by two gypsies to murder an old woman who lived in a remote cottage. He was executed in Newcastle in 1791 and his body hung here in a cage until the skeleton collapsed. Although there is a tradition that his bones were buried beneath the gibbet it has been suggested that they were taken to a less obvious place. It may be significant that Winter's ghost is usually seen by the trees close to the cattle grid, about a hundred yards from the gibbet.

Epworth Humberside

8 miles SW of Scunthorpe

The rectory was the birthplace of John Wesley who, as a boy, witnessed the remarkable poltergeist behaviour that bedevilled the Wesley household here in 1716.

Everingham Humberside

13 miles SE of York

A ghostly lady cyclist, killed in an accident, haunts the road near the entrance to the hall. Coincidentally the same area is haunted by the spirit of a lady cook from the hall, who drowned herself in a nearby pond.

Fatfield Tyne & Wear 🍺

6 miles SW of Sunderland

The Havelock Arms is haunted by a ghost which is seldom seen but often seems to be moving things (a common complaint of landlords about supernatural residents).

Featherstone Castle Northumberland

3 miles SW of Haltwhistle

 The thirteenth-century castle has a traditional spectre in Sir Reginald FitzUrse from whom emanates the sound of rattling chains and agonised moans. He was starved to death at the castle early in its history. Featherstone's famous haunting, however, is the Ghostly Bridal. Abigail, the daughter of Lord Featherstone, loved a young man of the neighbouring Ridley family. Unfortunately they were Catholics while the Featherstones were Protestants and Abigail's father forbade the match, engaging her to a suitor of his liking whom she despised. The marriage took place and was a lavish occasion. Midway through the

Featherstone Castle

feast it was decided that the entourage should parade through the estate, returning to the banquet later with renewed appetites. Lord Featherstone was left at table with his cronies. When night began to fall he became worried and was distraught by the time midnight arrived, sitting alone surrounded by the abandoned feast. Then he heard the drawbridge being lowered and the clatter of hooves. Soon after the party returned, but silently and without joy for their eyes were fixed in the stares of death and their faces were pallid. Worse still, their bodies were disfigured by terrible bloody wounds. Seeing this Lord Featherstone made the sign of the cross whereupon the whole scene vanished with a gust of wind. The Ghostly Bridal is still seen here, especially in Pinkeyn Clough, the ravine where the party was ambushed and slain by affronted supporters of the Ridleys.

Flamborough Humberside ⚓

5 miles NE of Bridlington

The north landing is haunted by the shades of smugglers trundling barrels of liquor from their phantom boats.

Flixton North Yorkshire 🐇

5 miles S of Scarborough

This village used to be dreaded for its werewolf which had enormous fangs, red eyes and a repulsive smell. In Saxon times a hostel was built in the village specifically to provide travellers with shelter against wolves.

Flodden Field Northumberland 👑 ✕

11 miles SW of Berwick

The Earl of Surrey's English army overwhelmed that of James IV of Scotland on 9 September 1513, the Scottish king himself falling and being hacked to death after three hours of unrelenting combat. In the eighteenth century two brothers from Cornhill swore that they had seen a re-enactment of the king being killed as they went out snaring rabbits early one morning. They were able to describe the features of the king as well as the banners and accoutrements of the fighting men and experts agreed that their accounts were amazingly accurate. Many local people have heard the sounds of battle from the site, and drivers on the A697 have seen soldiers of the sixteenth century cross the road in front of them.

Fountains Abbey North Yorkshire 👞

3 miles SW of Ripon

A ghostly choir has been heard chanting plainsong in the abbey's Chapel of the Nine Altars (open to the public), but the most interesting ghost resides in nearby Fountains Hall, built around 1611 by the greedy Sir Stephen Proctor. He was so ruthless in extracting fines from practising Catholics that in the end he was murdered by one of them at the threshold of the hall. His daughter witnessed this and haunts the area as a Blue Lady. An Elizabethan man has been seen emerging from the panelling in the stone hall.

Frodingham Humberside

5 miles SE of Driffield

A ghostly horseman haunts the road here and has been known to climb on to a saddle behind the rider. Sometimes this phantom is headless, sometimes its cowl partly conceals a grinning skull.

Gillamoor North Yorkshire 💀

8 miles NW of Pickering

The naked ghost of Kitty Garthwaite is seen by the River Dove. She was left pregnant by her suitor and drowned herself two hundred years ago. Now she seeks revenge by attempting to lure other young men to a similar watery death.

Gunthorpe Humberside 🐇

4 miles N of Gainsborough

The road on the east bank of the Trent is haunted by a ghostly cat as big as a pig.

Haltwhistle Northumberland

Bellister Castle, on the south bank of the South Tyne, is the haunt of a Grey Man, an ancient who bears the terrible wounds that caused his death in the sixteenth century. He was an itinerant minstrel who used to pay regular calls at the castle. The Lord of Bellister began to suspect that the old man was a spy, and the idea so took hold on his mind that he set his hounds on the minstrel.

Haworth West Yorkshire

The ghost of Emily Brontë has been seen walking on the moorland path near the waterfall. On 19 December 1978, the anniversary of her death, she appeared at Weaver's restaurant, where she climbed a staircase that had been removed years before.

Hepple Northumberland

5 miles W of Rothbury

A man seated on a black horse clutching his stomach is a ghostly portent of danger to the village and he usually appears by the river to warn of a flash flood.

Hickleton South Yorkshire

6 miles W of Doncaster

The village is frequented by a phantom highwayman (sometimes appearing to be headless) who approaches the main road from the lane opposite the church. Terence Whitaker, author of *North Country Ghosts & Legends*, saw him in 1953 and described the sight of the cloaked figure with the tricorn hat (obviously in this case he wore his head) as the most terrifying encounter with the supernatural he had experienced. Some think that the three skulls displayed in the church porch once belonged to executed highwaymen and that one of them accounts for the ghost.

Holy Island Northumberland 🐇

11 miles SE of Berwick-on-Tweed

The ruins of Lindisfarne Priory (open to the public) are haunted by the spectre of St Cuthbert whose most celebrated appearance was to King Alfred to reassure him (a fugitive at the time) that he would eventually be monarch. St Cuthbert was abbot of Lindisfarne in the seventh century and his is the ghost heard hammering at an anvil on the shore during stormy nights. A phantom white dog prowls the abbey ruins and the decomposed face of a drowned man is seen at a window of the coastguard station overlooking the priory.

Howick Hall Northumberland

4 miles NE of Alnwick

The unusual apparition at the hall (open to the public) is that of an old lady who wears long skirts and a large Victorian bonnet. Her method of disappearing is clever: she gathers herself up into the hues of a rainbow before disappearing, feet first, into the ground.

Hylton Castle Tyne & Wear

3 miles W of Sunderland

The ruins of the small fifteenth-century castle were haunted by the Cauld Lad, a spectre of a naked boy who in bygone days helped in the running of the place, but was mischievous if not given work to do. The naked, shivering ghost was that of Robert Skelton, a stable lad murdered by Baron Robert Hylton in 1609, who threw a hayfork at the sleeping boy for not having his horse ready. The Cauld Lad ceased to haunt after servants left out a cloak and hood for him to wear, and when bones found in a nearby pond (where the wicked baron had thrown the body) were properly buried.

Hylton Castle

Ilkley West Yorkshire 🐇

The moorland to the south of the town is a favourite lair of the spectral black dog of the north, known here as Gytrash. It is also an area of frequent UFO activity.

Ivelet North Yorkshire 🐇 💀

15 miles W of Richmond

The quaint old bridge over the River Swale near Muker is haunted by a headless Black Dog, a token of tragedy to follow. The bridge is part of a Corpse Way (the route taken by funeral processions from remote farms) and there is a stone by the bridge where the wickerwork coffins were laid while the bearers rested.

Kettleness North Yorkshire 🐾

4 miles NW of Whitby

Bram Stoker allowed Count Dracula to disembark from the doomed ship here in the shape of a demonical black dog, and phantom Black Dogs of amazing size have been seen at Kettleness ever since the publication of *Dracula*.

Kippax West Yorkshire 🍺

8 miles E of Leeds

The Old Tree Inn has the ghost of a former landlord described as a white haze with a smiling face. He was held responsible for turning off the gas taps to the beer servers. Obviously a real ale fanatic.

Knaresborough North Yorkshire

The phantom of Eugene Aram haunts the locality of St Robert's chapel on the north bank of the Nidd. He hid the body of William Houseman, whom he murdered in 1744, in a cave still known as Eugene Aram's cave.

Langley Park Durham

3 miles NW of Durham

The remains of Langley Hall, once a magnificent Tudor mansion, stand on the northern side of the A691. The drive to the hall past Coalpark Gill is frequented by a phantom hearse which appears at midnight drawn by headless horses and with a headless driver.

Leeds West Yorkshire

Kirkstall Abbey

The ethereal figure of an abbot has been seen in the gatehouse, now a museum.

Temple Newsam

The 'Hampton Court of the North' (open to the public) has a variety of ghosts but no one knows any longer why these lost souls linger here. Lord Halifax met a Blue Lady here in 1908; the noisy phenomenon that besets the upper floor is known as the Phantom Ball, and the ghosts of a young boy who steps from a cupboard and a Knight Templar haunt the Darnley Room. Finally, unearthly screams occasionally emanate from the south wing.

Leeming North Yorkshire ✈

5 miles SW of Northallerton

The airfield is well seen from the Great North Road and was a bomber station during the Second World War. The bomb store used to be at the remote southern extremity of the field and close by was a mound of earth concealing the wreckage of aircraft that came to grief at Leeming. This area is haunted by wartime aircrew in flying kit and their ghostly voices have also been heard.

Leven Humberside

6 miles NE of Beverley

A headless lady climbs up on to the saddle of horsemen at White Cross, sometimes playfully clipping their ears with bony fingers as she rides behind. (See Frodingham, above, for a neighbouring ghost with similar habits.)

Lindholme South Yorkshire 🥾

9 miles NE of Doncaster

The wartime airfield was constructed on featureless marshland which is now intensively cultivated. It is haunted by an apparition in flying gear named Willy, a Polish Lancaster pilot who died when his aircraft crashed on Hatfield Moors. Willy seems to have taken over Lindholme from an earlier ghost – a hermit named William de Lindholme (another Willy?).

Lissett Humberside 🥾

6 miles S of Bridlington

The appearance of the 'Reaper's Bomber' brought apprehension to airmen at RAF Lissett when it was a bomber base in 1943–4. The ghostly Halifax foretold losses to the flight leaving that day but only appeared if all the crew were to be killed on any individual aircraft. The airfield is now farmland again and the Halifax has not been seen since 16 August 1944, when a Halifax with a Canadian pilot crashed at Foston. However, its engines are sometimes heard droning over the lonely fields.

Long Marston North Yorkshire

6 miles W of York

Cromwell's ghost is supposed to haunt the Old Hall (his headquarters during the battle in 1644). Spectral stragglers from the defeated Royalist army were run through by motorists in 1932.

Loxley South Yorkshire

4 miles W of Sheffield

The village of Robin Hood's birth is haunted by the wraith of Mary Revill who was murdered on the common on 31 December 1812. The murderer was never discovered.

Marsden Grotto Tyne & Wear 🍺

5 miles N of Sunderland

A pub occupies the caves once used by smugglers. One of them, nicknamed Jack the Blaster, betrayed his colleagues to revenue men and it is his ghost that haunts the pub. He has his own tankard hanging behind the bar which, if it is ever moved, triggers poltergeist activity.

Mitford Castle Northumberland

2 miles W of Morpeth

A terrifying spectre is guardian of the ruined castle. A portly old warrior suddenly appears waving a sword in one hand and holding a bloody head in the other. Fearsome screams come from the mouth of the detached head.

Mortham Tower Durham

3 miles SE of Barnard Castle

A headless lady who trails a length of silk walks at the medieval tower house which belonged to the Rokeby family. She was the beautiful wife of an insanely jealous husband who, wrongly believing her to be unfaithful, cut off her head and threw the body into the river. His dagger dripped the usual indelible drops of blood on to the steps of a spiral staircase. An eighteenth-century parson met the ghost beneath the bridge over the River Greta and had a conversation with her in Latin, though he did not reveal where her voice came from.

Newburgh Priory North Yorkshire 💀

8 miles SE of Thirsk

The stones of the medieval monastery were incorporated into the mansion built on the site for the Lords Fauconberg. The evil-looking man in silk breeches and wig is the ghost of a duellist who once fought here, and the White Lady who walks by the lake is a harbinger of death.

Newcastle upon Tyne Tyne & Wear ✚

The clanking ghost of a knight in armour haunts the cathedral church of St Nicholas, usually appearing in an aisle close to the tomb of a crusader.

North Kilvington North Yorkshire

2 miles N of Thirsk

The White Lady that occasionally appears here is the ghost of the young daughter of Roger Meyell of Kilvington Hall, killed in the chapel there by soldiers at the time of the Dissolution.

Norton South Yorkshire 🐾

7 miles S of Sheffield

Bunting Nook is the haunt of a boggart that usually appears as a Black Dog with eyes the size of saucers but can also manifest as a green mist that seems to flow into human shapes.

Otterburn Northumberland ✗

20 miles N of Hexham

In 1388 there was a battle on the lonely moors here when the Scots defeated the English. There have often been reports of this conflict being re-enacted as a battle in the sky, though some are inclined to believe that the phenomenon is really UFO activity.

Preston Northumberland 🐾

6 miles N of Alnwick

A terrible phantom dog belongs to this small hamlet. It is as big as a donkey and as ferocious as a Doberman, having been bred for its ferocity as a guard dog many generations ago. When it became too dangerous for its keeper, it was fed poisoned meat. Instead of dying, the hound suddenly gained unnatural strength. It burst from its kennel, set upon its master and tore his limbs asunder. Only then did the dog expire.

Raby Castle Durham

6 miles NE of Barnard Castle

The castle itself (open to the public) is haunted by Old Hell Cat, the spirit of a long-dead Lady Barnard who got the name for being so disagreeable. She is seen sitting on top of the battlements knitting so furiously that her needles glow red-hot. The district around the castle is haunted by the spectres of the victims of mass-murderer Maria Cotton, executed at Durham in 1873. The victims pursue a ghoulish game of tag, chasing each other over fields and hedges.

Ripley North Yorkshire

3 miles NW of Harrogate

The castle (open to the public) is haunted by a polite nun who knocks on the bedroom doors of guests but enters only if asked.

Ripon North Yorkshire 🍺

The shade of Tom Crudd haunts the Unicorn Hotel on the marketplace, where he was the boot boy until his death in 1762. Also known as Old Boots, he looked a little like Mr Punch, and had the unusual ability of being able to hold a coin between his chin and his nose.

Rochester Northumberland

20 miles SE of Jedbergh

Roman masonry and decoration is incorporated into the fabric of houses in the village. This came from the settlement of Bremenium just to the north where the semi-naked ghost of a woman has been seen weeping at dusk on summer evenings.

Rock Hall Northumberland 🕐

4 miles N of Alnwick

The hall is presently a school and has a ghostly Cavalier as well as a Grey Lady who is said to walk from South Charlton to Rock on 15 August each year, the anniversary of her husband's death.

Rossington South Yorkshire

4 miles SE of Doncaster

The ghost of a man in top hat and frock coat has been seen at the stables of Rossington Hall. He is thought to be a Victorian owner of the estate.

Rothbury Northumberland

10 miles SW of Alnwick

A spectral black cat haunts the river's edge below the bridge over the River Cocquet. It may be seen from the corner of an eye but invariably disappears when looked at directly.

Ruswarp North Yorkshire

1 mile SW of Whitby

The shade of a village idiot known as Goosey, because he once ate a whole goose at one sitting, haunts the Sleights Road out of the village. He was murdered, and the appearance of his ghost has been known to cause accidents. A spectre carrying his head beneath his arm haunts the footpath to Whitby at Fitz Steps where it begins its climb to Prospect Hill.

Saltergate Inn North Yorkshire 🍺

7 miles N of Pickering

A fire has been kept burning at the pub continuously for two hundred years so that the ghost of a man does not escape. He was killed in a fight between smugglers and excise men and was buried beneath the hearth.

Sand Hutton North Yorkshire 💀

3 miles W of Thirsk

The Busby Stoop Inn takes its name from an incident in 1702 when Tom Busby killed his father-in-law at the pub by hitting him with a hammer. The murderer was hanged and gibbeted on gallows put up opposite the inn and his ghost may be seen on moonless nights with the noose around its neck and the head at an unnatural angle. However, it is best to keep watching the road, as a glimpse of Tom's ghost is said to bring disaster before the next full moon.

Scarborough North Yorkshire 🐴 💀

The ghost of Edward II's favourite, Piers Gaveston, haunts Scarborough Castle (open to the public). Gaveston was captured here and taken to Warwick for execution. (See also Guy's Cliffe, South Midlands.) His headless ghost is malicious. It haunts the broken battlements and rushes at trespassers foolhardy enough to visit the castle at night. The resort also has a Pink Lady, Lydia Bell, who haunts the street where she was murdered in 1804, and a black horse that has haunted here since Norman times, appearing out of a thundercloud.

Seaton Delaval Hall Northumberland 🐴

9 miles NE of Newcastle

The hall, built by Vanbrugh for Lord Delaval in 1728, is haunted by the ghost of an early member of the family who lived in the castle that first occupied the site. With a child in her arms she frequents the chapel, as does the hall's other ghost, a headless dog.

Selside North Yorkshire 🚂

7 miles N of Settle

Signalmen operating remote boxes on the Settle and Carlisle line used to know of many ghosts. One was Big John, whose bulky figure was often seen ahead by a man walking to his signalbox but which would vanish unaccountably and, in winter, leave no footprints in the snow. Salt Lake Cottages are a terrace of railway housing between Selside and Ribblehead. Number 1 is haunted by the ghost of a platelayer killed on the track, who has been known to climb into bed alongside a mortal occupant in the front bedroom, but more often manifests in the form of a chilly presence.

Sheffield South Yorkshire 👑

The Turret House (open to the public) is the only part of the great hunting lodge of the Earls of Shrewsbury to survive intact. Mary, Queen of Scots was held here for part of the fourteen years of her confinement, which ended with execution at Fotheringhay. Her ghost has been seen at the Turret House, usually as a Grey Lady.

Simonside Northumberland

3 miles SW of Rothbury

This lovely outlier of the Cheviot Hills provides a magnificent viewpoint for all of Northumberland. It is the haunt of a deugar, a cannibalistic hunchbacked dwarf, who cooks his victims over a stick fire before eating them.

Skipsea Castle Humberside

7 miles S of Bridlington

Lady de Bevere was the niece of William the Conqueror and her wraith haunts the earth ramparts. She was killed by her mad husband who denied his wife proper burial by hiding her body. All she wants is for someone to follow her apparition to the hiding place and then to exhume her bones and give them a Christian resting place.

Snape Castle North Yorkshire 👑

8 miles NW of Ripon

The happy spirit of Catherine Parr, last wife of Henry VIII, haunts the castle where she lived when she was married to Lord Latimer until his death in 1542. Her ghost is seen as a young girl with blonde hair wearing a blue dress.

Spofforth Castle North Yorkshire

3 miles NW of Wetherby

A unique ghost haunts this ruined castle (open to the public). It is the figure of half a woman (presumably the top half) which throws itself from the battlements.

Staithes North Yorkshire

9 miles NW of Whitby

The ghost of a young girl is sometimes seen on Boulby Cliff. She died when the edge crumbled away in the nineteenth century and her ghost walks on thin air following the cliff line of her era.

Stanbury West Yorkshire 🍺

2 miles W of Haworth

The Old Silent Inn has the ghost of a kindly old lady who was once landlady and a great cat-lover. She used to attract neighbourhood strays by ringing a silver bell at the back door (now blocked up), which is where her ghost appears. The inn takes its name from having served Bonnie Prince Charlie as a refuge after 1745.

Stockton on the Forest North Yorkshire ✕

4 miles NE of York

A ghostly army in the sky was seen here in 1812. The battlefield of Stamford Bridge is nearby (where King Harold gloriously vanquished Norse invaders in 1066 before being defeated by William of Normandy) so this may have been a re-enactment. Alternatively it could have been a UFO sighting.

Staithes

Swinton South Yorkshire 🐗

7 miles W of Doncaster

The village has the bizarre ghost of a farmer's wife named Mary who was killed when, pursued by her drunken husband enraged because she had slaughtered a pig he particularly prized, she was chased into the river and drowned. The haunting is of Mary riding on the back of a large black pig.

217

Tees-side Airport Cleveland 🖾📷

2 miles E of Darlington

During the Second World War the airfield was used as a bomber base with first Halifaxes and then Lancasters being used by the Canadian squadrons, the most famous of these being number 428, appropriately nicknamed the Ghost Squadron because of its death's head insignia. A hero of this unit haunts the Tees-side Airport Hotel which was formerly the officers' mess. The figure walking its corridors may be the ghost of a Canadian pilot named Mynarski who won a posthumous Victoria Cross for trying to rescue the rear gunner from his burning aircraft (he died in the attempt), or that of J. McMullen, another Canadian pilot who guided his doomed aircraft away from Darlington and stayed with it to crash in open countryside.

Thirlwall Northumberland

4 miles W of Haltwhistle

As at Hylton Castle (see above), Thirlwall has the ghost of a Cauld Lad. This one is said to be that of an orphan cast out by a wicked uncle. He haunts the common but may well have lived in the castle, now uninhabited for four hundred years and in ruins. A ghostly dwarf is said to stand guard over a golden table hidden at the bottom of a well and sealed with a curse that can only be broken by 'the coming of one who is the only son of a widow'.

Thornton Abbey Humberside

11 miles NW of Grimsby

Thomas de Gretham was an abbot of the Augustinian Abbey who dabbled in Black Magic. The skeleton found seated at a table in a walled-up room was supposed to be his, and so it is probably his ghost that walks the ruins (open to the public). After the dissolution of the monastery Sir Vincent Skinner built a mansion here which, upon completion, collapsed overnight. Material from the abbey was also used to build Ferriby Sluice, which turned out to be equally unsuccessful.

Todmorden West Yorkshire 🐇

6 miles SE of Burnley

The Gabriel Hounds, Yorkshire's version of the Wild Hunt, fly down the Cliviger Gorge to vanish at Mankinholes, just to the east of the town – they are likely to appear at Hallowe'en but also fly as an omen of death. Over the years many UFOs have been sighted on and above the moorland around Todmorden.

Tynemouth Tyne & Wear 🐇

7 miles E of Newcastle

The ruins of the priory are haunted by Prior Olaf, a Viking who was wounded when his fleet attacked the priory. The monks tended his injuries and he joined their order, rising to become prior. The Viking attacks continued, however, one of them led by Olaf's brother, who was killed besieging the priory. Olaf was heartbroken, and died of grief praying in the chapel. His ghost looks towards the sea from the crumbling walls and is most likely to be seen in daylight, on fine days when the wind is from the east.

Wandering Willie is the ghost of a border collie whose master crossed the river each day in the ferry. One day his master failed to return to the northern shore and the faithful dog waited at the ferry stage for several years until he died of old age (his body was preserved and may be seen at the Turk's Head inn). His ghost is most likely to be seen near the Collingwood statue.

Wadsley South Yorkshire ●

4 miles NW of Sheffield

Look for a White Lady on the Common between nine and eleven p.m. She looks very distressed, raising her arms in the air. Some believe her appearance to be due to the leakage of natural energy from the earth, others say it is due to the release and ignition of methane gas – a Will o' the Wisp.

Wallington House Northumberland 🐾

15 miles NW of Newcastle

The journals of Augustus Hare are a useful source of Victorian ghost stories and when he stayed at this house (now open to the public) he was so terrified that he barricaded himself in his room. In 1862 he wrote of ghostly birds beating against the windows and phantasms that could be heard packing and unpacking their valises all night long. His host was Sir Walter Trevelyan, a miserly and unkempt man never known to laugh. Even today, with Wallington a National Trust property, there is a slightly forbidding atmosphere about the house, perhaps due to the Victorian murals in the vast central hall.

Walworth Castle Durham 🍺

4 miles NW of Darlington

The building, now a hotel, incorporates part of the castle built in 1189, and has been a home of the Hansard family and, more recently, a school. Its Grey Lady was often seen by a headmaster of the school who was able to describe her on the radio in detail. She is the ghost of a maidservant who proved bothersome to one of the lords of Walworth – maybe he had made her pregnant. He had her bricked up in a spiral staircase on one of the many occasions when the castle was being modernised. The staircase still exists and ascends behind the library to one of the turrets – footsteps are sometimes heard climbing the stone stairs, and a psychic wedding guest once caught a glimpse of the ghost on the outside of the present building, halfway up a wall. As the hotel proprietor remarked, this killed the party stone dead. The other ghost here is that of a young stableboy who was also murdered. His used to be a malevolent ghost that pulled bedclothes off guests as they slept and so harassed the servants that it was difficult to keep staff. However, he has been quiet since the new west wing was built.

Warkworth Castle Northumberland

6 miles SE of Alnwick

The path from the castle to the hermitage (both open to the public) is haunted by the ghost of Margaret Neville. She was the wife of the first Earl of Northumberland and mother of the Hotspur immortalised by Shakespeare.

Washington Tyne & Wear

6 miles SE of Newcastle

The Old Hall belongs to the National Trust (and is open to the public) and was the home of George Washington's ancestors. It is haunted by a Grey Lady who walks an upstairs corridor.

Watton Humberside

6 miles N of Beverley

Only fragments remain of the abbey, haunted by the ghost of Elfrida (a nun made pregnant by a monk and executed for her trouble) and by curious figures that seem to be phantasms of people without heads. The ghostly woman and child also seen here are the spirits of two people killed by Roundhead troops as they scoured the countryside after the battle of Marston Moor.

West Auckland Durham

3 miles SW of Bishop's Auckland

A ghostly rider on a grey horse gallops over the countryside towards Hamsterley, his face bloody and and terror-fraught.

Westgate Durham

4 miles W of Stanhope

Weardale was a remote place in the eighteenth century, populated only by lead-miners and a few hill farmers. It was necessary to engage guides to penetrate into the upper parts of the valleys and cross from one hill to another. In the middle years of the century a merchant was collecting debts from his clients in Weardale but found himself without guides when he wished to cross into Teesdale. He pressed on regardless and arrived on a wild and lonely road as night began to fall. He was last seen to the west of Stanhope at a spot called Park House Pasture. Suspicion fell upon three ne'er-do-wells who had become wealthy overnight and were seen disposing of a horse in a quarry. However, there was no other proof to account for the man's disappearance until a skeleton was discovered in Park House Pasture a generation later. This also confirmed the reason for a ghost haunting the spot – that of a phantom horseman bearing hideous wounds who rides across the fields, vanishing at the place where the skeleton was found.

Whitby North Yorkshire ✠ ● ☙

St Mary's Church

A spectral coach is driven along Green Lane to the churchyard. Here the passengers alight and gather around the grave of a newly buried seaman. He rises up and joins them in the coach which then clatters down Church Steps and turns sharp right at the bottom to plunge into the sea from Haggerlythe. This coach is the bargheist coach, which the spirits of the sea send out for the souls that rightly belong to them. (Bargheist should not be confused with barguest, the ghostly hound; see Appletreewick, above.)

West Cliff
People glancing up towards Captain Cook's statue from the beach have seen a misty form drifting down from the clifftop. This wraith appears on clear days when there is no trace of fog about.

Whitby Abbey
The abbey (open to the public) is haunted by the ghost of its founder St Hilda, which appears framed by one of the northern windows wearing a shroud. Heavenly choirs may be heard here at dawn on Christmas Day (use the ancient calendar for the correct date) singing the music of Caedmon, who was a monk of Whitby. A third haunting is by Constance de Beverley, a nun at the abbey who loved Marmion, the brave but faithless knight immortalised by Scott. She was immured for breaking her vows and her ghost is seen and heard on a twisting staircase leading down to a dungeon.

Wigglesworth North Yorkshire
4 miles S of Settle

The ghost of a young woman has caused accidents on the road west from the village past the lane to Tosside. She drowned when fetching water from the stream and maliciously dodges in front of cars at night.

Wold Newton Humberside
9 miles S of Grimsby

A farm in this remote village has a barn haunted at harvest time. It is lit up by flickering light and the sound of the flails of yesteryear is heard as the grain is threshed.

Woodhorn Northumberland ✚ 🖊
6 miles E of Morpeth

St Mary's churchyard is haunted by the ghost of Tom Chalkley, a naval rating killed in action in the First World War. The first appearance of the ghost (showing the terrible wounds that killed him) occurred before the official telegram arrived informing the parents of their son's death. A particularly unnerving ghost is seen in the lane outside the church. It is a skeleton, its teeth chattering, dressed in miner's clothing, who rides an old-fashioned bicycle.

Wyke West Yorkshire
4 miles S of Bradford

High Fernley Hall was troubled by a headless ghost after one of the two brothers who occupied the hall in 1742 was rejected by a girl for the other brother. The rejected sibling took the unusual step of announcing that he would kill himself by decapitation and then return to haunt the hall. The intriguing part of this story is how he managed to chop his own head off. Hell Fire Corner, just to the south of the village at the intersection of the A58 with the Brighouse road, has a thoroughly unsavoury reputation, being visited by a headless horseman (perhaps the suicidal brother), as well as phantom cars and UFOs.

York North Yorkshire 🏮 ⊕ 🕐 🍴

Angler's Arms

The pub stands next to Marmaduke's in Goodramgate and has three ghosts, only one of which is ever seen. There is something very nasty in the cellar – an entity described as being of great age and utter evil – while in contrast the apparition seen on the stairs is a friendly little girl. The strong smell of lavender water that sometimes engulfs the pub is also held to be supernatural.

Cock and Bottle

The pub is in Skeldergate, built on land that once belonged to the disreputable George Villiers, second Duke of Buckingham. It is conjectured that his is the ghost that troubles landlords and customers here. An apparition of an ugly man with a large nose has been seen, and there is also something that dislikes people wearing crucifixes and snatches them from their necks.

Holy Trinity Church

The church was once attached to a convent and its ghost is that of the abbess who was in charge at the time of its dissolution. She defied Henry VIII's soldiers and was killed. Her wraith is often seen, a figure that glides across the church wearing a hood and a trailing gown, especially likely to be seen on Trinity Sunday. The churchyard is haunted by the headless shade of Thomas Percy, Duke of Northumberland, who led an uprising against Elizabeth I. When the uprising failed he was beheaded at York; his head is said to be buried here.

Marmaduke's Restaurant

The establishment in Goodramgate takes its name from a crippled boy who lived in the house until his death in 1715, when he hanged himself in his garret room. Marmaduke is a helpful presence but has never been seen.

The Minster

Dean Gale, who died in 1702 and is buried in the Minster, haunts the choir, his ghost sitting in the Dean's pew.

Museum

Early in 1954 the library of the York Museum was disturbed by a regular series of hauntings which always seemed to follow the same pattern. Every fourth Sunday, at 8.40 p.m., an unseen hand would draw a book entitled *The Antiquities and Curiosities of the Church* from the shelves and drop it to the floor. There was a marked drop in temperature before the occurrence and on at least two occasions the caretaker reported seeing the spectral outline of an elderly man searching for a book.

St William's College

A clergyman was robbed and killed by two brothers, scholars of the college, in Tudor times. The elder brother advised the younger to hide and then went to the authorities and blamed him for the crime. The younger brother was soon caught, found guilty, and executed at the castle. The remorse subsequently felt by the elder, guilty brother brought about his early death, and his spirit has proved restless ever since, his footsteps frequently being heard in empty corridors at the college.

Theatre Royal

The theatre is haunted by a Grey Lady, believed to be the ghost of a nun who worked in the medieval St Leonard's Hospital which was replaced by the theatre in 1744. A greyish shape distracted a rehearsal of *Dear Octopus* in 1974, but whether this was ectoplasm or the Grey Lady is unknown. A few years ago a service of exorcism was held to banish the Grey Lady. It may be too early to know if the exorcism was successful, for there was also the ghost of an actor killed in a stage duel and the sound of supernatural organ music.

Treasurer's House

This is a favourite venue for York's ghost tours, famous for the appearance of phantom Roman legionaries first reported nearly fifty years ago.

York, Theatre Royal

Scotland

Clamis Castle

Few visitors to Glamis Castle today arrive without knowing a little of its famous ghost story – how an heir to the laird was born, severely physically and mentally disabled, whom his father considered a monster. The laird, who later became Earl of Strathmore, kept the boy captive, out of sight, where he daily grew more wretched and violent, eventually reaching adulthood. When the earl died his brother succeeded to the title and was told the secret of the monster, still confined to a hidden room. Eventually the poor son died but the family still closely guarded the information that he had ever existed, successive stewards confiding it to each new earl. Today the public regards the wretched son as a ghost though there is scant evidence for its haunting the castle, which has other, better authenticated ghosts, such as that of Lord 'Beardie' Crawford who chose to throw dice against the Devil.

Edinburgh, Scotland's capital, is, like York, a city that makes a living from its ghosts. Its most celebrated ghost story, that of Major Weir at West Bow, combines strong elements of witchcraft with a spectacular haunting, the Major riding a headless black horse.

Britain's most remote ghost story comes from Sandwood Bay near Cape Wrath, where two ghostly seamen roam the shore, the pain of their loneliness eased by the mermaids who call to them from beyond the breakers.

Abbotsford House Borders

2 miles W of Melrose

George Bullock was Sir Walter Scott's steward and it is presumed to be his ghost that disturbed Sir Walter in 1818, when building work was going on in the house. Bullock was not known to be dead at the time. He was away from the house (now open to the public), and it was subsequently discovered that he had died at two in the morning – the same time that the violent noises disturbed Scott.

Aberdeen Grampian

Jake was a stagehand at His Majesty's Theatre when he was killed by the stage hoist. His ghost haunts the theatre. Some time after his death colleagues remarked that his ghost was a lot more active than he had been during his lifetime.

Abergeldie Castle Grampian

2 miles E of Balmoral

Queen Victoria and Prince Albert often rented this small, picturesque castle, built in the sixteenth century for the head of Clan Gordon, and used it as an annexe to Balmoral. Several young princes stayed at the castle in the summer months and learned about its ghost, a witch named Kittie Rankie, who had been imprisoned in its dungeon before she was burned on the hill overlooking Abergeldie.

Airlie Castle Tayside ✆

6 miles W of Kirriemuir

A phantom drummer, sometimes accompanied by the wailing of ghostly pipes, heralds the death of the chief of the Airlie family even if they are abroad at the time.

Ardchattan Priory Strathclyde

2 miles NE of Connel Bridge

There is a legend that a nun from Kilmaronaig Convent on the opposite shore of Loch Etive was once enticed into the priory by the monks and concealed in a hiding place beneath the floor of the oratory. The prior discovered her and had her immured alive. Her spirit haunts the scanty remains of the monastery.

Ardvreck Castle Highland

1 mile N of Inchnadamph

Montrose was betrayed by Neil McLeod of Assynt, the laird of Ardvreck, and captured at the castle in 1650 before being taken to Edinburgh for execution. Soon after Ardvreck was burned down in revenge and all its inhabitants killed. The ghost of a giant is sometimes seen in the romantic ruins on the shore of Loch Assynt.

Ashintully Castle Tayside

11 miles NW of Blairgowrie

There are three ghosts here. Crooked Davie is a hunchback who was cruelly mistreated and then killed by a wicked member of the Spalding family, lairds of Ashintully. A Green Jean walks among the trees in the family graveyard behind the castle. She was murdered by her uncle for her inheritance. The third ghost is that of a tinker summarily executed for trespassing. As he was about to die, he cursed the Spaldings, saying that the family would become extinct within a generation. The prophesy was fulfilled.

Balcomie Castle Fife 🍺

9 miles SE of St Andrews

A common story of a forgotten prisoner left to die comes from this ancient tower house. At Balcomie the man was put in the dungeon because his persistent playing of the fife irritated the colonel of troops garrisoned at the castle. The colonel left to visit Dunbar and returned four days later to find the musician dead. The plaintive sound of the fife has often been heard around the castle.

Baldoon Castle Dumfries and Galloway

2 miles S of Wigtown

The phantom of Janet Dalrymple haunts the ruined tower clad in a bloodstained white gown. She was in love with her bridegroom's uncle and rejected the overtures of her husband on the wedding night, ending up by stabbing him. He recovered but Janet became mad and died nineteen years later. Scott used the story in *The Bride of Lammermuir*, which in turn inspired Donizetti's opera.

Ballechin House Tayside 🐾

3 miles S of Pitlochry

In the latter years of the nineteenth century this was reckoned to be the most haunted house in Britain and the Marquess of Bute rented it in order that the Society for Psychical Research might investigate its ghosts. They catalogued a wide variety of phenomena and some of these may survive today, even though little remains of the house except a portion of the east wing. Look for a ghostly nun who walks the grounds with a companion, and a spectral black spaniel (said to be the spirit of Major Steuart in the shape of his favourite dog – the major owned the house in the 1870s and his housekeeper died in suspicious circumstances).

Balnagown Castle Highland

5 miles S of Tain

The turreted castle dates from the thirteenth century and was once the home of the earls of Ross. It is haunted by the ghost of Black Andrew who was thrown out of a tower window with a rope round his neck after being found guilty of rape.

Bedlay Castle Strathclyde

7 miles NE of Glasgow

The twelfth-century castle near the northern end of the M73 was once the palace of the bishops of Glasgow, one of whom, Bishop Cameron, came to an unhappy end in the fourteenth century, being found drowned in the fishpond. His ghost still haunts the ancient building.

Ben Macdhui Grampian 💀

12 miles NW of Braemar

This is the second-highest mountain in Britain and it has its very own ghost, one which resembles the yeti of the Himalayas or Bigfoot of North America. Known as Am Fear Liath Mhór, the Big Grey Man, he is most often seen just below the skyline near the Larig Ghru Pass – a twenty-foot-tall swaggering figure with a large head and covered with short brown hair like an ape's. The BGM's presence is frequently felt to be malign. It infests the mind, attempting to divert the climber to the precipitous drop at Lurcher's Crag.

Borthwick Castle Lothian ♛

12 miles SE of Edinburgh

A haunt of Mary, Queen of Scots, who escaped from the castle disguised as a boy during her honeymoon with Lord Bothwell. The slight, boyish spectre that walks between the castle and the churchyard is presumed to be her ghost.

Braemar Castle Grampian

In Victorian times a honeymoon couple came to the castle (now open to the public). The bride woke one morning to find herself alone and, thinking that she had been abandoned by her husband, she took the extreme step of killing herself. In fact he had risen early to go hunting. Her ghost is only active when newly-weds are at the castle and she restricts her appearances to the bridegroom. The castle was burned down by John Farquharson, the Black Colonel of Inverey, in 1689, and it may be his ghost that also haunts the present building, sometimes leaving a candle burning as a reminder of his visitation.

Brodick Castle Isle of Arran

The National Trust for Scotland now owns the mansion that was formerly the family home of the Dukes of Hamilton (and of the Dukes of Montrose for one generation) and it is open to the public. Brodick's Grey Lady haunts the oldest part of the house and is the spectre of a servant who was seduced by an officer of the Cromwellian garrison which occupied (and enlarged) the castle in the mid-seventeenth century. When she found herself to be pregnant she committed suicide by jumping from the Old Quay. The ghost of a man in a green velvet coat is seen in the library.

Buckholm Tower Borders 🐾

1 mile NW of Galashiels

An evil man named Pringle lived here in Covenanting times, when the Presbyterians were fighting to protect their religion. Pringle murdered two of their supporters and in June spectral hounds visit the house in eternal pursuit of his soul. There is poetic justice in this: Pringle was fond of setting his own dogs on ordinary people.

Cairngorm Range Grampian 🐾 ✋

The Cairngorms are haunted by the Famh – a ghostly creature that resembles a mole but is the size of a large dog with an enormous head. Ghostly music and voices are often heard in the wild parts of the mountains. (See also Ben Macdhui, above.)

Carleton Castle Strathclyde

6 miles SW of Girvan

Terrible screams occasionally issue from the ruined building, sited on top of a rocky crag. They are said to derive from the time when the laird disposed of seven wives by pushing them from the Gamesloup Crag. The eighth wife, May Cullean, proved more canny than the rest when it came to her turn to strip off her clothes and jewellery. She feigned shyness and made him turn his back as she took off her gown. Then she pushed him to his death.

Castle of Mey Highland

15 miles N of Wick

Also known as Barrowgill Castle, this is the home of a Green Lady. The daughter of a former laird (the Queen Mother is the present one), she was thwarted in her love for a ploughboy by her father, and committed suicide by jumping from an upper window. (Open to the public when the Queen Mother is not in residence.)

Cawdor Castle Highland

5 miles SW of Nairn

The handless girl who walks the environs of this castle (open to the public) is the ghost of a daughter of an earl of Cawdor. She defied her father's will by courting a young man who was the son of the chief of an enemy clan. When the earl discovered his daughter's disloyalty he chased her to a chamber in the highest tower of the castle. She lowered herself from the window, clinging to the sill and defying her father to send her to her death below. His response was to sever her hands with one blow of his sword. (See Rait Castle, below, for a similar story.)

Clachtoll Highland 🐾 ☠

4 miles NW of Lochinver

The Western Highlands, like most other parts of Britain, have Black Dog stories, one of which comes from this township. This beast has gleaming eyes that burn like sods of peat and a face that is part-human but has horns resembling antlers. As it disappears it gives a terrible cackle of laughter. Should the animal overtake you, or bark more than twice, you are doomed.

Corgarff Castle Grampian

10 miles SE of Tomintoul

This was built as a hunting lodge in 1537 but became a residence of the Forbes family. In 1571 Adam Gordon of Auchindoun besieged the castle and burned it down with its defenders inside. Margaret Forbes, the chief's wife, and twenty-six others died. Their screams may be heard on the occasions when the tragedy is supernaturally re-enacted.

Corsock Dumfries and Galloway 🎺

13 miles W of Dumfries

A spectral piper plays demonically on Corsock Hill and the apparition is all the more frightening for having no head.

Cortachy Castle Tayside 🎺

7 miles NW of Forfar

The ghostly drummer of Cortachy is heard when a member of the Ogilvy family is to die at the castle. The boy drummer betrayed the family by failing to warn them of an approaching enemy force. He suffered their revenge by being thrown from the battlements inside his drum.

Cortachy Castle

Crathes Castle Grampian

7 miles W of Ballater

The Green Lady is the ghost of a young woman killed when her father found that she was carrying an illegitimate child. Her body remained hidden for a hundred and fifty years, though throughout that time, and ever since, the Green Lady has made frequent appearances at Crathes Castle (open to the public).

Cullen House Grampian

11 miles W of Banff

This archetypal Scottish baronial house is haunted by the Mad Earl, the sixth earl of Findlater, who was the victim of bouts of insanity when he became dangerously violent. In the course of one of these fits he killed his trusted factor. When the earl discovered what he had done he cut his own throat, and his spirit has remained restless since that time. Occasionally the whole tragic episode is re-enacted. One of the bedrooms, named the Church Room, is particularly susceptible to the Mad Earl's ghost.

Culloden Highland ✕

6 miles E of Inverness

This barren moor retains an eerie flavour of the massacre that took place in 1746 and there are numerous reports of ghosts being seen. As in so many accounts of clashes between ghostly armies, the fighting is often described as taking place in the sky.

Culzean Castle Strathclyde ⚓

8 miles N of Girvan

The phantom piper of Culzean pre-dates the building of the castle (open to the public) in the eighteenth century. His music heralds the marriage of the chieftain of the Kennedy clan and is usually heard on stormy nights on Piper's Brae, within the castle demesne.

Cupar Fife 🍺

9 miles W of St Andrew's

The Royal Hotel is haunted by a hooded monk who usually appears in the functions room, where there is often poltergeist activity as well. The nineteenth-century hotel is built on the site of a monastery graveyard.

Dean Castle Strathclyde

1 mile N of Kilmarnock

The fourth Earl of Kilmarnock's bloody head rolled across the floor in front of a horrified housemaid. It proved to be an apparition, warning of the fate the earl would suffer a year later, when he was beheaded at the Tower of London for supporting the Jacobites.

Dornoch Highland

The Witch's Stone is situated on the edge of the golf course and marks the spot where in 1772 Janet Horne was burned to death for witchcraft. Her ghost haunts the place when the moon is waning on autumnal nights.

Drumlanrig Castle 🐎

3 miles NW of Thornhill

An enormous yellow ape has haunted this palatial castle (open to the public) for three hundred years. A female ghost that walks with a fan in one hand and her head in the other is supposed to be the wraith of Lady Anne Douglas.

Dumfries Dumfries and Galloway ♛

A headless horseman haunts the district between Castle Street and the riverside. This is the ghost of young MacMilligan who literally lost his head to a young girl. Pursued by her brothers he fled on horseback but failed to see a low bough which struck his head from his shoulders. A plaque in Castle Street marks the site of the Minorite Friary where in 1306 Robert the Bruce killed Red Comyn, the English king's representative in Scotland. However, it is Bruce's ghost that is seen here, with that of his supporter Roger de Kirkpatrick whose dirk made sure of Comyn's death.

Dunphail Grampian 🚂

6 miles S of Forres

There are stories of a ghost train that runs on the old Highland Railway line here even though the tracks were lifted many years ago. The train runs through Dunphail station suspended a few feet above the ground.

Dunrobin Castle Highland

1 mile NE of Golspie

A comparatively humble medieval stone keep lies at the heart of the palace created for the Dukes of Sutherland in the eighteenth and nineteenth centuries (now open to the public). The upper part of the original building is haunted by Margaret, the daughter of the fourteenth Earl, who fell in love with Jamie Gunn, a young groom. When the earl found out about the affair he was enraged and had Jamie expelled from the estate and his daughter confined to the topmost chamber of the ancient tower. Jamie's love was undaunted, however, and he arranged for the escape of his sweetheart, smuggling a length of rope to her room. Unhappily his plans were betrayed to the earl's steward who arrived with his master as his daughter was about to descend the rope. Seeing that all hope of escape was lost she fell to her death rather than endure further unhappiness. Her sobbing ghost remains in the disused room she occupied at the top of the old tower.

Duntrune Castle Strathclyde ⚓

6 miles NW of Lochgilphead

The twelfth-century stronghold guards the entrance to Loch Crinan. Its ghost is an Irish piper who was sent to the castle by Coll Ciotech, his chieftain, to spy out its defences. The Campbells, who held the castle, were suspicious of the Irishman and imprisoned him in a room high in a tower. From here he could see the approaching Irish force, and knowing that they would be defeated should they attack he took his pipes and played a pibroch to warn his chief of the danger. The Campbells were angry at their carelessness in leaving him the pipes and cruelly cut off the piper's fingers before killing him. On many occasions thereafter the melancholy sound of ghostly pipes echoed across the still waters of the loch, and the story was given credence about a hundred years ago when a fingerless skeleton was discovered in the walls of the castle. After the bones were given a Christian burial the haunting ceased, though in the 1970s there were reports of further ghostly activity at Duntrune.

Edinburgh Lothian ☞ ♛

Castle

The phantom drummer at the castle (open to the public), a well-known haunting dating from the mid-seventeenth century, is able to play in both the Scottish and English styles.

Charlotte Square

This is the best-haunted part of the New Town, having a spectral monk, the ghost of a woman dressed in Georgian style, a sad beggar and a phantom coach.

Holyroodhouse

In *Haunted Royal Homes*, Joan Forman writes of her investigations into psychic activity at Holyroodhouse (open to the public). She met people who claimed to have seen the ghost of Mary, Queen of Scots, while a window cleaner described seeing the ghost of a man in Tudor costume who might have been the shade of her secretary, David Rizzio, brutally murdered at the palace in 1566.

West Bow

The story of Major Weir is a classic tale of the supernatural. Weir was the commander of the City Guard and a passionate Presbyterian lay-preacher. He never married but lived with his elder sister, Grizel, in an old house in West Bow. After a lifetime of respectability his reputation suddenly crumbled in 1669 when all manner of strange stories were told about him – how he had entered into a pact with the Devil, that he never knelt in church, that the strange, twisted stick he carried was his familiar and acted as his servant, and that you could smell brimstone coming from him as he passed. Suddenly at a prayer meeting the major confessed that all the accusations were true and implicated his sister in his diabolical activities, saying that he had also committed incest with her. Both were arrested and charged with sorcery. Their fate was a foregone conclusion, Weir being burned alive (with his stick, which resisted the flames for longer than he did) on 11 April 1670 and his sister hanged the following day at the scaffold in Grassmarket. The house at West Bow stood empty for over a century before anyone was brave enough to defy its ghosts. It was demolished in 1878. Weir's ghost, mounted on a headless black horse, gallops down the High Street to West Bow, surrounded with flames. The shape of Grizel is also seen, her flesh blackened and her face stretched in a terrible grimace, and the tapping of Weir's diabolical stick is a further reminder of a Scottish warlock.

Eilean Donan Castle Highland

8 miles E of Kyle of Lochalsh

The meticulous reconstruction of this archetypal Highland castle (now open to the public) was inspired by a vision experienced by a local stonemason, Farquhar MacRae. Later research confirmed that the restoration was historically correct. The castle is haunted by the ghost of a Spanish mercenary who died in a siege in 1719.

Ethie Castle Tayside

4 miles NE of Arbroath

The castle was the home of the wicked Cardinal Beaton (1494–1546) who had hundreds of Protestants burned at the stake. He was eventually murdered at St Andrew's but his ghost belongs to Ethie and may be heard rather than seen, the laboured steps of an old man suffering from gout, who drags a bandaged leg. A Green Lady acts as a banshee at the castle, her ghost appearing to warn of the impending death of an earl of Northesk. She did so quite recently, even though the Northesks have left the castle, just before the earl died in London.

Fyvie Castle Grampian ☞

24 miles NW of Aberdeen

The discovery in the 1920s of a skeleton behind panelling at Fyvie Castle (open to the public) triggered numerous appearances of a Grey Lady. Her spirit was calmed when the bones were replaced in their original position though there are still reports of sightings. Fyvie also has a ghostly drummer boy, and a Green Lady whose appearance used to warn of the death of the head of the family (the Gordons of Fyvie, who were enticed by the Green Lady to die in the room known as the Gordon bedroom).

Glamis Castle Tayside

5 miles SW of Forfar

This is the ancestral home of the earls of Strathmore (now open to the public) who, on coming of age, were entrusted with Scotland's best-kept secret – the identity of the Monster of Glamis. The mystery seems to date from 1821 when a son was born to Lord Glamis, himself the heir to the eleventh earl of Strathmore. According to records this child died soon after being born, but legend maintains that in fact he lived on despite being hideously deformed, mentally as well as physically. The family expected this 'monster' to live only a short time but he outlived his father, dying during the time when his brother, Claude, was earl. The fourteenth earl was the last to be told the secret when he came of age in 1876 and the knowledge of it changed his personality – he became gloomy and reclusive. The Monster is just one ghost of Glamis: there are at least four others.

Lord 'Beardie' Crawford played dice with the Devil in one of the high, turreted towers and died soon afterwards. The room where the game took place is never used because the game will continue there eternally, the enormous, lavishly bewhiskered Beardie perpetually stamping his feet and cursing his lack of fortune as he sits before an empty firegrate.

The ghost of a small black boy appears on a chair at the door of the sitting room, the shade of a young servant who died from ill-treatment long ago.

A Grey Lady is the most active ghost at Glamis: she appears in the chapel and may be the spirit of the beautiful Janet Douglas who, falsely accused of plotting against King James V, was burned at the stake in Edinburgh in 1542.

The Haunted Chamber is where the Strathmores' personal executioner used to reside. Like Beardie's tower it is kept empty.

Glasgow Strathclyde 🚂

Shields Road Station

Glasgow's underground system provides several ghost stories, the most famous being that of the Grey Lady who haunts Shields Road station. She was killed when she fell on the track in 1922, while her little girl was heroically rescued by the stationmaster.

Theatre Royal

The Theatre Royal, home of Scottish Opera, is haunted by the spirit of a cleaning lady named Nora.

Haddington Lothian

16 miles E of Edinburgh

St Mary's church has the grim-faced ghost of John, first Duke of Lauderdale, who died in 1682 and is buried in the family vault here. He was an ardent enforcer of the laws of the Covenanters which brought great suffering to those who opposed them. The coffin containing his embalmed body was also restless, always being found in a different position whenever the vault was opened.

Hermitage Castle Borders

12 miles S of Hawick

Few buildings are more sinister, more redolent of evil. The castle (open to the public) is haunted by Lord Soulis, 'Terrible William',

Hermitage Castle

who kidnapped children and used them in demonic rituals, aided by an ugly dwarf named Robin who was said to be his familiar. Soulis was eventually put to death by local people who threw him into a cauldron of boiling lead (because of his pact with the Devil he could not be killed by steel or rope). His screams are heard in and about the castle, while Robin remains as a ghostly guardian of his master's treasure.

Hopetoun House Lothian
11 miles W of Edinburgh

There is a certain path in the grounds of the house (open to the public) that seems to generate a feeling of menace and is disliked by dogs. A dark-robed figure has been seen and this apparition usually heralds a death in the Marquess of Linlithgow's family.

Houndwood Borders
10 miles NW of Berwick

Chappie o'Houndwood (Houndwood House is on the north bank of the River Eye) is a rare spectre in that only the lower part of his body is seen, up to his knees. This makes him difficult to identify.

Inveraray Strathclyde ✕ ⚓

An astonishing account of a spectral army 'more numerous than the armies of both sides at the battle of Culloden' dates from between 1746 and 1753 and was written down on the orders of the Duke of Argyll. The troops were dressed in red and were accompanied by women and children as they marched from the bridge at Glen Shiray to the one close to the castle at Glen Aray, where they all disappeared. The haunting took place on a summer's afternoon and was witnessed by two men, neither of whom had been drinking or suffered from hallucinations. The castle itself (open to the public) has the ghost of a piper whom Montrose hanged nearby before the present castle was built. The piper is seen and heard on the stairs as well as in the Blue Room, Archie's Room and the Green Library.

Inverawe House Strathclyde
1 mile E of Taynuilt

Green Jean is a helpful spirit who lends a hand with the housekeeping but appears only to members of the Clan Campbell.

Inverness Highland

The Eden Court Theatre is part of the riverside arts complex and was opened in 1974. It was built on the site of the Bishop's Palace and its Green Lady is said to be the ghost of the wife of a bishop who hanged herself in the chapel at the turn of the century. Appropriately this is now the theatre's Green Room.

Iona Strathclyde ⚓

The beautiful island, where St Columba established Christianity in Scotland, is the spiritual heart of the nation and possesses a special atmosphere of tranquillity. Ghostly monks are seen on the island accompanied by bells and other-worldly music and some people have witnessed re-enacted episodes from Iona's history, including the sacking of the monastery by Viking invaders.

Jedburgh Castle Borders

A tall hooded figure wearing a dark cloak and a mask is a harbinger of death at Jedburgh Castle. Its most famous visitation was in 1285 at the wedding feast of King Alexander III. The sinister figure's sudden appearance brought the festivities to an end and within six months the king was dead, drowned when his horse stumbled and pitched him into the Firth of Forth. Similarly, James IV was warned by an apparition at Jedburgh about his impending defeat and death at Flodden, Northumberland.

Kenovay Isle of Tiree

The ghost of a seaman haunts the tranquil churchyard here. Remarkably his ghost seems to have been seen both before and after his body was washed up on the shore and then buried in the churchyard.

Killiecrankie Tayside ✗ ☠

3 miles NW of Pitlochry

A strange, other-worldly light bathes the battlefield at dusk on the anniversary of the English defeat, 27 July. A ghost to beware of in the pass itself is what appears to be a monk dressed in a white robe – if he touches you it means death within the year. Another ghost that may be encountered at the northern end of the pass is that of a Mrs Hays who was murdered here two hundred years ago. Hers is a terrible phantom, a disembodied head that glows with a sinister green light and shows its repulsive features before joining with a misty body and disappearing.

Kylesku Hotel Highland 🍺

25 miles N of Ullapool

The former snug of this lovely old hostelry is now the pool room and this may account for the present shyness of the ghost. There are two differing stories to account for Kylesku's haunting. Many think the phantom is that of Mr Mackay, the brother of Miss Mackay who as landlady in the 1890s was tricked into losing her licence by a policeman from Stoer. Miss Mackay was a formidable lady and her brother enjoyed escaping into the snug where he was safe from her temper. The alternative story tells of a barrel of whisky washed up on the shore and taken to the inn, which was then known as the Old Ferry House. A marathon drinking session ensued in a secluded upper room until one of the party tried to bring it to an end before the dawning of the sabbath. In the resulting fracas he was tumbled down the ladder which gave access to the room and broke his neck. The famous broadcaster Professor Joad saw the ghost in the 1950s. Soon afterwards the room was converted into a ladies' lavatory, where many of its patrons felt uneasy, as though someone or something was watching them. Now that it is a lively pool room there is even less scope for ghostly activity.

Lanark Strathclyde 🍺

The Cartland Bridge Hotel, a country-house hotel occupying a Georgian building, is haunted by an old lady wearing a veil and a pale blue dress.

Larkhall Strathclyde 🍺

7 miles NW of Lanark

The Applebank Hotel has a lintel that was formerly at the family home of the McNeils. Their house was burned down but the lintel survived, carrying its psychic memory of one of the McNeil brides, an Indian princess. She was desperately unhappy in Scotland and one day simply disappeared, leaving behind a ghost to haunt the house and then the pub.

Lauriston Castle Lothian

3 miles NW of Edinburgh

It is surprising that only one story of the supernatural comes from this beautiful castle (open to the public): the shuffling sound of slipper-clad feet that is a reminder of an old butler who once worked at Lauriston.

Leith Hall Grampian

6 miles S of Huntly

A big man with a bushy black beard is the phantom of this property, which belongs to the National Trust for Scotland (and is open to the public). His head is bandaged, and this suggests that he is the ghost of John Leith who died in 1763, shot in the head by Abernethy of Mayen, a fellow guest at a dinner party in Aberdeen.

Linlithgow Palace Lothian 🕐 👑

14 miles W of Edinburgh

An apparition of an old man in a long blue gown appeared in the church here to James IV of Scotland to warn that he would shortly be killed in battle, as indeed he was, at Flodden. The ghost of his wife, Margaret Tudor, is also dressed in blue and is first seen near the entrance to the palace. She then walks towards the church where she vanishes. This royal ghost is often seen on April mornings, around nine o'clock. It has been suggested that the queen manufactured the ghost that appeared to her husband, hoping to dissuade him from going to battle.

Littledean Tower Borders

6 miles E of Melrose

The countryside is haunted by a figure on horseback who rides the wind on stormy nights. He is supposed to be an erstwhile laird of Littledean who killed a stable boy.

Loch Morlich Highland

5 miles E of Aviemore

The sandy beach of this small loch is the haunt of Red Hand, a giant warrior also known as Big Donald of the Ghosts, who is reputed to make visits across the Atlantic to haunt his descendants there too.

Loch Mullardoch Highland

20 miles E of Kyle of Lochalsh

In the 1980s two hill walkers were surprised to see a cottage on the lonely shore of this loch that was not marked on their map. As they descended towards it, higher ground hid it from view for a while, and when they climbed the next ridge it had inexplicably vanished. Later it was pointed out that the water level in the loch had been raised thirty years before and submerged a hunting lodge near the shore they had seen.

Meggernie Castle Tayside

8 miles N of Killin

The fifteenth-century stronghold has a most unusual ghost – one that appears in two halves. The upper part of the spectre (a beautiful woman) haunts the top floors, while the ghost from the waist down visits the ground floor and the lime avenue leading up to the castle. This lower part is the most frightening for the long skirt is soaked with blood. It is said that when Meggernie was the seat of the Clan Menzies the chief killed his lovely wife in a fit of jealous rage. He attempted to hide the body by cutting it in half, burying half in the churchyard and half beneath the floor of the north tower, a place particularly favoured by the ghost. (Another account gives a murder date of 1862, after the time of the Menzies.) If the woman's ghost touches you there will be an intense feeling of burning, yet there is no blister.

Melrose Abbey Borders

Unsurprisingly, it is a monk whose ghost haunts the eastern side of the ruins (open to the public). He does not walk but rather creeps along the ground in a snake-like way, perhaps his punishment for pursuing a wicked lifestyle. Some think that he may be a vampire, others that he is the ghost of the medieval scholar Michael Scot who is buried here. Even though he wrote against the practice of magic local people believed him to be a wizard because of his interest in science.

Muchalls Castle Grampian

4 miles N of Stonehaven

A Green Jean, the Scottish form of Green Lady, haunts the drawing room of the seventeenth-century stronghold which originally belonged to the Burnetts of Leys. She is said to have drowned in a sea cave below the castle where she had gone (via a secret passageway) to meet her sailor lover. However, in one of the more recent sightings of the ghost, the girl was wearing a yellow dress and appeared in a bedroom. (The castle is open to the public.)

New Galloway Dumfries and Galloway

Glenlee House, just to the north-west of the town (and shown as Glenlee Park on maps), has an intriguing story of a Lady Ashburton who killed her husband because he was infested with lice. She, in turn, was murdered by the butler and her ghost walks dressed in a grey dress of rustling silk.

Newark Castle Borders ✕ ◉

3 miles W of Selkirk

In 1645 this border keep was the scene of a terrible massacre when five hundred of Montrose's supporters, survivors of the Battle of Philiphaugh, were butchered along with their wives, children and camp followers by the victorious Covenanters. Echoes of this slaughter are heard on its anniversary (13 September).

Newstead Borders

1 mile E of Melrose

The Romans established a camp on the banks of the Tweed here and called it Trimontium after the three peaks of the Eildons that overlooked it. In the evenings there are ethereal sounds of marching soldiers (surely muted if they wear sandals?) as well as bugle calls and building noises such as sawing and hammering.

Pencait Castle Lothian ♛

7 miles SW of Haddington

The spirit of a sorcerer, Alexander Hamilton, is just one of the ghosts that dwell here (the castle is also known as Fountainhall House). Refused hospitality at Pencait, he cast a spell on the household which brought death to the chatelaine and her eldest daughter. Hamilton was foolish enough to boast of his success and consequently was arrested, tried for witchcraft, and hanged at Edinburgh. There is also the ghost of John Cockburn who committed a murder in the castle (there are sounds of the body being dragged across the floor) and that of Charles I (sources do not say whether this is of Scotland or England).

Rait Castle Highland

3 miles S of Nairn

This was built for the Comyns and is haunted by a girl in a bloodstained dress who has had her hands chopped off. The Comyns planned to massacre their rivals, the Mackintoshes, at a feast they arranged at Rait. However, the Mackintoshes had been warned of the plan and were able to escape the trap. The Comyn chief believed that it was his daughter who had betrayed his plan (she was betrothed to a Mackintosh) and he cut off her hands, whereupon she jumped to her death from the battlements. (A handless girl also haunts Cawdor Castle, above.)

Roslin Chapel Lothian ✠

8 miles SE of Edinburgh

The chapel, with its amazing Prentice Pillar, appears to be on fire when one of the St Clair Erskine family (that of the ancient earls of Rosslyn) is on their deathbed.

Ruthven Castle (Barracks) Highland

1 mile S of Kingussie

A Green Lady apparently warns of imminent death, and there is also the re-playing of an infernal game of chess in which the infamous Wolf of Badenoch, Robert II's son Alexander, took on the Devil and, needless to say, lost.

Saddell Abbey Strathclyde

9 miles NE of Campbeltown

Antony Hippisley Coxe, visiting Saddell in the early 1970s, found it an intensely atmospheric place. Since his visit the castle has been restored and now looks less sinister. Its ghosts are monks because material from their monastery was used in the building of the castle, even gravestones being utilised as firebacks.

St Andrew's Fife

A veiled Grey Lady haunts the area of the round tower within the precincts of the ruined cathedral.

Sandwood Bay Highland

6 miles S of Cape Wrath

The location is remote and necessitates a two-hour walk across peat bogs and sand dunes but it is well worth the effort. The beach is the haunt of a bearded man in seaboots as well as the spectre of a headless sailor, cast ashore from the wreck of a Polish boat more than three hundred years ago. Sandwood is also famous for its mermaids, but they are more likely to turn out to be seals. I have stumbled over a seal here – it was hidden by wind-driven sand and glowered indignantly before taking itself off to the sea.

Sanquhar Castle Dumfries and Galloway

10 miles NW of Thornhill

The blonde-haired White Lady here is the ghost of Marion of Dalpeddar who disappeared in 1590 (some people believed that she was murdered by Lord Sanquhar). In 1875 the skeleton of a woman with golden hair was found buried head-down in the masonry of the castle.

Schiehallion Tayside 🐾

9 miles NW of Aberfeldy

This conical peak has magical significance in the Highlands with evil water horses living in its lochs and a ghostly Black Dog lurking among the deep gulleys.

Scone Palace Tayside

3 miles N of Perth

The south passage of the palace (open to the public) is the haunt of a ghost enigmatically known as the 'Boring Walker'. The sound of footsteps in rooms known to be empty is a common phenomenon in thousands of old houses, but at Scone it is given an odd twist in that the footsteps echo from a stone floor, whereas the south passage has a creaky wooden floor.

Skene Grampian 🐇 🕒

9 miles W of Aberdeen

Alexander Skene was laird here and died in 1724. He was a famous warlock who, it was said, had lost his shadow in escaping from the Devil. Skene had four familiars, a jackdaw, hawk, magpie and crow, which always sat beside him when he went out in his coach, drawn by headless black horses. He would drive to the village graveyard to obtain the unbaptised bodies of babies which he fed to his feathered fiends. The Wizard Laird is still to be seen on the night of Hogmanay, driving across the loch in his spectral carriage.

Solway Firth Dumfries and Galloway ⚓

The Firth was a favourite haunt of pirates and smugglers in bygone days and the smugglers may have invented the stories of phantom ships which sail the treacherous waters of the estuary. The *Betsy Jane* was a slave ship wrecked on the Gilstone Rock one Christmas Day. Her captain and crew were all drowned but the vessel is doomed to sail on, into eternity. The *Rotterdam* was a larger sailing ship that also sank in the Firth with the loss of all crew and passengers. This ghost ship appears to forewarn of another disaster at sea.

Spedlin's Tower Dumfries and Galloway

5 miles NW of Lockerbie

The tower dates from 1480 and soon after became the home of the Jardine family. One of the Jardines became exasperated by the behaviour of the local miller, a man named Porteous, and locked him in the dungeon. He then rode off to Edinburgh, forgetting that he had the key in his pocket. Porteous suffered an agonising death from thirst and hunger but before dying cursed the Jardine family. Thus his ghost haunted the tower and caused endless trouble until it was exorcised, being committed instead to the dungeon where Porteous died. The Bible used in the service was left in a niche at the foot of the stairs to make sure that the spirit did not escape. For all this the cries of the starving man were often heard and if anyone pushed a twig through the door its bark would be immediately stripped off, so ravenous was the ghost. In time the Jardines prospered from the tea trade and moved to a new mansion on the other side of the river. Soon afterwards the old Bible was sent to Edinburgh for restoration, whereupon Porteous's ghost escaped from the dungeon and wrought havoc on the family in their new home, even tipping the newly created baronet and his wife from their bed. The disturbance ceased when the Bible was returned to its niche, where it remained until the Jardines moved with it to Cumbria. By then the Tower was in decay, but recently it has been restored as a home. Its owner has so far seen no sign of the miller's ghost.

Stirling Central

The castle has the ghost of a beautiful woman dressed in pink who has most often been seen walking from the castle to Ladies' Rock, a viewpoint once used by the ladies of the castle who wanted to watch the jousting tourneys.

Traquair House Borders ♛

6 miles SE of Peebles

Bonnie Prince Charlie stayed at Traquair (open to the public) shortly before his disastrous battle with the English at Culloden. At the end of his visit he passed through the main gates (known as the Bear Gates because of the family emblem borne on the pillars) and asked that they be kept closed until a Stuart sat on the English throne. They have remained closed ever since, and the ghost of the Prince haunts the 'spooky room' of the mansion, one of the cellars, as well as the avenue leading up to the disused gates.

Wormit Tayside 🚂

2 miles S of Dundee

The Tay Bridge disaster occurred on 28 December 1879 and a ghostly train crosses the Tay by a non-existent bridge on the anniversary, its tail-lamps receding until they suddenly vanish as the carriages come to the missing girders.

South West England

Cornwall, Devon

1 **Aveton Gifford**
  Devon
2 **Beer** Devon
3 **Berry Pomeroy**
  Castle Devon
4 **Bolventor** Cornwall
5 **Boscastle** Cornwall
6 **Brixham** Devon
7 **Buckfastleigh** Devon
8 **Buckland Abbey**
  Devon
9 **Buckland**
  Monachorum Devon

10 **Burgh Island** Devon
11 **Camborne** Cornwall
12 **Chardstock** Devon
13 **Colebrooke** Devon
14 **Dartington** Devon
15 **Dartmouth** Devon
16 **Dozmary Pool**
  Cornwall
17 **Exeter** Devon
18 **Falmouth** Cornwall
19 **Frithelstock** Devon

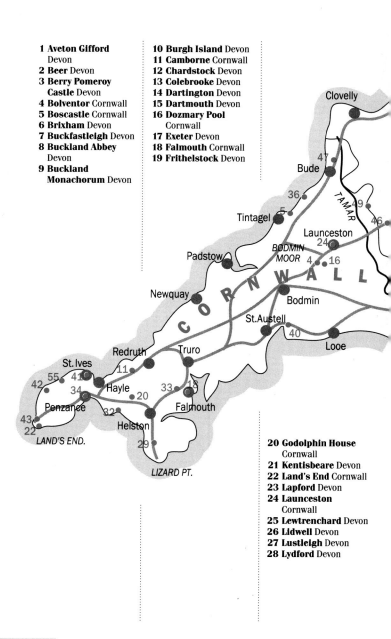

20 **Godolphin House**
  Cornwall
21 **Kentisbeare** Devon
22 **Land's End** Cornwall
23 **Lapford** Devon
24 **Launceston**
  Cornwall
25 **Lewtrenchard** Devon
26 **Lidwell** Devon
27 **Lustleigh** Devon
28 **Lydford** Devon

South West England

Somerset, Avon, Dorset

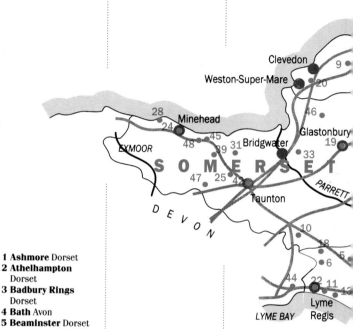

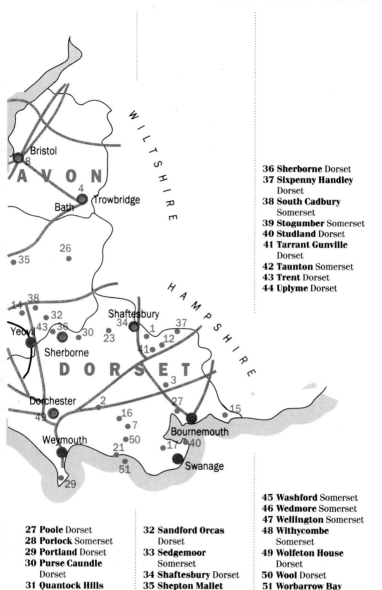

36 Sherborne Dorset
37 Sixpenny Handley Dorset
38 South Cadbury Somerset
39 Stogumber Somerset
40 Studland Dorset
41 Tarrant Gunville Dorset
42 Taunton Somerset
43 Trent Dorset
44 Uplyme Dorset

45 Washford Somerset
46 Wedmore Somerset
47 Wellington Somerset
48 Withycombe Somerset
49 Wolfeton House Dorset
50 Wool Dorset
51 Worbarrow Bay Dorset

27 Poole Dorset
28 Porlock Somerset
29 Portland Dorset
30 Purse Caundle Dorset
31 Quantock Hills Somerset

32 Sandford Orcas Dorset
33 Sedgemoor Somerset
34 Shaftesbury Dorset
35 Shepton Mallet Somerset

Southern England

Wiltshire, Hampshire, Berkshire

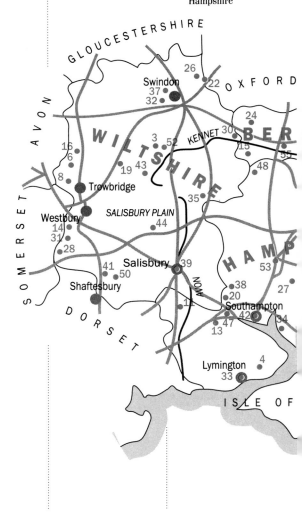

11 Breamore House Hampshire
12 Brimpton Berkshire
13 Cadnam Hampshire
14 Chapmanslade Wiltshire
15 Combe Berkshire
16 Corsham Wiltshire
17 Crondall Hampshire
18 Datchet Berkshire
19 Devizes Wiltshire

20 East Wellow Hampshire
21 Eton Berkshire
22 Faringdon Wiltshire
23 Gosport Hampshire
24 Great Shefford Berkshire
25 Havant Hampshire
26 Highworth Wiltshire
27 Hinton Ampner Hampshire
28 Kilmington Wiltshire

29 Liphook Hampshire
30 Littlecote House Wiltshire
31 Longleat House Wiltshire
32 Lydiard Millicent Wiltshire
33 Lymington Hampshire
34 Netley Hampshire
35 North Tidworth Wiltshire
36 Portsmouth Hampshire
37 Rodbourne Cheney Wiltshire
38 Romsey Hampshire
39 Salisbury Wiltshire
40 Selborne Hampshire
41 Semley Wiltshire
42 Southampton Hampshire
43 Stanton St Bernard Wiltshire
44 Stonehenge Wiltshire
45 Sunninghill Berkshire
46 Tidmarsh Berkshire
47 Totton Hampshire
48 Vernham Dean Hampshire
49 Warblington Hampshire
50 Wardour Castle Wiltshire
51 Waterlooville Hampshire
52 West Kennett Wiltshire
53 Winchester Hampshire
54 Windsor Berkshire
55 Yattendon Berkshire

Southern England

Surrey, Sussex, Kent, Isle of Wight

1 **Angmering** West Sussex
2 **Arundel** West Sussex
3 **Balcombe** West Sussex
4 **Battle Abbey** East Sussex
5 **Bayham Abbey** Kent
6 **Bearsted** Kent
7 **Billingham Manor** Isle of Wight
8 **Bluebell Hill** Kent
9 **Bramber Castle** West Sussex
10 **Brighton** West Sussex
11 **Burwash** East Sussex
12 **Buxted** East Sussex
13 **Canterbury** Kent

14 **Chanctonbury Ring** West Sussex
15 **Chatham** Kent
16 **Chilham** Kent
17 **Cobham** Surrey
18 **Cuckfield** West Sussex
19 **Dover** Kent
20 **Dunnose Point** Isle of Wight
21 **East Cowes** Isle of Wight
22 **Eastbourne** East Sussex
23 **Eastwell** Kent

24 **Farnham** Surrey
25 **Faversham** Kent
26 **Gatcombe** Isle of Wight
27 **Golden Hill Fort** Isle of Wight
28 **Goodwin Sands** Kent
29 **Guildford** Surrey
30 **Hastings** East Sussex
31 **Herstmonceux** East Sussex
32 **Hever Castle** Kent
33 **Icklesham** East Sussex

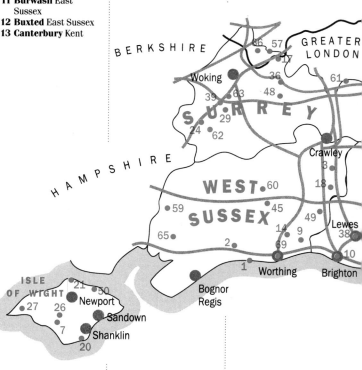

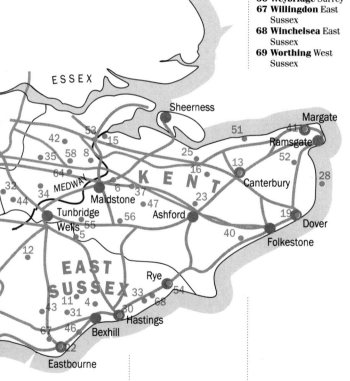

Greater London

1 **Acton** W3
2 **Addington**
3 **Bellingham** SE6
4 **Bexley**
5 **Biggin Hill**
6 **Blackheath** SE3,
   SE9
7 **Bruce Castle** N17
8 **Camberwell** SE5

9 **Canonbury** N1
10 **Charlton House** SE7
11 **Chiswick** W4
12 **Cockfosters**
13 **Colindale** NW9
14 **Croydon Airport**
15 **Crystal Palace** SE19

16 **Docklands** E14
17 **Enfield**
18 **Greenwich** SE10
19 **Ham House**
20 **Hammersmith** W6
21 **Hampstead** NW3

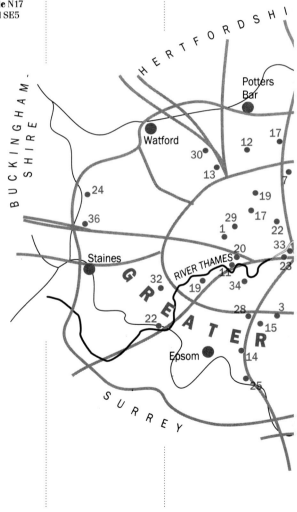

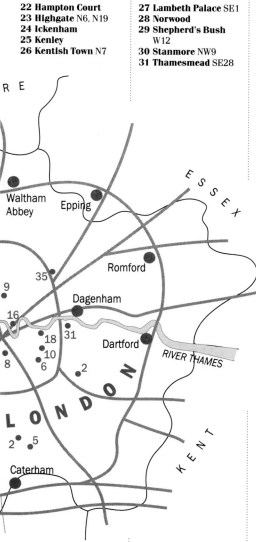

Greater London

1 Baker Street NW1	**6 Buckingham Palace** SW1	**10 Clerkenwell** WC1
2 Bank of England EC2	**7 Buckingham Street** WC2	**11 Drury Lane** WC2
3 Berkeley Square W1	**8 Chelsea** SW3	**12 Gower Street** WC1
4 Bow Road E3	**9 Cleopatra's Needle** WC2	**13 Haymarket** SW1
5 British Museum WC1		**14 Kensington Palace** W8
		15 Kensington: **St Mark's Road** W11

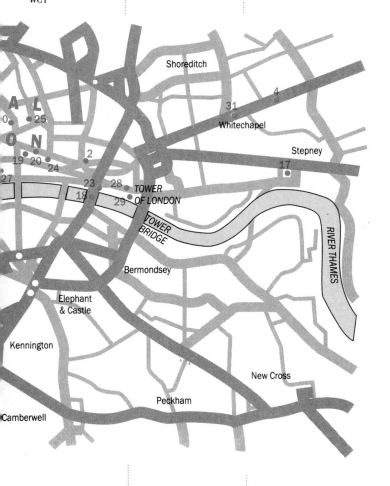

Eastern England

Norfolk, Suffolk, Essex

THE WASH

CAMBRIDGESHIRE

51

HERTFORDSHIRE

Bishop's Stortford

56

54   50

G R E A T E R

L O N D O N

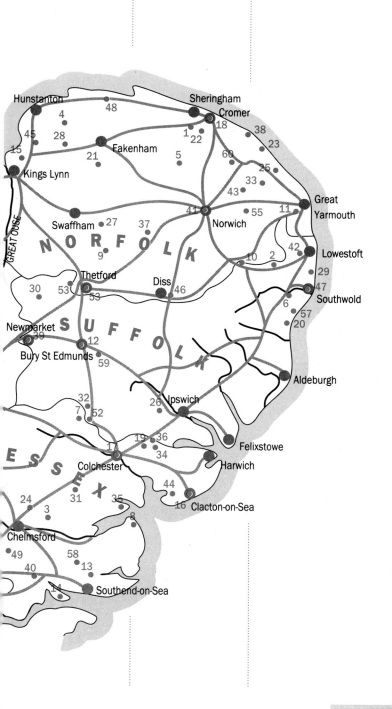

Hunstanton
4
48
45
28
15
21   Fakenham
Kings Lynn
Sheringham
Cromer
18
1 22
38
23
5
60
25
33
43
55   11   Great Yarmouth
41
Norwich
GREAT OUSE
Swaffham 27   37
9
NORFOLK
10   2   42   Lowestoft
Thetford   Diss
30   53   46   29
53   6   47   Southwold
SUFFOLK   57
20
Newmarket
39   12
Bury St Edmunds   59
Aldeburgh
32
7 52
26   Ipswich
19 36
I   34   Felixstowe
Colchester   Harwich
ESSEX
24   31   44
3   35   16   Clacton-on-Sea
8
Chelmsford
49   58
40   13
14   Southend-on-Sea

Eastern England

Lincolnshire, Cambridgeshire, Hertfordshire, Bedfordshire

1 **Abbot's Langley**
Hertfordshire
2 **Ashwell**
Hertfordshire
3 **Aspley Guise**
Bedfordshire
4 **Ayot St Lawrence**
Hertfordshire
5 **Balsham**
Cambridgeshire
6 **Bishop's Stortford**
Hertfordshire
7 **Boston** Lincolnshire
8 **Bovingdon**
Hertfordshire
9 **Caistor** Lincolnshire
10 **Cambridge**
11 **Cammeringham**
Lincolnshire
12 **Caxton Gibbet**
Cambridge-
shire
13 **Conington**
Cambridge-
shire
14 **Crowland**
Lincolnshire
15 **Doddington Hall**
Lincolnshire
16 **East Kirkby**
Lincolnshire
17 **Eynesbury**
Cambridgeshire
18 **Fillingham**
Lincolnshire
19 **Grantchester**
Cambridgeshire
20 **Grayingham**
Lincolnshire
21 **Gunby Hall**
Lincolnshire
22 **Hatfield House**
Hertfordshire
23 **Haverholme
Priory** Lincolnshire
24 **Hinxworth**
Hertfordshire
25 **Hitchin**
Hertfordshire

26 **Holywell**
Cambridgeshire
27 **Huntingdon**
Cambridgeshire
28 **Irby Dale Wood**
Lincolnshire
29 **Kensworth**
Bedfordshire
30 **Kimbolton Castle**
Cambridgeshire
31 **Knebworth House**
Hertfordshire
32 **Lincoln** Lincolnshire
33 **Little Gaddesden**
Hertfordshire
34 **Louth** Lincolnshire
35 **Madingley**
Cambridgeshire
36 **Markyate**
Hertfordshire
37 **Metheringham**
Lincolnshire
38 **Minsden Chapel**
Hertfordshire

39 **Murrow**
Cambridgeshire
40 **Offord Cluny**
Cambridgeshire
41 **Owmby** Lincolnshire
42 **Ravensden**
Bedfordshire
43 **St Albans**
Hertfordshire
44 **St Ives**
Cambridgeshire
45 **Salisbury Hall**
Hertfordshire
46 **Sawston Hall**
Cambridgeshire
47 **Scampton**
Lincolnshire
48 **Soham**
Cambridgeshire
49 **Stanbridge**
Bedfordshire
50 **Studham**
Bedfordshire
51 **Tydd St Giles**
Cambridgeshire

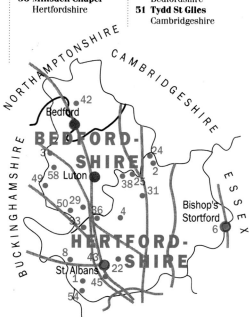

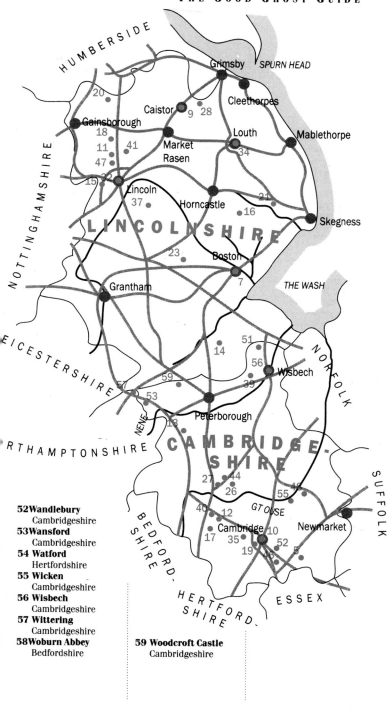

HUMBERSIDE

Grimsby
SPURN HEAD
Cleethorpes
20
Caistor 9 28
Gainsborough
18
11 41
47
15 32
Market Rasen
Louth 34
Mablethorpe

NOTTINGHAMSHIRE

Lincoln
37
Horncastle
21
16
Skegness

LINCOLNSHIRE

23
Boston
7
THE WASH

Grantham

LEICESTERSHIRE

51
14
56
Wisbech
NORFOLK
59
39

NENE
53
13
Peterborough

NORTHAMPTONSHIRE

CAMBRIDGE-
SHIRE

27 44
26
55 48
40 12
GT OUSE
SUFFOLK

BEDFORD-
SHIRE

17 35
Cambridge 10
Newmarket
19 52 5

HERTFORD-
SHIRE
ESSEX

South Midlands

Gloucestershire, Hereford & Worcester, West Midlands, Warwickshire

1 **Aconbury** Hereford and Worcester

2 **Alcester** Warwickshire

3 **Alfrick** Hereford and Worcester

4 **Ashton-under-Hill** Hereford and Worcester

5 **Astley** Warwickshire

6 **Avenbury** Hereford and Worcester

7 **Aylton** Hereford and Worcester

8 **Baddesley Clinton** Warwickshire

9 **Beoley** Hereford and Worcester

10 **Bidford on Avon** Warwickshire

11 **Birmingham** West Midlands

12 **Brailes** Warwickshire

13 **Bretforton** Hereford and Worcester

14 **Broadway** Hereford and Worcester

15 **Burton Dassett** Warwickshire

16 **Callow** Hereford and Worcester

17 **Callow End** Hereford and Worcester

18 **Canley** West Midlands

19 **Cheltenham** Gloucestershire

20 **Childswickham** Hereford and Worcester

21 **Cirencester** Gloucestershire

22 **Coughton Court** Warwickshire

23 **Coventry** West Midlands

24 **Croft Castle** Hereford and Worcester

25 **Cropthorne** Hereford and Worcester

26 **Curdworth** Warwickshire

27 **Dudley** West Midlands

28 **Dunsmore Heath** Warwickshire

29 **Eardisley** Hereford and Worcester

30 **Edge Hill** Warwickshire

31 **Erdington** West Midlands

32 **Ettington Park** Warwickshire

33 **Gloucester** Gloucestershire

34 **Goodrich Castle** Hereford and Worcester

35 **Guy's Cliffe** Warwickshire

36 **Hampton Bishop** Hereford and Worcester

37 **Harborne** West Midlands

38 **Harbury** Warwickshire

39 **Harvington Hall** Hereford and Worcester

40 **Hereford** Hereford and Worcester

41 **Hergest Court** Hereford and Worcester

42 **Hoarwithy** Hereford and Worcester

43 **Huddington** Hereford and Worcester

44 **Ilmington** Warwickshire

45 **Kenchester** Hereford and Worcester

46 **Leigh** Hereford and Worcester

47 **Lenchwick** Hereford and Worcester

48 **Little Compton** Warwickshire

49 **Little Lawford** Warwickshire

50 **Mickleton** Warwickshire

51 **Napton-on-the-Hill** Warwickshire

52 **Netherton** West Midlands

53 **Owlpen** Gloucestershire

South Midlands
Buckinghamshire, Oxfordshire, Northamptonshire

1 **Althorp**
Northamptonshire
2 **Amersham**
Buckinghamshire
3 **Boughton**
Northamptonshire
4 **Burford** Oxfordshire
5 **Clifton Hampden**
Oxfordshire
6 **Colnbrook**
Buckinghamshire
7 **Cumnor** Oxfordshire
8 **Fawsley Park**
Northamptonshire
9 **Fotheringhay**
Northamptonshire
10 **Harrington**
Northamptonshire
11 **Henley-on-Thames**
Oxfordshire
12 **High Wycombe**
Buckinghamshire
13 **Loughton**
Buckinghamshire
14 **Mapledurham**
Oxfordshire

15 **Minster Lovell**
Oxfordshire
16 **Naseby**
Northamptonshire
17 **Oundle**
Northamptonshire
18 **Oxford** Oxfordshire
19 **Ringstead**
Northamptonshire
20 **Rycote Chapel**
Oxfordshire
21 **St Leonards**
Buckinghamshire
22 **Stanton Harcourt**
Manor Oxfordshire

23 **Thame** Oxfordshire
24 **West Wycombe**
Buckinghamshire
25 **Weston-on-the-**
Green Oxfordshire
26 **Wolvercote**
Oxfordshire
27 **Woodstock**
Oxfordshire

WARWICK

GLOUCESTERSHIRE

THAMES

Wales

Clwyd, Gwynedd, Powys

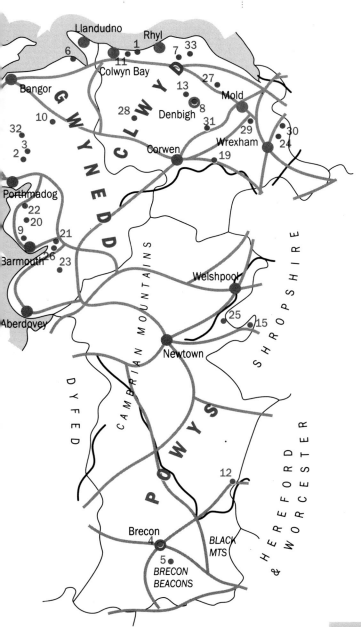

Wales

Gwent, Dyfed, Glamorgan

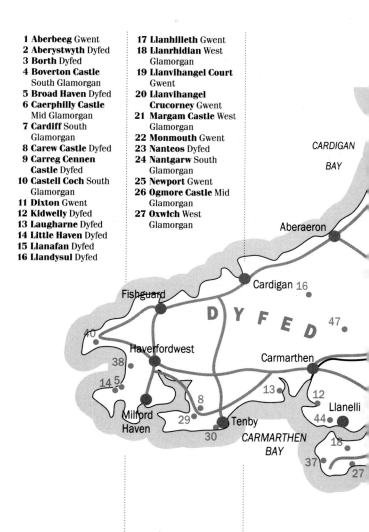

28 Oystermouth Castle West Glamorgan
29 Pembroke Dyfed
30 Penally Dyfed
31 Penhow Castle Gwent
32 Pentre Meyrick South Glamorgan
33 Plynlimon Dyfed
34 Pontypool Gwent
35 Pwyllywrach Manor South Glamorgan
36 Raglan Castle Gwent
37 Rhossili West Glamorgan

38 Roch Castle Dyfed
39 St Athan South Glamorgan
40 St David's Dyfed
41 St Donat's Castle South Glamorgan
42 Sker House Mid Glamorgan
43 Southerndown Mid Glamorgan
44 Stradey Dyfed
45 Strata Florida Abbey Dyfed
46 Swansea West Glamorgan
47 Talley Dyfed
48 Tintern Abbey Gwent
49 Usk Gwent

North Midlands

Shropshire, Staffordshire, Cheshire, Derbyshire, Nottinghamshire, Leicestershire

1 **Albrighton** Shropshire
2 **Alderley Edge** Cheshire
3 **Annesley Hall** Nottinghamshire
4 **Ashford in the Water** Derbyshire
5 **Astley Abbots** Shropshire
6 **Atcham** Shropshire
7 **Attenborough** Nottinghamshire
8 **Barrow** Shropshire
9 **Beckbury** Shropshire
10 **Bleaklow Hill** Derbyshire
11 **Blithfield Hall** Staffordshire
12 **Bosley** Cheshire
13 **Bottesford** Leicestershire
14 **Bradgate Park** Leicestershire
15 **Bradwell** Derbyshire
16 **Braunstone** Leicestershire
17 **Bridgnorth** Shropshire
18 **Broughton Astley** Leicestershire
19 **Broughton Hall** Staffordshire
20 **Burtonwood** Cheshire
21 **Buxton** Derbyshire
22 **Capesthorne Hall** Cheshire
23 **Castleton** Derbyshire
24 **Checkley** Staffordshire
25 **Chester** Cheshire
26 **Chesterfield** Derbyshire
27 **Christleton** Cheshire
28 **Combermere Abbey** Cheshire
29 **Crewe** Cheshire
30 **Croft** Leicestershire
31 **Darley** Derbyshire
32 **East Stoke** Nottinghamshire
33 **Easthope** Shropshire

34 **Eyam** Derbyshire
35 **Farndon** Cheshire
36 **Fradley** Staffordshire
37 **Gawsworth** Cheshire
38 **Glossop** Derbyshire
39 **Gonalston** Nottinghamshire
40 **Grace Dieu Priory** Leicestershire
41 **Grindleford** Derbyshire
42 **Handforth** Cheshire
43 **Harlow Wood** Nottinghamshire
44 **Hassop** Derbyshire

45 **Hathersage** Derbyshire
46 **Hockenhul Hall** Cheshire
47 **Holwell** Leicestershire
48 **Hope** Derbyshire
49 **Hopton Castle** Shropshire
50 **Husbands Bosworth** Leicestershire
51 **Ipstones** Staffordshire
52 **Ironbridge** Shropshire

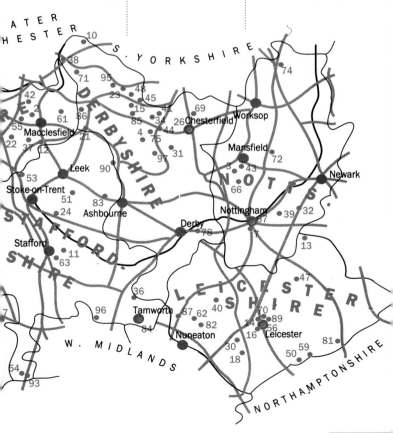

269

North West England

Cumbria, Lancashire, Greater Manchester, Merseyside

1 **Appleby** Cumbria
2 **Ashton-under-Lyne** Greater Manchester
3 **Askerton Castle** Cumbria
4 **Astley** Greater Manchester
5 **Barrock Fell** Cumbria
6 **Bebington** Merseyside
7 **Beetham** Cumbria
8 **Blackpool** Lancashire
9 **Blease Hall** Cumbria
10 **Bramhall Hall** Greater Manchester
11 **Brampton** Cumbria
12 **Brindle** Lancashire
13 **Burnley** Lancashire
14 **Caldbeck** Cumbria
15 **Carlisle** Cumbria

16 **Cartmel** Cumbria
17 **Chingle Hall** Lancashire
18 **Claife** Cumbria
19 **Clayton-le-Moors** Lancashire
20 **Coniston** Cumbria
21 **Corby Castle** Cumbria
22 **Crackenthorpe** Cumbria
23 **Croglin** Cumbria
24 **Dent** Cumbria
25 **Dunham Massey Hall** Greater Manchester

26 **Egremont** Cumbria
27 **Elterwater** Cumbria
28 **Formby** Merseyside
29 **Godley** Greater Manchester
30 **Greystoke Castle** Cumbria
31 **Hall i th' Wood** Greater Manchester
32 **Hawkesdale Hall** Cumbria
33 **Heskin Hall** Lancashire
34 **Hob Stones** Lancashire
35 **Hoghton Tower** Lancashire

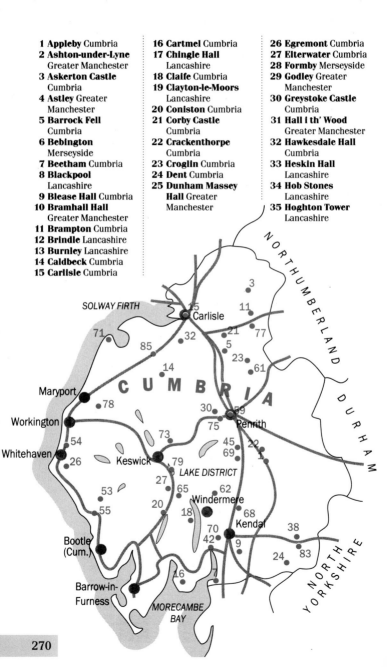

North East England
Yorkshire, Humberside

1 **Appletreewick** North Yorkshire
2 **Askrigg** North Yorkshire
3 **Aston** South Yorkshire
4 **Attercliffe** South Yorkshire
5 **Batley** West Yorkshire
6 **Beauchief Abbey** South Yorkshire
7 **Beverley** Humberside

8 **Birstall** West Yorkshire
9 **Bolton Abbey** North Yorkshire
10 **Boroughbridge** North Yorkshire
11 **Bradford** West Yorkshire
12 **Burton Agnes** Humberside

13 **Burton Constable** Humberside
14 **Byland Abbey** North Yorkshire
15 **Calverley** West Yorkshire
16 **Coverham** North Yorkshire
17 **Drighlington** West Yorkshire

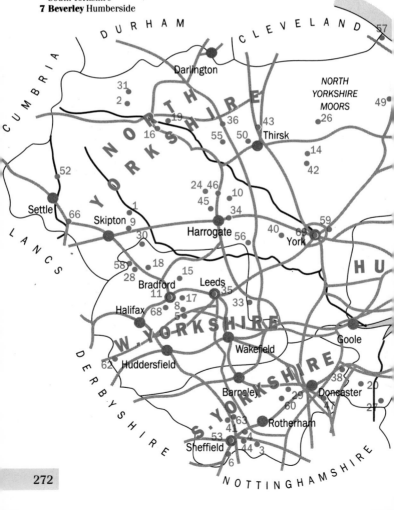

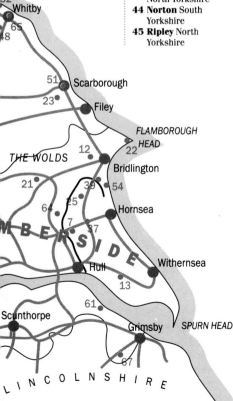

North East England

Northumberland, Durham, Tyne & Wear, Cleveland

1 **Alnwick Castle**
Northumberland
2 **Alwinton**
Northumberland
3 **Bamburgh Castle**
Northumberland
4 **Barnard Castle**
Durham
5 **Barrasford**
Northumberland
6 **Belsay**
Northumberland
7 **Berwick-on-Tweed**
Northumberland
8 **Blanchland**
Northumberland
9 **Blenkinsopp Castle**
Northumberland
10 **Capheaton**
Northumberland
11 **Carter Bar**
Northumberland
12 **Catcleugh Reservoir**
Northumberland
13 **Chillingham Castle**
Northumberland
14 **Cresswell**
Northumberland

15 **Darlington** Durham
16 **Dilston Castle**
Northumberland
17 **Dunstanburgh
Castle**
Northumberland
18 **Durham** Durham
19 **Ellingham**
Northumberland
20 **Elsdon**
Northumberland
21 **Fatfield** Tyne & Wear
22 **Featherstone Castle**
Northumberland
23 **Flodden Field**
Northumberland
24 **Haltwhistle**
Northumberland
25 **Hepple**
Northumberland
26 **Holy Island**
Northumberland
27 **Howick Hall**
Northumberland
28 **Hylton Castle** Tyne &
Wear
29 **Langley Park**
Durham
30 **Marsden Grotto**
Tyne & Wear
31 **Mitford Castle**
Northumberland
32 **Mortham Tower**
Durham
33 **Newcastle upon
Tyne** Tyne & Wear

34 **Otterburn**
Northumberland
35 **Preston**
Northumberland
36 **Raby Castle** Durham
37 **Rochester**
Northumberland
38 **Rock Hall**
Northumberland
39 **Rothbury**
Northumberland
40 **Seaton Delaval Hall**
Northumberland
41 **Simonside**
Northumberland
42 **Tees-side Airport**
Cleveland
43 **Thirlwall**
Northumberland
44 **Tynemouth** Tyne &
Wear
45 **Wallington House**
Northumberland
46 **Walworth Castle**
Durham
47 **Warkworth Castle**
Northumberland
48 **Washington** Tyne &
Wear
49 **West Auckland**
Durham
50 **Westgate** Durham
51 **Woodhorn**
Northumberland

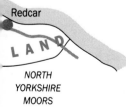

Redcar

LAND

NORTH
YORKSHIRE
MOORS

Scotland

Grampian, Tayside, Highland, Fife, Central

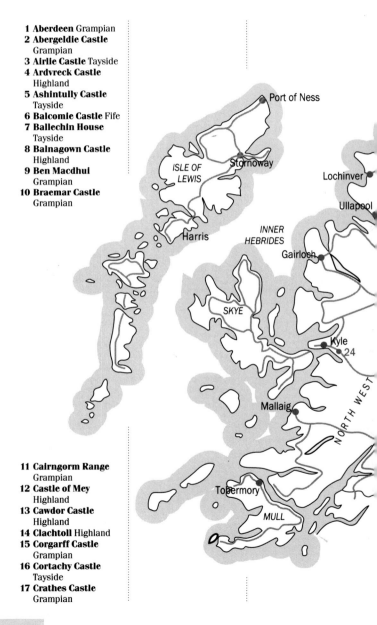

18 Cullen House Grampian
19 Culloden Highland
20 Cupar Fife
21 Dornoch Highland
22 Dunphail Grampian
23 Dunrobin Castle Highland
24 Eilean Donan Castle Highland
25 Ethie Castle Tayside

26 Fyvie Castle Grampian
27 Glamis Castle Tayside
28 Inverness Highland
29 Killiecrankie Tayside
30 Kylesku Hotel Highland
31 Leith Hall Grampian
32 Loch Morlich Highland

33 Loch Mullardoch Highland
34 Meggernie Castle Tayside
35 Muchalls Castle Grampian
36 Rait Castle Highland
37 Ruthven Castle Highland
38 St Andrew's Fife
39 Sandwood Bay Highland

40 Schiehallion Tayside
41 Scone Palace Tayside
42 Skene Grampian
43 Stirling Central
44 Wormit Tayside

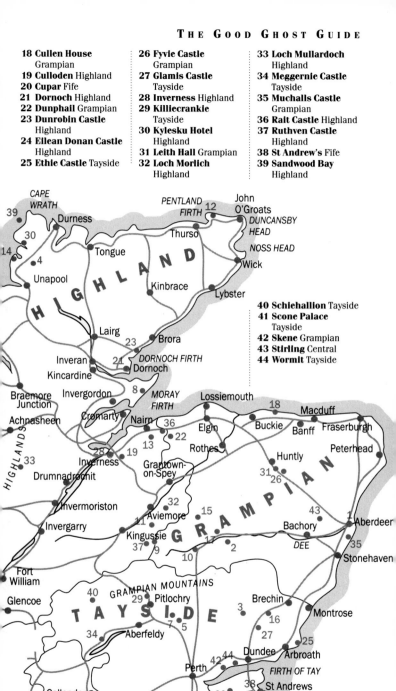

Scotland

Borders, Strathclyde, Dumfries and Galloway, Lothian, Isle of Arran,
Isle of Tiree

1 Abbotsford House
Borders
2 Ardchattan Priory
Strathclyde
3 Baldoon Castle
Dumfries and
Galloway

4 Bedlay Castle
Strathclyde
5 Borthwick Castle
Lothian
6 Brodick Castle Isle
of Arran
7 Buckholm Tower
Borders

8 Carleton Castle
Strathclyde
9 Corsock Dumfries
and Galloway
10 Culzean Castle
Strathclyde
11 Dean Castle
Strathclyde

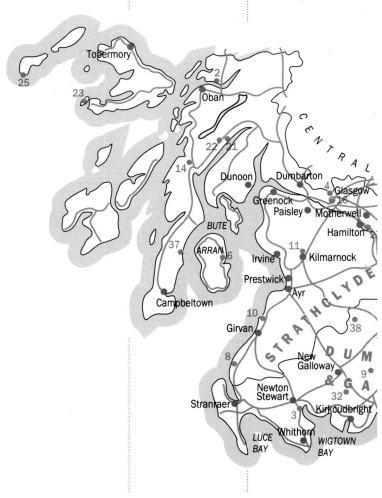

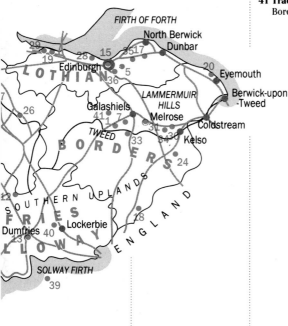

Selected bibliography

Abbot, G.	Ghosts of the Tower of London	1980
Alexander, Marc	Legendary Castles of the Border	
Armand, Muriel	The Ghosts of Cheshire	1989
Barber, Sally & Chips	The Ghosts of Exeter	1990
Bardens, Dennis	Ghosts & Hauntings	1965
Bell, David	Leicestershire Ghosts & Legends	1992
Bord, Janet & Colin	Atlas of Magical Britain	1990
Brooks, J.A.	Britain's Haunted Heritage	1990
	Ghosts & Witches of the Cotswolds	1981
	Ghosts of London	1982
	Ghosts of the Lake District	1988
	Ghosts & Legends of Wales	1987
Brown, Richard S.	The Folklore, Superstitions & Legends	
	of Birmingham and the West Midlands	1992
Brown, Theo	Devon Ghosts	1982
Bulwer-Lytton, Edward	The House & the Brain	1859
Bunn, I. & M. Burgess	Haunted Lowestoft	1988
Clarence, Daniel	Haunted Derbyshire	
Clarke, David	Ghosts & Legends of the Peak District	1991
Cliffe, Steve	Shadows: A Northern Investigation of	
	the Unknown	1993
Devon Folk Life Register	Shades & Spectres	
Downes, Wesley H.	The Haunted Colchester Area	1992
Evans, Alan & William Willis	Ghosts & Legends of	
	the Vale of Neath	1987
Eyre, Kathleen	Lancashire Ghosts	
Forman, Joan	Haunted East Anglia	1974
	Royal Hauntings	1987
	The Haunted South	1978
Fox, Ian	The Haunted Places of Hampshire	1993
Goss, Michael	The Evidence for Phantom Hitch-Hikers	1984
Guiley, Rosemary Ellen	Guinness Encyclopaedia of	
	Ghosts and Spirits	1994
Halpenny, Bruce B.	Ghost Stations	1986
Hassall, Keith & Mike Firth	Haunted Halls of Lancashire	1990
Hippisley-Coxe, Antony D.	Haunted Britain	1973
Holland, Richard	Haunted Clwyd	1992
	Supernatural Clwyd	1989
Howat, Polly	Norfolk Ghosts & Legends	1993
James, M.R.	Twelve Medieval Ghost Stories	1922
Kristen, Clive	Ghost Trails of Northumbria	
Legg, Rodney	Mysterious Dorset	1987
	Guide to Dorset Ghosts	

Matthews, Rupert	*Haunted Chester* 1992
	Haunted Oxford 1993
McCarthy, Christine	*Some Ghostly Tales of Staffordshire* 1988
McDermott, Paul	*Whitby Ghost Book* 1987
Middleton, Judy	*Ghosts of Sussex* 1988
Moakes, Len	*Haunted Nottinghamshire* 1987
Payne, Jessie	*Ghosthunters' Guide to Essex* 1987
Pipe, Marian	*Ghosts and Folklore of Northamptonshire*
Playfair, Guy Lyon	*Haunted Pub Guide* 1985
Poole, Keith	*Ghosts of Wessex* 1976
Prince, Rosalind	*Some Ghosts of Staffordshire* 1981
Pugh, Jane	*Welsh Ghostly Encounters* 1990
Reynolds, Hazel	*Ghosts & Legends of Northumbria* 1992
Robb, Rosemary	*Ghost Hunting* 1992
Roberts, Andy	*Ghosts & Legends of Yorkshire* 1992
Robinson, P.H. & Paul Hesp	*Ghosts & Hauntings in Beverley & the East Riding* 1987
Roderick, Alan	*Ghosts of Gwent* 1987
Royal, Margaret & Ian Girvan	*Bristol Ghosts* 1977
	Local Ghosts 1976
Scott-Davies, A.	*Shrewsbury Ghost Book* 1989
	The Ironbridge District Ghost Book 1990
	Haunted Shropshire 1992
Solomon, Phillip	*Ghosts of the Midlands*
Spencer, John & Anne	*The Encyclopaedia of Ghosts and Spirits* 1992
Taylor, Keith	*Ghosts of Wollaton* 1990
Thresher, Muriel & Beryl Carrington	*St Albans Ghost Lore* 1987
Underwood, Peter	*A - Z of British Ghosts* 1971
	Ghosts of Dorset 1988
	Ghosts of Kent 1985
	Ghosts of Wiltshire 1989
	This Haunted Isle 1986
Ward, Cyril	*Ghosts of Leigh*
Wentworth-Day, James	*Haunted Essex*
Whitaker, Terence	*North Country Ghosts & Legends* 1988
	Scotland's Ghosts & Apparitions 1991
Wiltshire, Kathleen	*Ghosts & Legends of the Wiltshire Countryside* 1973
Woods, Frederick	*Cheshire Ghosts & Legends* 1990
(No author credited)	*Guide to the Haunted Castles of Scotland* 1981

Glossary

Banshee
A female spirit that is an omen of death in Scotland and Ireland but may also visit England. In Wales the banshee is known as the Gwrach-y-rhibyn. *See East Riddlesden, NE England; Ethie Castle, Scotland; Caerphilly and St Donat's castles, Wales.*

Barguest
The term for the spectral black dog used in northern England. See *Appletreewick, NE England.*

Battles
The ghostly re-enactments of battles are a common feature of supernatural stories in Britain. They vary from minor skirmishes to major conflicts and witnesses are able to describe details of the weapons and accoutrements of the time. In some instances the fighting takes place in the sky above the battlefield. *See Flodden Field, Stockton on the Forest, and Otterburn, NE England; Edge Hill, South Midlands; Culloden, Scotland.*

Black Dog
Ghostly black dogs may be encountered throughout Britain but are particularly likely where Scandinavian influence most prevails. In Norfolk, where there are many Norse-based place names, the phantom hound is known as Black Shuck. He is as big as a calf and has fearsome saucer-sized eyes that glow yellow or red. In northern England the dog is called by a variety of different names, such as Barguest, Cappel, Gytrash (or Guytrash, or plain Trash), Padfoot, Skriker or Galleytrot. In Wales it is the Cwn (occasionally Ci) Annwn. Some specimens appear headless. Black Dogs represent evil, having derived from Odin's black hound in Viking mythology, and they are invariably omens of death.

Boadicea, Queen (also known as Queen Boudicca)
The warrior-queen of East Anglia who waged a brave, but ultimately disastrous, war against the Roman colonisers, killing at least seventy thousand of them. When she was finally defeated in AD62 she took poison to avoid capture. *See Cammeringham and Theydon Bois, Eastern England.*

Boleyn, Anne
Henry VIII's passion for this spirited young girl lead to his separating the English church from that of Rome. Thus he was able to obtain his divorce from Catherine of Aragon. However, the action failed to bring the happiness he desired, and three months after the marriage Anne herself was doomed once he suspected her of

adultery. She was beheaded on Tower Hill on 9 May 1536 and her ghost walks at many places she lived in girlhood. *See Blickling, Eastern England; Lambeth Palace and the Tower of London.*

Boggart
A hobgoblin common in northern England which could be mischievous or helpful to the household where it dwelt. Only a few were malevolent and these were usually easily banished by exorcism. Their demise in modern times has been put down to their fear of motor traffic. *See, for example, Brindle, NW England.*

Brocken Spectre
This is a trick of the light witnessed on mountain ridges when the sun is low. The shadows of climbers may be projected on to banks of cloud or mist as enormous figures, and these shadows have perhaps given rise to tales of the Monarch of the Mist (the Brenin Llywd of Snowdon, Wales) and the Big Grey Man (Am Fear Liath Mhór of Ben Macdhui, Scotland).

Civil War
Although England has had more than one Civil War in its history the term is usually applied to the 1642–48 conflict between King Charles I with his Cavaliers, and the supporters of Parliament under Oliver Cromwell (the Roundheads). After a series of savage battles King Charles's army was defeated in 1648, and the king was beheaded in January 1649. More than 100,000 men may have died in the long war, one in ten of the male population.

Covenanters
Protestant reformers in Scotland who established the Presbyterian Church in 1638 and challenged the divine right of the monarch. They were brutally persecuted for this until 1690 when a Protestant king restored the legality of the Presbyterian Church.

Cromwell, Oliver
An able soldier who began by fighting against a corrupt despot (as he considered King Charles I), Cromwell later became a despot himself, autocratically ruling as Lord Protector from 1653 until his death in 1658. Two years later the monarchy was restored and his body was exhumed from Westminster Abbey and hanged. Afterwards his head was cut from his body and began its travels around the country, only finding its resting place at Cambridge three hundred years later. *See Long Marston, NE England; Red Lion Square, London; Sidney Sussex College, Cambridge, and Murrow, Eastern England.*

Dissolution
The term given to Henry VIII's requisitioning of all the monasteries and their treasures when he split with the Church of Rome in 1534. The Pope had refused to condone his divorce from Catherine of Aragon when Henry wished to marry the young Anne Boleyn.

Doppelgänger

The ghost of a person still alive, literally his or her double. It is often a death-omen, and the person whom it represents may be on their deathbed when the doppelgänger is seen, often hundreds of miles away. In rare cases someone sees their own doppelgänger: Percy Bysshe Shelley did, just before he drowned. *See Moorseats Hall at Hathersage, and Bridgnorth, both in the North Midlands.*

Dracula

The Transylvanian count made his landfall in England on the coast of North Yorkshire. *See Kettleness, NE England.*

Drake, Sir Francis

As a young man Drake gained a reputation as a buccaneering seaman, adept at capturing treasure from the Spanish. His privateering endeared him to Queen Elizabeth, and she supported his expeditions, notably that of 1577 when he reached the Pacific Ocean in the *Golden Hind*. Soon after his return he was knighted and in 1588 played a prominent role in the defeat of the Spanish Armada. In 1593 he set out on his final voyage, which many believe took him to a landfall in California. However, it seems more likely that he died of dysentery off a small West Indian island. Drake's epic voyages and his bravery gave him a standing among English seamen rivalled only by Nelson. Some uncharitably believed that this charisma derived from a pact he made with the Devil. This may help to explain why his ghost haunts so many places in the West Country which had only tenuous links with him in his lifetime. *See Buckfast Abbey, Stogumber and Exeter's Ship Inn, SW England.*

Ectoplasm

A strange, jelly-like substance that floats in the air, produced from the bodies of mediums at seances. It has also been seen at some haunted sites: *see York's Theatre Royal, NE England; Wilton Row, London; Lyme Regis, SW England.*

Exorcism

The ritual that banishes restless spirits from places where they disturb the earthly occupants. Some spirits are persuaded to leave by friendly conversation; others are more stubborn, in which case an elaborate service is performed, usually by a priest. In bygone times the ghosts were consigned to boxes or bottles which were hidden in inaccessible places, such as beneath a waterfall. A time limit was placed on this commitment which in many instances will soon expire. The spirits, by now enraged by the lengthy enforced captivity, may present considerable problems to exorcists in the future. *See Little Lawford, South Midlands.*

Familiar spirit

A tame demon helpful to witches or wizards, sometimes taking animal form, usually as a cat or toad. *See Leeds Castle, Southern England; Hermitage Castle, Scotland; British Museum, London.*

Fetch
An archaic term for a wraith, still used in Norfolk for a friendly, homely ghost, usually of a person not long dead or sometimes a doppelgänger (see above).

Ghoul
A ghost with a taste for human flesh that usually inhabits a churchyard. *See Stanmore, London; Launceston, SW England.*

Glyndwr, Owain (also known as Owen Glendower)
A chieftain of North Wales who rebelled against Henry IV in 1401 proclaiming himself Prince of Wales. Although his army was defeated at Shrewsbury in 1403 he continued a guerilla campaign against the English, often fighting heroically against larger forces. He died in 1416. *See Nannau and Ruthin Castle, Wales.*

Gunpowder Plot
When James I succeeded Elizabeth I in 1603 English Catholics hoped that there might be greater tolerance for their faith since his mother (Mary, Queen of Scots) had been a Catholic. It soon became apparent that James's ministers maintained the opposition to catholicism of the previous regime and consequently a group of disaffected Catholics lead by Robert Catesby embarked on a conspiracy centred on blowing up the king and Parliament. The day chosen for this was 5 November 1605, when King James was to go to the Palace of Westminster for the opening of Parliament. A key figure in the plot was Guy Fawkes, a recent convert to the faith. He rented a cellar beneath the House of Lords and filled it with twenty barrels of gunpowder. The plot failed because the conspirators unwisely told their plans to a further eight Catholics opposed to the king, and one of them warned his brother-in-law, Lord Monteagle, to stay away from the opening of Parliament. This message was passed on to the authorities by a disloyal servant, and they discovered the gunpowder when they searched the basement of the Palace of Westminster on 4 November. Fawkes was arrested immediately and the remaining conspirators were rounded up in the weeks that followed. Catesby died at his home at Wombourne, Staffordshire, resisting arrest with a handful of supporters. Eight of the others involved in the plot were executed together in January 1606. The fifth of November was originally dedicated as a day for the nation to give thanks for the preservation of king and Parliament, but celebrants on Bonfire Night do not always observe this.

Gytrash (also Guytrash)
A northern name for the spectral black dog. *See Ilkley, NE England.*

Hallowe'en (All Hallows Eve)
This is the night of 31 October, when earth-bound spirits return to their homes and witches fly out. In pagan times this was the last day of the year when the boundary between this world and that of

the spirits was considered particularly fragile. The Christian Church dedicated the day as All Saints' Day in an attempt to rid it of its ancient significance.

Hitch hikers
Stories of phantom hitch hikers have proliferated throughout the world since the advent of the motor car (though in these pages there are also examples from earlier times where ghosts have materialised as unwanted pillion passengers to horse riders). *See Bluebell Hill, Southern England; Wellington, SW England.*

Isabella, Queen
The daughter of Philip IV of France, who married the English king, Edward II, in 1308. Finding that he preferred the company of handsome male courtiers, she became the mistress of Roger Mortimer and together they had her husband cruelly murdered at Berkeley Castle in 1327. Their plan to gain the throne failed and Mortimer was executed in 1330. Isabella was held prisoner until her death in 1358. *See Newgate Street, London; Nottingham Castle, East Midlands; Castle Rising, Eastern England.*

Jacobites
The name given to the supporters of the Catholic English king, James II, who was deposed by William, Prince of Orange (who thus became William III) in 1688. The Jacobites continued to try to restore a Stuart king to the English throne, first with the Old Pretender (James's son whose rebellion was quashed in 1715), and then with the Young Pretender, better known as Bonnie Prince Charlie. The latter made a brave attempt at invading England in 1745, reaching Derby before realising that English support for his uprising was not forthcoming. Forced to retreat northwards, his army was finally annihilated at Culloden in 1746. The prince, after many adventures in the Highlands, managed to escape to France and in 1788 died in Rome, still calling himself King Charles III of Great Britain.

Jeffreys, Judge
The Lord Chief Justice in Jacobean times who imposed savage sentences on those convicted of opposing the king. During the 'bloody assizes' which followed the Battle of Sedgemoor he sentenced 320 of Monmouth's erstwhile supporters to death as he presided over a series of courts in the West Country. When William III came to the throne in 1688 Jeffreys was imprisoned in the Tower of London where he died the following year. *See Lydford and Taunton, SW England.*

Mary, Queen of Scots
A tragic figure of Scottish history (and heir to the English throne) who was forced to flee to England in 1568 where she sought Elizabeth I's protection. But Mary was a Catholic (as well as being Elizabeth's heir) and the English queen kept her in captivity until,

discovering Mary to be involved in a plot to unseat her, she had her executed at Fotheringhay in 1587. Mary's ghost is seen at many of the places where she was held prisoner. *See Sheffield, NE England, and Borthwick Castle, Scotland.*

Montrose, James Graham, first Marquis of
As a young man Montrose supported the Reformation and helped draw up the Covenant of Presbyterianism. Later he deserted the Covenant army to fight for Charles I but after initial success his Scots troops were among the Royalists routed at Naseby in 1645. Montrose fled abroad to regroup his forces and attempted another campaign in 1650. He was taken prisoner and executed at Edinburgh in the same year. *See Ardvreck Castle, Scotland.*

Phantom army
Ghostly armies on the march have been reported from many localities and they seem to be remembrances from many widely different eras. *See Attercliffe and Long Marston, NE England; Dent and Souther Fell, NW England; Naseby, South Midlands; Sedgemoor, SW England; Pevensey Castle, Southern England; Inveraray, Scotland.*

Poltergeist
An invisible ghost with the ability to move objects. *See Cirencester, South Midlands.*

Reformation
The setting up of a Protestant Church separate from the Church of Rome, instigated in England by Henry VIII (in 1549, when the Book of Common Prayer was published) and in Scotland by John Knox (in 1560, with the creation of the Presbyterian Church).

Silkie
The name given to some White Ladies in northern England. *See Belsay, NE England.*

Spectral army
See Phantom army, above.

Troll
A mischievous (sometimes malevolent) dwarf of Scandinavian origin. *See Appletreewick, NE England.*

Vampire
A re-animated corpse which obtains its nourishment by sucking blood from the living while they sleep at night. The earliest stories of vampires come from Eastern Europe and the name was first used in England in 1732, although there are accounts of similar undead creatures from early medieval times. *See Croglin, NW England; Alnwick and Berwick-on-Tweed, NE England.*

Warlock
A male witch, or wizard. *See West Bow, Edinburgh, Scotland.*

Werewolf

The wolfman of ancient mythology and more recent horror films is seldom encountered in British ghost stories, *but see Flixton, NE England.*

Wild Hunt

In Norse mythology the god Odin leads his fearsome pack of hounds across the night sky seeking the souls of the damned. The myth was adapted by later storytellers to suit their own religious ends; thus after the Reformation the Hunt was said to be seeking the souls of unbaptised children who had not been allowed churchyard burial. Later, when witches were blamed for misfortunes, they were believed to follow the hounds on their broomsticks. Legends concerning the ghostly hunt are confusing, for although to see it usually proves fatal, sometimes it appears to give warning of national disaster. Further, it is known by a variety of names, such as the whisht hounds in the West Country (*see Buckfastleigh, SW England*), and the Gabriel hounds in Yorkshire (*see Todmorden, NE England*).

Will o' the Wisp

A ghostly light that flickers mysteriously across low-lying ground. It is usually taken to be caused by methane gas ignited by a natural agency, and it is also known as Jack o' Lantern or Jenny Burnt Tail (*see Thurlton, Eastern England; Burton Dassett, South Midlands*). In Wales the same phenomenon is known as the Canwyll Corph, or corpse candle (*see Plynlimon*).